Ageing and Employment Policies

Working Better with Age: Korea

OECD

BETTER POLICIES FOR BETTER LIVES

Please cite this publication as:
OECD (2018), *Working Better with Age: Korea*, Ageing and Employment Policies, OECD Publishing, Paris.
https://doi.org/10.1787/9789264208261-en

ISBN 978-92-64-06483-6 (print)
ISBN 978-92-64-20826-1 (pdf)

Series: Ageing and Employment Policies
ISSN 1990-102X (print)
ISSN 1990-1011 (online)

Photo credits: Cover © iStockphoto.com/MirekP

Corrigenda to OECD publications may be found on line at: *www.oecd.org/publishing/corrigenda*.

Foreword

The average age of the population of OECD countries is increasing fast, and the average age of the labour force is also increasing. In such a context, giving older people better work choices and incentives and access to good jobs is crucial for promoting economic growth and improving the sustainability of public social expenditures. Older people offer tremendous potential value to businesses and the economy but public policies and private workplace practices continue to pose barriers to work or fail to provide good work.

To respond to the continued disadvantage older people are facing in the labour market, the OECD Employment, Labour and Social Affairs Committee decided to carry out a new series of policy reviews on *Working Better with Age* to encourage greater labour market participation at an older age, through the fostering of employability, job mobility and labour demand. It builds upon earlier work of the OECD on Ageing and Employment Policies, summarised in *Live Longer, Work Longer*, published in 2006.

This report on Korea is one in a series of country case studies on this matter. It points to areas where changes are needed to improve employment opportunities, working conditions and work incentives at an older age, including measures to adapt wage-setting practices, tackle age discrimination, improve job skills of older people and their working conditions, and better activate older job seekers. It also reviews Korea's policies against the *Recommendation of the Council on Ageing and Employment Policies* which was formally endorsed by ministers of employment from all OECD countries in January 2016 (see https://legalinstruments.oecd.org/en/instruments/OECD-LEGAL-0419).

This review was carried out by OECD's Directorate for Employment, Labour and Social Affairs. This report on Korea was prepared by Anne Saint-Martin, Veerle Miranda, Christopher Prinz (project leader), Marko Stermsek, Hyeongso Ha and Anne Sonnet. Dana Blumin provided the statistical work and Monica Meza-Essid provided technical assistance. The report also includes comments to an earlier version from Mark Keese and from a number of Korean ministries and authorities.

Table of contents

Tables

Figures

Boxes

Acronyms and abbreviations

AARP	American Association of Retired Persons
ALMPs	Active Labour Market Programmes
BLSP	Basic Livelihood Security Programme
CLA	Collective Labour Agreement
CHAMP	National Human Resources Development Consortium programme
DB	Defined Benefit
DC	Defined Contribution
DRA	Default Retirement Age
EI	Employment Insurance
EITC	Earned Income Tax Credit
ESPP	Employment Success Package Programme
GDP	Gross Domestic Product
HRM	Human Resources Management
IRP	Individual Retirement Pension
ITA	Individual Training Accounts
KFTU	Korea Federation of Trade Unions
KOSIS	Korean Statistical Information Service
KRW	Korean Won
MOEL	Ministry of Employment and Labor
NCS	National Competency Standards
NHRC	National Human Rights Commission
NPS	National Pension Scheme
PES	Public Employment Service
PIAAC	OECD Survey of Adult Skills
SMEs	Small and Medium-sized Enterprises
TWAs	Temporary Work Agencies
VET	Vocational Education and Training

Executive summary

Korea is experiencing much faster population ageing than any other OECD country. If nothing is done to improve the labour market situation of older workers, this could put a brake on the trend of rising living standards observed in recent decades. There is no time for complacency: the median age of the population is projected to increase from 41 years today to 55 years in the mid-2050s, and the old-age dependency ratio (population aged 65 plus over the population aged 15-64) is projected to increase from 20% today to around 70% in 2050, 20 percentage points above the then OECD average.

In a nutshell, the key challenge is to increase the quality of life and work of older workers whilst maintaining their high employment rate. Unlike in many other OECD countries, there is little choice but to work for older workers in Korea; yet work is not an effective antidote against poverty when getting old. Most people end up in poor quality jobs after ending their core career in their early 50s, with low and insecure earnings and little or no social protection. Structural reforms are needed to reduce labour market duality, which affects older workers disproportionally. Measures should be taken to reduce i) the gap between wages and productivity, which increases with age and contributes to push older workers out of regular jobs, and ii) the gap in job quality between regular and non-regular jobs. This requires tackling employers' practices with respect to early retirement plans while at the same time moving away from seniority-based practices for setting wages and granting promotions, reforming the hiring and dismissal rules for regular and non-regular work, and strengthening social protection. Providing good opportunities for workers to upgrade their skills and learn new ones throughout their working careers is also a key requirement for fostering longer working lives in good quality jobs.

All these issues are at the heart of the policy debate in Korea. While the Tripartite Agreement, signed in September 2015 by the government, trade unions and employers associations, was a big step forward, a number of important aspects – such as employment regulations for permanent and temporary jobs – are still under discussion and have not yet received approval from the National Assembly, newly formed in June 2016. Likewise, recent government initiatives, e.g. to postpone the age of mandatory retirement, promote a job- and competency-based system for setting wages and reduce working time, could help increase workers' productivity and improve working conditions, but questions remain as to whether these measures will be forcefully implemented. And while the gradual implementation of the National Competency Standards could help to better recognise, use, manage and reward the actual skills and competencies of the workforce, this will take time to materialise.

The aim of this report is to identify what further measures could be taken to promote more and better jobs for older workers in Korea. To respond to the policy challenges, the OECD recommends that policy makers in Korea take further action to: i) make work rewarding for older workers; ii) encourage employers to retain and hire older workers; and iii) promote the employability of workers throughout their working lives.

Measures to make work rewarding for older workers could include:

- Raising payments for persons over 50 provided by the earned income tax credit and improving the coverage among older self-employed workers.
- Broadening the coverage and increasing the generosity of the Basic Livelihood Support Programme, Korea's social assistance measure.
- Targeting the Basic Pension to the most needy and increasing benefit amounts.
- Improving the pension scheme coverage among self-employed and non-regular workers and making the scheme financially sustainable.
- Fostering the implementation of retirement pension plans, especially in small and medium-sized enterprises.

Measures to encourage employers to retain and hire older workers could include:

- Fostering the introduction of wage peak systems to ease the postponement of the age of mandatory (early) retirement.
- Proactively promoting the implementation of job- and skill-based professional appraisal measures, instead of seniority-based practices.
- Reducing the uncertainties surrounding dismissal costs to reduce the incentive for employers to have recourse to precarious forms of employment.
- Providing additional employment rights for temporary agency workers as well as new business opportunities in the temporary work agency sector.

Measures to promote the employability of workers could include:

- Rigorously implementing the new National Competency Standards.
- Refocusing active labour market expenditures on the most effective support measures and phasing-out direct job-creation measures.
- Strengthening second-career guidance for middle-aged and older workers.
- Monitoring closely the implementation of the new guidelines on working time.
- Introducing employer-paid sick leave and a statutory cash sickness benefit to facilitate the return to the main job of workers experiencing health problems.

Assessment and recommendations

Korea's population is ageing faster than any other OECD country's

Korea is currently in the midst of an unprecedented demographic transformation, with population ageing progressing faster than in any other OECD country. The median age of the population is projected to reach around 55 years by the mid-2050s, compared with a median age below 20 years back in the 1970s. There are currently less than 200 residents in Korea aged 65 and above for every 1 000 of the working-age population (ages 15-64) – well below the OECD average of 246 in 2015. The Korean figure, however, is projected to quadruple over the coming decades, exceeding the OECD average quickly and peaking at a projected 760 by around the year 2065 – the highest ratio of any OECD country.

Such sweeping demographic changes are likely to have important consequences for Korea's fiscal institutions and social cohesion, as labour resource utilisation remains a key engine of economic growth. Population ageing thus presents a major challenge for Korea, requiring a comprehensive and decisive policy response.

Shortcomings around job quality are a particular issue for older workers

At almost 70%, Korea's employment rate of older workers aged 50-64 is relatively high – 6.6 percentage points above the OCED average. However, many workers retire early from their main job (most of them before reaching age 55) and find new employment in poor quality, highly insecure and low-paid jobs or become self-employed. Older workers in Korea effectively retire at an average age of 71-73 years – the oldest of any OECD country. Almost two out of every five workers aged 55-64 in Korea hold a non-permanent job, compared with an OECD average of just one in every ten. Precarious work is even more common among still older workers, with three out of every five of those aged 65-69 in non-permanent positions – roughly three times the OECD average.

For a majority of workers, early retirement from the main job results in lower earnings and potential hardship. Poverty is very high among Korea's elderly population, despite the fact that such a large proportion of them are economically active. Korea has one of the highest rates of relative income poverty among those aged 51-65 among all OECD countries – second only to Mexico. Work is therefore not an effective antidote against poverty for a sizeable number within Korea's elderly population.

Structural reforms and better social protection are needed

When labour regulations that govern hiring and firing are ill-adapted to businesses' needs, they may end up being bypassed in practice. In Korea, many non-typical salaried workers – including those in bogus forms of self-employment – enter into a regulatory grey area, holding jobs that are in practice neither strongly regulated nor coverable under social protection measures. This provides a great deal of flexibility for firms but at workers' expense in terms of greater insecurity and higher risk of poverty – most notably among older workers after early retirement from their main job.

Human resource management practices in Korea rely predominantly on a seniority-based approach to setting wages and granting promotions. As a result, long working hours, mandatory early retirement, and voluntary "honorary retirement" practices widely encompass older workers as employers seek to reduce labour costs within their rigid seniority-focused workplace structures. Such outcomes are ultimately detrimental for employers and workers alike. Introducing worker appraisal and wage-setting mechanisms that are less rigidly tied to individuals' seniority – and more weighted towards their actual skills and competencies or the demands of the particular role they fulfil – would align Korea more closely with the norms in other OECD countries and benefit all economic stakeholders alike. In particular, such a move could help older workers to retain their main jobs until their effective retirement.

Policy makers have few direct tools to intervene in wage-setting arrangements agreed between social partners. Nevertheless, policy makers should make direct efforts to challenge the status quo in order to improve both economic growth and social cohesion within the context of population ageing.

Recent reforms are well-directed but could go further

Korea's Tripartite Agreement, signed in September 2015 by the government, trade unions and employers' representatives, marked an important step forward in developing a modern regulatory framework. Likewise, recent government initiatives such as regulating mandatory early retirement, promoting wage-setting mechanisms based on job and skill requirements and reducing working hours should help increase workers' productivity and improve working conditions. Questions remain around the extent to which these measures will finally be implemented. The aim of this report is to identify what more could be done to promote more and better jobs for older workers in Korea. It focuses on policies along three key areas: a) making work attractive for older workers and tackling old-age poverty; b) encouraging employers to retain and hire older workers, including in core-career jobs; and c) promoting the employability of workers throughout their working lives.

Making work more rewarding for older workers and tackling old-age poverty

Korea is still relying heavily on labour regulations and collective agreements to protect jobs instead of social protection measures capable of protecting workers themselves throughout their career plus under any spells of unemployment or underemployment. Shortcomings with this approach are evidenced through the prevalence of precarious work that results, for many, in insufficient income security. Workers outside of regular salaried employment often face a double penalty of poor working conditions and little or no social protection. While such dualities are a somewhat general feature of Korea's labour market, they affect older workers disproportionately.

The main pillars of a comprehensive system of social protection are in place, but many components of the system are still very young and, thus, only gradually capturing the entitled population. Public pension measures are not yet fully mature while other branches of social protection could be further aligned or expanded to better protect individuals against common risks – notably unemployment, sickness and poverty. Older workers currently remain underserved by existing social protection measures.

Reducing in-work poverty among older workers

Among Korea's salaried employees aged 55-64, 45% are either working part-time or engaged on a non-permanent or non-typical basis; a share that goes up to over 60% for those aged 65-74. Well-designed in-work benefit measures and unemployment insurance programmes have proven effective in reducing poverty among disadvantaged groups of workers in a number of OECD countries. While Korea has both such types of benefits in place, they do not protect older workers effectively.

Korea's Earned Income Tax Credit (EITC) covers couples with and without children as well as single household members aged 50 and over with very low wages. EITC presents rather strict eligibility criteria – notably around the real estate and financial assets requirements contained in the means test – and relatively low benefit amounts equivalent to roughly 2% of Korea's average wage (even though EITC payments for single-earner couples may reach a maximum value of 5.3% of the average wage). For EITC to be a more effective instrument to tackle in-work poverty, notably among older workers in second careers, eligibility criteria and benefit amounts need to be revised.

For Korea's Employment Insurance (EI) measure, the main priority going forward will be to extend the actual coverage for various groups of non-salaried and non-typical workers currently not formally encompassed by the measure and ensure that all employers including very small businesses comply with the mandatory requirement to register their workers and to contribute towards the EI fund. This issue was discussed extensively in a recent OECD report.

Reducing post-retirement poverty without impairing work incentives

In Korea, in 2015 just under four in ten individuals aged 65-76 had an income lower than 50% of the national mean – the common threshold used for defining relative income poverty in a population. This was significantly higher than the equivalent share of 11% among OECD countries on average. In large part, this reflects the fact that Korea's public pension system is not yet fully mature. More broadly, however, it points towards the need for social protection measures to provide increased support for older people.

Steps have been taken to broaden the coverage and increase the value of benefits under Korea's social assistance scheme, the Basic Livelihood Security Programme (BLSP), though more could still be done. While recent reforms have successfully put an end to the "all or nothing" nature of previous BLSP benefits, the benefit level itself remains low by OECD standards and eligibility conditions – notably the family support obligation by way of which people whose close relatives (children, siblings, parents) would in principle be in a position to provide financial support – still affect older persons disproportionately.

Building an employment-friendly and cost-effective pension system is a key requirement for ensuring those entering retirement have an adequate standard of living while those who still want to work may be rewarded in doing so. Korea's Basic Pension could be better targeted and the payment value increased in order to provide a more solid safety net. This is all the more important as retirement benefits paid under Korea's National Pension have been significantly reduced to ensure the measure's financial sustainability.

Measures could also be taken to extend both institutional and effective coverage of the National Pension. For many non-regular workers, employers are still managing to evade their obligations to document their workers formally and pay into the measure, similar to EI. Moreover, employers are required to insure employees only up until the age of 60, although the pensionable age varies from 61 to 65 (and will be 65 for all workers from

2033 onwards). Past age 60, employees can decide themselves whether they want to continue paying into the National Pension. Those deciding to do are effectively obliged to double their contributions to the measure in order to compensate for the absence of employers' contributions, which puts off many low-wage earners. Many older workers thus work for a decade or more without extending their pension rights.

Further measures could also be taken to foster the implementation of retirement pension plans, notably among small and medium-sized enterprises (SMEs). Despite several government initiatives over the past decade to encourage the conversion of the mandatory retirement allowance into a retirement pension, the allowance continues to be used as severance payment throughout workers' careers. More radical measures need to be taken to transform the allowance into a second pillar of the pension system. First, the age when the retirement pension can be drawn should be aligned with the National Pension pensionable age, and therefore should increase progressively up to age 65 (from 55 currently). Second, retirement pension plans could be made mandatory for all workers irrespective of their contract type and in all firms irrespective of their size. Early withdrawals should be possible but limited to specific circumstances (e.g. the purchase of a principal residence or expenditure on children's education) and, upon retirement, workers should be given strong fiscal incentives to convert their entitlements into an annuity instead of claiming a cash payment.

The following policy actions could be considered:

- *Broaden the coverage and increase the value of EITC*. For EITC to be effective in reducing poverty for older workers, eligibility criteria and benefit amounts need to be revised. In particular, means testing criteria relating to real estate and financial assets are currently too restrictive for older workers and could be relaxed.
- *Consider raising EITC payments for persons over 50 and improve the coverage of the EITC scheme among older self-employed workers.* The very high poverty rate among older people relative to the rest of the population – and especially among those who are working – calls for a stronger focus on this target group.
- *Take further steps to broaden the coverage and increase the generosity of BLSP*. Benefit amounts remain low by OECD standards and the family support obligation still prevents many poor older persons from receiving BLSP benefits.
- *Better target the Basic Pension and increase benefit amounts*. These adjustments are essential to ensure a solid safety net for at-risk groups in the older population.
- *Improve the coverage of the NPS among self-employed and non-regular workers and raise the contribution rate to achieve financial sustainability of the scheme*. NPS coverage could be improved by increasing the penalties for employers who do not formally document and enrol their workers and by expanding the resources and mandate of the labour inspectorate to control compliance of employers.
- *Foster the implementation of retirement pension plans, notably in SMEs*. Retirement pension plans should be made mandatory for all workers irrespective of their contract type and in all firms irrespective of their size. In addition, the age when retirement pension benefits can be drawn should be aligned with the National Pension pensionable age, and therefore should increase accordingly.

Encouraging employers to retain and hire older workers

The willingness to work at old ages is very high in Korea, yet older workers bear the brunt of important inefficiencies in the labour market in terms of common wage-setting practices. A recent survey among Korean workers aged 20-50 years found that over 80% of respondents would like to work at least up to age 65, with over 30% of them seeking to retire at around age 70. Strikingly, respondents also expressed strong worries about their effective retirement age from their main job: over 80% have concerns that they will be coerced into retiring before age 60, and 56% even before age 55.

Addressing wage rigidities and mandatory early retirements

For older workers in Korea, the seniority-based wage-setting mechanism creates a gap between wage and productivity that, in turn, nurtures a culture of forced early retirement. Coupled with insufficient investment in skills development, such wage-setting practices are a major driver of early exits from the main job that also largely help to explain the precarious employment situation of older workers. However, this system does provide workers with the guarantee that they will receive relatively high earnings at a time when they will have to pay for the education of their children, provide financial support to their parents, and make pension contributions for their own retirement. High education costs coupled with weaknesses around social protection currently result in strong support among workers and trade unions for maintaining the *status quo*.

Various measures have been taken recently to prevent employers from setting mandatory retirement at ages lower than 60 years. While this is a big step forward, problems remain. First, this will put additional burden on firms by increasing the gap between the wage bill and their workers' labour productivity, due to the high prevalence of seniority-based wage-setting practices. In the absence of any wage adjustments, the (overall) employment impact of this law is unclear and could even be negative. Second, "honorary retirement" which is formally voluntary can still be used by firms to bypass the new regulation.

In the short run, these issues can be addressed by the introduction of wage-peak systems whereby the employer commits to maintaining older workers in their jobs in exchange for a wage cut that is partly compensated by government subsidies granted to the employee. To foster the take-up of such systems, these subsidies could be higher for low-wage earners. The redistributive effect of wage-peak systems needs to be evaluated; fine-tuning measures may be necessary to ensure vulnerable workers can benefit from the system. A well-designed system of in-work benefits is likely to be more effective in this respect while also being sustainable in the long term, unlike wage-peak systems that should remain transitory measures until reforms of wage-setting practices are rolled out.

From a longer-term perspective, the progressive implementation of a job-based system for setting wages and granting promotions is a key requirement for improving the labour market situation of older workers in Korea. The government is providing information and free counselling for helping companies to engage in a respective dialogue with the trade unions and the employers' representatives. But compensating measures may be needed to find broader acceptance for reform among workers. The transition towards a job-based system may cause a loss in lifetime earnings for those who have been hired before that transition and paid according to a seniority-based system for a number of years. A rather simple response for firms to redistribute the accrued amount of deferred wages is to further postpone the age of mandatory early retirement. Hence, there is scope for the social partners to agree on a win-win strategy.

The roots of the problem may also include a lack of knowledge from key stakeholders regarding the market wage that could be applied for a given job that requires certain specific and/or general skills. In this respect, the progressive revamping of the National Qualifications System, based on the National Competency Standards, should provide an effective tool for recognising and validating the skills workers have acquired throughout their careers. This is essential for using, managing and rewarding the actual skills and competencies of the workforce more effectively and could support the transition towards more job-oriented wage-setting practices.

Easing employment protection regulation and labour market duality

Improving the set of rules that govern layoffs and hiring is also essential to reduce Korea's labour market dualities and improve the labour market situation of older workers. Although there are no statutory severance payment requirements in place and also no particular regulations around collective dismissal, individual dismissals of permanent workers are quite strictly regulated. This can be a strong barrier for vulnerable groups – including older workers – to retain quality work or to (re)enter the labour market.

Individual dismissals are allowed for urgent managerial reasons, an ill-defined criterion that is difficult to prove in front of a court. Therefore, layoff costs are difficult to predict for employers and can be high due to long and complex judicial procedures. Furthermore, if a dismissal is recognised as unfair, reinstatement into the old job is generally offered to the worker; this regulation is also likely to affect employers' hiring behaviour.

At the other end of the spectrum, many non-regular workers are deprived of basic social protection and employment rights, as regulations and legal requirements are often not respected or well-enforced, most notably among SMEs. There is scope for reducing labour market dualities by improving the quality of non-regular jobs and other forms of precarious employment. This may require new regulations around fixed-term contracts, temporary work agencies (TWAs) and non-typical work. In particular, the use of in-house subcontracting should be restricted, while TWA regulations should be improved. TWA employment can open opportunities to improve the quality of non-standard forms of work, provided legal provisions are backed up with collective agreements. Experience from the Netherlands suggests that providing additional rights to TWA workers while opening up new business opportunities for TWAs can constitute a win-win strategy. But achieving this requires collective, well-coordinated efforts by public authorities, employer representatives and trade unions. It also requires the TWA sector to be large enough to be well structured and organised, and led by large firms that are unionised.

Combating age discrimination

Korea has enacted laws to combat age discrimination. This should be complemented by other initiatives to promote age diversity, such as positive and affirmative actions. As the enforcement of legal rules is essentially based on discriminated workers' willingness to claim their rights, public awareness and incentives for victims of discrimination to lodge complaints are crucial elements of an effective anti-discrimination policy.

In Korea, very few cases are brought before the relevant bodies, the National Human Rights Commission (NHRC), the adjudicative body, and the Ministry of Employment and Labor (MOEL), the enforcement body. Legal rules could be a stronger vehicle of cultural change if enforcement is not exclusively dependent on individuals deprived of their rights. NHRC and MOEL are empowered to investigate companies and organisations, but they cannot take legal actions against employers who operate discriminatory practices, their scope for action being limited to providing administrative guidance and making recommendations. The extent to which such non-binding measures are effective is rather unclear, also because the split of responsibilities and insufficient co-ordination between the two bodies complicate the task further. More should be done in this respect.

The following policy actions could be considered:

- *In the short run, foster the introduction of wage peak systems by increasing the amount of subsidies for low-earners*. This is crucial to help employers coping with the new legal requirement to postpone the age of mandatory early retirement in order to ensure that workers can retain their main jobs for longer.
- *Proactively tackle the seniority-centred professional appraisal culture*. This could be achieved by promoting the gradual implementation of job- and skill-based professional appraisal measures. To achieve broader acceptance among workers, the government could continue its support through compensatory measures.
- *Reduce the uncertainty surrounding dismissal costs*. Clarifying the definition of unfair dismissal and the modalities of reinstatement in case of unfair dismissal would make protection for regular workers more efficient, in turn reducing the incentive for employers to have recourse to precarious forms of employment.
- *Restrict the scope for using lawful in-house subcontracting, while improving TWA regulations*. A balanced reform that provides both additional rights for TWA workers and new business opportunities in the TWA sector could benefit workers and employers alike.
- *Complement legal provisions against age-discrimination with an effective implementation body*, which can take legal actions against employers who operate discriminatory practices. Legal rules could be a vehicle of cultural change if enforcement is not exclusively dependent on individuals deprived of their rights.

Promoting the employability of workers throughout their working lives

Maintaining the employability of workers throughout their working lives is essential to ensure that they can stay longer in their main jobs and retain good-quality work right up until retirement. For Korea, the challenge is threefold. First, as many workers begin a second career after retiring early from their main job, employment services and active labour market policies have an important role to play in helping them to make successful employment transitions or, at the very least, to minimise the implied costs. Second, from a longer term perspective, building an effective system of lifelong learning is critical to ensure that workers can use and upgrade their core competencies and skills throughout their working lives and stem the widespread practices of forced early retirement. Third, efforts to improve working conditions must continue to make working longer with full work capacity possible for older workers.

Expanding vocational education and training

The main challenge faced by Korea is to better link the education system, including vocational education and training programmes, with labour market needs. Driven by rapid technological advances and strong economic growth, business needs have changed dramatically over the past few decades. But older workers in Korea are not well equipped to deal with the new skill requirements, compared with both their counterparts in other OECD countries and younger adults in their own country. While this is partly due to Korea's rapid economic growth, this also indicates that vocational education and training policies have not been responsive enough to this fast-changing environment. Nearly two out of three persons aged 55-65 in Korea have either no experience with the use of computers or (at most) very low familiarity with computer devices and applications. This is by far the highest proportion in OECD countries, raising concerns on the employability of older workers in productive and rewarding jobs.

Strikingly, the willingness to learn among older workers is very high in Korea compared to other OECD countries, as survey data demonstrate. Slightly more than one in five persons aged 55-64 report unmet demands for training, more than twice the OECD average for this age group. Korea would rank among the best-performing countries with respect to education and training for older workers if all these demands were met, whereas the actual participation rate is significantly below the OECD average.

Time-related constraints are a major obstacle to training participation in Korea (for all age groups), where being too busy at work is the most prevalent reason reported by workers to explain why they did not participate in any work-related training although they wanted to do so – at almost 40%, Korea's share is the highest among the OECD countries.

The new guidelines on working time can contribute to ease these time constraints, but additional measures should be taken, notably for SMEs that often face labour shortages making it difficult for them to free up time for their employees to take training. In addition, SMEs often lack experience and training facilities to provide their employees with adequate opportunities to upgrade their skills and acquire new ones.

The National Human Resources Development Consortium (CHAMP) programme addresses a number of organisational and technical constraints faced by SMEs, as it provides financial incentives for large companies, business associations and universities to set up consortia for sharing know-how, equipment and training facilities with SMEs. Another important strength of the CHAMP programme is the provision of training that is relevant to the labour market, with a clear focus on practical and relevant work problems, since in essence this programme is based on a win-win strategy between training providers – most often a large firm – and beneficiaries.

Steps could be taken to further extend the CHAMP programme through specific measures, in close collaboration with the PES or Job Hope Centres for middle-aged and elderly people. For instance, the CHAMP programme could be backed up with support and assistance measures for SMEs to recruit a replacement worker for an employee on training, including public subsidies for hiring an unemployed person.

From a longer-term perspective, it is crucial to develop effective tools for measuring and recognising skills and competencies that workers acquire throughout their careers. The national qualification system has remained too focused on technical skills and does not constitute anymore an adequate screening device for employers, a proper signalling device for employees or a relevant policy tool for public authorities to evaluate skill developments and anticipate skill needs. The development of new National Competency Standards (NCS) is an important step forward as this is designed to provide a better picture of the skills and abilities that are required for various jobs and occupations at the industry level, in line with the competencies actually used and needed in the labour market. The big remaining challenge for the government is to operationalise and promote the effective use of the NCS. This requires a comprehensive package of measures to reflect the NCS in both vocational education and training provisions and qualifications frameworks to improve their labour market relevance. The reform process is underway, but more could be done to mobilise all relevant stakeholders, including training providers, employers' organisations and trade unions, who will ultimately be responsible for the successful implementation of the NCS.

Strengthening public employment services and active labour market policies

The Public Employment Service (PES) provides a range of outplacement services and training opportunities to older workers. It mainly focuses on facilitating the matching between jobseekers and job vacancies, with less attention paid to monitoring job-search activities. As in many OECD countries, this matching function relies increasingly on online services, with public portals offering integrated employment services (Work-Net) and guidance for skill development (HRD-Net).

In addition, specialised employment services are offered for vulnerable individuals aged 40 and over. These Job Hope Centres for middle-aged and elderly people provide a wide range of re-employment services tailored to individual needs. Going beyond the matching function, counselling and guidance services are provided to older workers who need (re)training before starting their job search, and often lack the basic ICT skills needed to use online services. In addition, subsidies and counselling services are made available to firms providing outplacement services to their pre-retired employees. The government's plan to make the provision of outplacement services mandatory for larger firms is commendable. Such change in legislation should affect medium-sized companies as well, maybe only excluding firms with less than 20 or 50 employees.

PES interventions, however, remain limited in scope. Korea's spending on active labour market programmes (ALMPs), at 0.37% of GDP in 2016, is only somewhat lower than the OECD average of 0.5%, partly because of a low level of unemployment. However, much of Korea's ALMP spending is for direct job creation while spending on training and employment subsidies is low. Moreover, spending on the administration of the PES, at 0.04% of GDP, is also just one-quarter of the corresponding OECD average. For the future, priory must be given to the most effective support measures for the unemployed, such as the Employment Success Package Programme. There is now compelling evidence that intensive job-search assistance coupled with targeted training can have large positive employment effects, while direct job creation is found to be less effective in terms of a sustainable transition into the labour market.

Steps should be taken to reduce spending on direct job-creation programmes in favour of expanding and strengthening ESPP and second-career guidance for mid-career and older workers. Alongside an expansion of ESPP, the income support provided to those ESPP participants who are not eligible for unemployment or social assistance payments should be increased while the screening process for participants should be made stricter to assess and monitor work motivation more closely and provide job-related training tailored to their needs. Likewise, steps should be taken to strengthen early intervention measures provided to mid-career and older workers by Job Hope Centres in order to help them prepare for their second careers after mandatory early retirement. In particular, these measures could include a comprehensive assessment of skills and work experience complemented by additional training sessions when necessary and, most importantly, by a formal recognition and validation of acquired skills and competencies.

Tackling working conditions

Progress has been achieved recently in terms of lowering working hours and establishing occupational health and safety systems, but further steps need to be taken to improve the working conditions especially for older workers. Many of them are still working long hours and this age group has been facing an increasing risk of occupational accidents in recent years.

While the new guidelines on working time are an important step forward, the government should assess their implementation closely to ensure the expected outcomes are achieved, also in SMEs. Reducing working hours of older workers is challenging since, in practice, older people need to work long hours to make ends meet before their retirement. Adequate income support is therefore critical, while employers would also need to be provided with guidance and consulting services.

Beginning in 2016, the Korean government introduced a new allowance system for older workers aged 50 or above, which subsidises 50% of their reduced income if they work 32 hours or less per week. This allowance could be a significant channel to promote the reduction of working hours and to retain older workers longer in their main job. It may also provide more time for older workers to participate in further training to enhance their productivity. In addition, the government should introduce a system which provides older workers with the right to request a reduction of working hours for health reasons if necessary. The combination of legal rights and financial supports could lay a solid foundation, thereby facilitating the reduction of working hours for older workers.

In order to reduce occupational accidents and improve the health of older workers, specific measures should be taken tailored to their labour market situation. It is essential to ensure older workers are aware of the risk factors they face in their job – especially any new job – and know how to deal with or avoid those risks before they start a new job. Employers should take into account the physical and mental health conditions of their older employees to ensure the overall work environment, including machinery, working tools, work methods, support from co-workers and supervisors, and working hours, is well adapted to their health conditions. The government could also consider establishing effective systems for monitoring the health of older workers, in cooperation with local health institutions. In addition, steps should be taken to introduce employer-financed paid sick leave and a statutory sickness benefit to facilitate the return to (main) jobs by workers facing temporary health problems.

The following policy actions could be considered:

- *Strengthen and expand the CHAMP programme through specific measures*, in close collaboration with the PES and Job Hope Centres. For instance, the CHAMP programme could be backed up with support and assistance measures for SMEs to recruit a replacement worker, coupled with public subsidies for hiring an unemployed person as a replacement for the employee on training.
- *Involve all relevant stakeholders in the implementation of the new National Competency Standards*. Vocational education and training providers, employers' associations and trade unions should be mobilised more effectively since they will be responsible for disseminating and implementing the new standards.
- *Refocus ALMP expenditure on the most effective support measures*. Steps should be taken to reduce spending on direct job-creation programmes, to strengthen

and expand ESPP and early intervention measures for workers nearing retirement.

- *Strengthen second-career guidance for middle-aged and older workers*. Support measures should include a comprehensive assessment of a worker's skills and work experiences, complemented by additional training sessions where necessary and alongside formal recognition and validation of acquired skills competencies.
- *Monitor closely the implementation of the new guidelines on working time* to ensure that the expected outcomes are achieved for all types of businesses, including SMEs. In addition, steps should be taken to provide older workers with a right to request reduced working hours if it is necessary for health reasons.
- *Explore possibilities to establish an effective system for monitoring the health conditions of older workers*, in cooperation with local health institutions. This would allow preventive actions whereby older workers could be informed about the risk factors they may face in their (new) job and provided with guidance on how to deal with or avoid those risk factors.
- *Introduce a period of employer-paid sick leave and a statutory cash sickness benefit as discussed at length in a recent OECD report.* Such measures would facilitate the return to the main job of workers experiencing health problems.

Chapter 1. The challenge of population ageing in Korea

This chapter evaluates the main demographic factors underpinning population ageing in Korea. It looks at some of the main impacts population ageing is likely to have on Korea's labour market and on social cohesion and, by extension, on the broader economy.

The statistical date for Israel are supplied by and under the responsibility of the relevant Israeli authorities. The use of such data by the OECD is without prejudice to the status of the Golan Heights, East Jerusalem and Israeli settlements in the West Bank under the terms of international law.

Korea is ageing more rapidly than any other OECD country

The population of Korea is ageing more rapidly than that of any other OECD country. This is expected to place an unprecedented economic burden on the working-age population and create a challenge for policy makers and fiscal institutions. The structure of Korea's population has transformed rapidly over the past generation or two and is projected to change even more within the forthcoming two generations (Figure 1.1). While the numbers of younger Koreans have contracted significantly and are due to contract further in the coming decades, the numbers of older people have multiplied.

Such transformational demographic change has already caused individual segments of Korea's working-age population to shrink in absolute terms (Figure 1.2, Panel A). The absolute number of children and adolescents in Korea (aged 0-14) reached a peak of 13.6 million in 1972 and has since declined to roughly half of that number. The number of young working-age adults (aged 15-29) peaked in 1989 at 13.2 million and has since fallen to less than 10 million. The number of prime working-age adults (aged 30-49) has also reached a peak at 17.2 million in 2006 and is now declining. According to the latest projections from the United Nations (UN-DESA), the older working-age population in Korea (aged 50-64) is forecasted to peak in 2024 while the number of those aged 65 and above will continue to expand until 2051 (Figure 1.2, Panel B).

The scale of demographic change is forecasted to make Korea's population the oldest among OECD countries in the 2050s. The median age has increased from less than 20 years before the mid-1970s to around 41 years today – just above the OECD average – and is projected to increase to nearly 55 years before stabilising at 50-55 years thereafter. This would place Korea's median age above the age of all other OECD countries.

Demographic developments taking place in Korea will also alter the balance in society between the working-age and elderly populations. A much higher proportion of retirees for every working individual is likely to place strain on the fiscal institutions and on the delivery of public services. Korea currently has 177 residents aged 65 and above for every 1 000 persons of working age. This ratio – known as the old-age dependency ratio – was considerably lower than the OECD average of 246 in 2015. The figure for Korea, however, is projected to quadruple in the coming decades, exceeding the OECD average by around the year 2025 and peaking at a projected 760 by around 2065 – the highest ratio of any OECD country – according to the latest UN projections (Figure 1.3, Panel B). This represents a sharp contrast to most of the 1980s, when Korea's dependency ratio was around 65-70 and thus one of the lowest in the OECD (Figure 1.3, Panel A).

Figure 1.1. The structure of Korea's population is changing significantly

Population in Korea by sex and age group, estimate for 2015 and comparison with one and two generations ago plus projections for one and two generations ahead (millions)

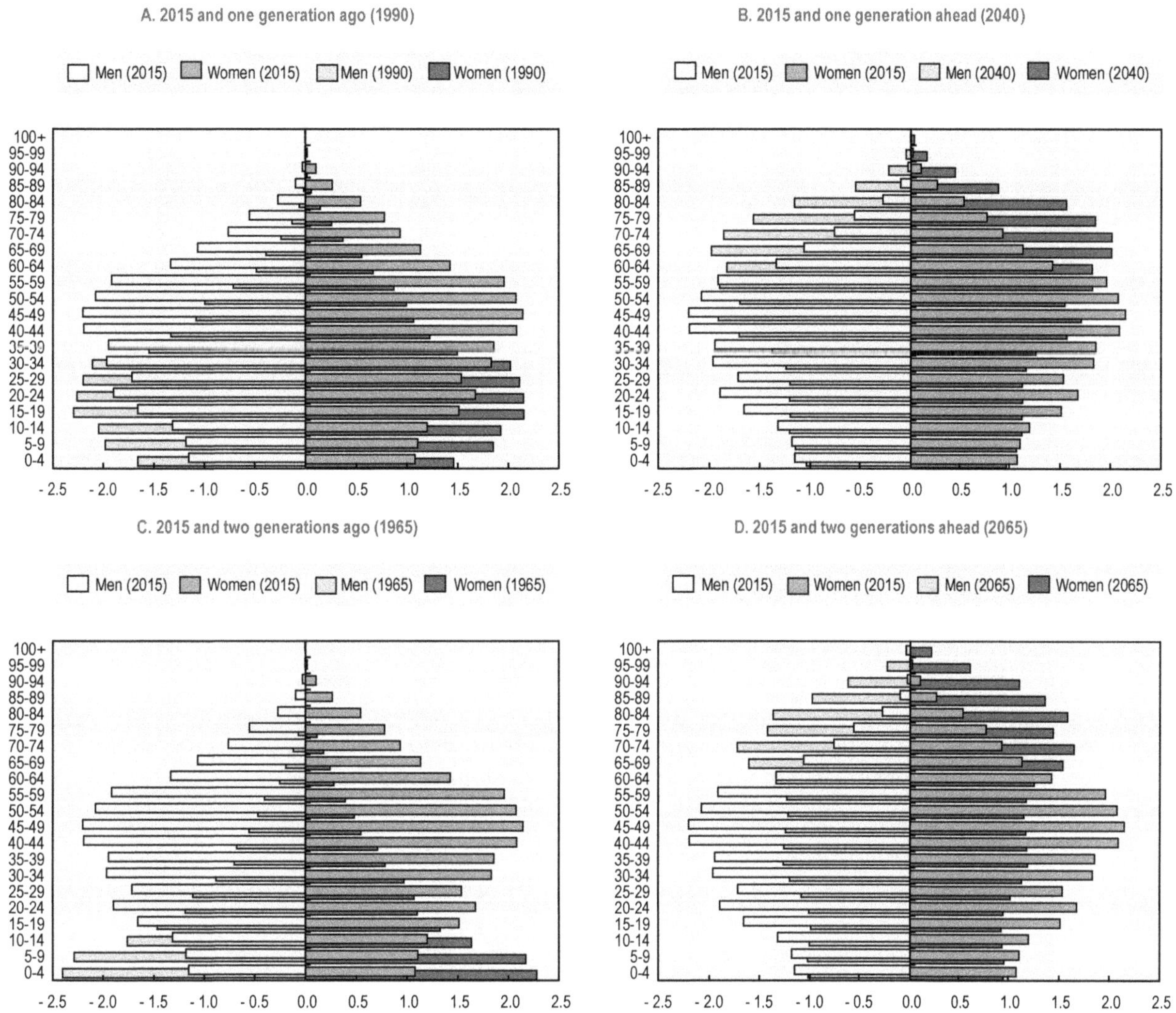

Note: One "generation" stands for a period of 25 years. Projections are based on the medium fertility variant. Estimates for age groups 80 and above in 1965 are missing.

Source: United Nations, Department of Economic and Social Affairs, Population Division (2017) *World Population Prospects: The 2017 Revision.*

StatLink http://dx.doi.org/10.1787/888933831564

Figure 1.2. Korea's youth and working-age population is already declining in absolute terms

Population in Korea by broad age group, estimates 1965-2015 and projections 2016-65 (millions)

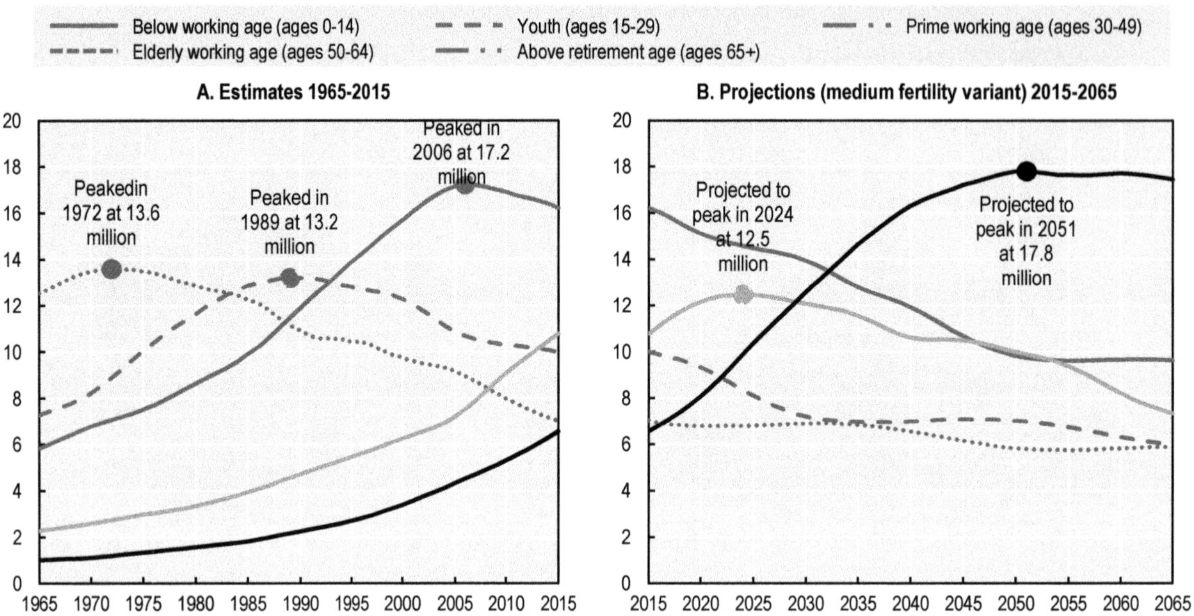

Note: Projections are based on the medium fertility variant.

Source: United Nations, Department of Economic and Social Affairs, Population Division (2017) *World Population Prospects: The 2017 Revision.*

StatLink http://dx.doi.org/10.1787/888933831583

Figure 1.3. Korea had the lowest dependency ratio of any OECD country during the 1970s and 1980s but is projected to have the highest by the 2060s

Number of people aged 65 or above in selected OECD countries for every 1 000 of the working-age population (ages 15-64), estimates 1965-2015 and projections 2016-65

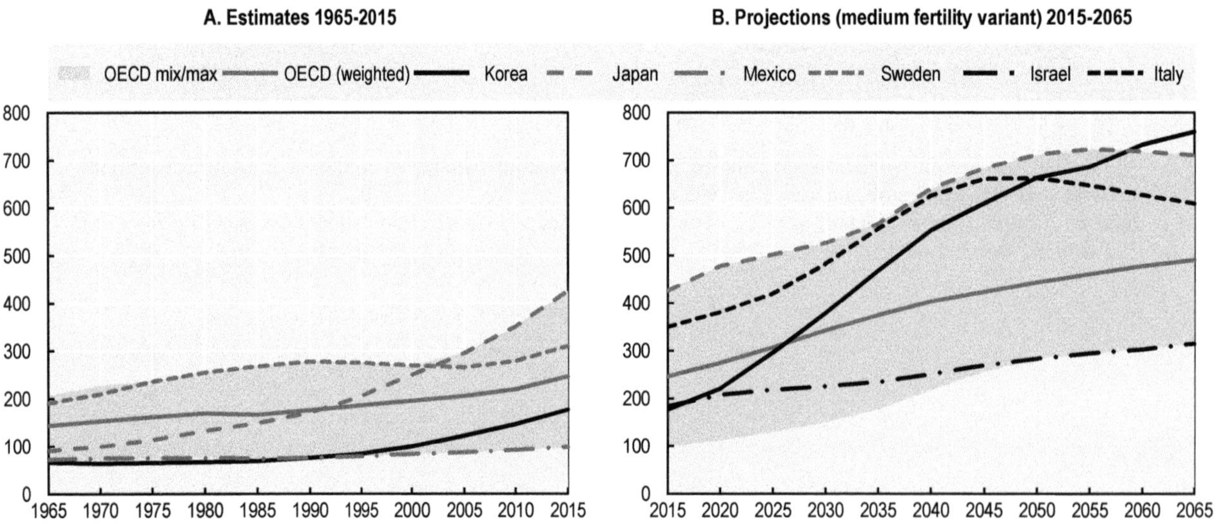

Note: Projections are based on the medium fertility variant.

Source: United Nations, Department of Economic and Social Affairs, Population Division (2017) *World Population Prospects: The 2017 Revision.*

StatLink http://dx.doi.org/10.1787/888933831602

The workforce itself is also ageing fast. Korea's older workers will soon play a major role in their country's economic performance. Workers aged 55-64 years are projected to make up 28.6% of Korea's 20-64 year-olds by 2050 – the highest proportion among all OECD countries (Figure 1.4, Panel B). Korea's potential labour force, meanwhile, is projected to shrink dramatically by 2050, losing 30% of its absolute number in 2015 – second only to Japan among OECD countries (Figure 1.4, Panel C).[1] In many OECD countries, including Japan and Korea but also many countries in the south and east of Europe, the number of people in the age group 65-69 – assuming people will work five years longer on average – will not be enough to compensate the potential rapid decline of the labour force (Figure 1.4, Panel A).

Population ageing might have consequences for economic performance

OECD countries' diverse experiences show that population ageing could, but need not, lead to worse economic outcomes. In Germany, for example, the working-age population has steadily declined in absolute terms over the past two decades, substantially increasing the financial burden on the workforce although Germany has managed to maintain a strong social model – though reformed under the "Hartz Reforms" of the early-2000s – and to maintain robust economic performance. Italy's experience, by contrast, has been somewhat gloomier: despite a more favourable demographic context, Italy has faced a prolonged period of economic stagnation, low productivity growth and rising public debt; maybe because labour market reforms have been postponed for too long, until the Jobs Act in 2012 and 2014.

The pace and extent of Korea's forthcoming demographic changes will likely have important consequences for economic performance given that labour resource utilisation is a key pillar of the Korean economy (Figure 1.5, Panel A). Labour productivity in Korea lags behind that of many other OECD countries. Korea's below-average level of GDP per capita reflects a productivity gap not fully compensated by its comparative advantage in terms of labour utilisation. While the number of hours worked per capita in Korea was 36% higher than the OECD average (and the highest among all OECD countries), labour productivity – measured as GDP per hour worked – was 37% lower than the OECD average (the fifth lowest after Mexico, Chile, Latvia and Poland). Rapid population ageing in Korea will gradually erode its comparative advantage in terms of labour inputs, even alongside higher labour force participation rates. Policies to support productivity growth are therefore crucial for Korea to sustain the trend of rising living standards observed in previous decades.

Figure 1.4. The potential labour force will shrink fast in Korea in the next 30 years

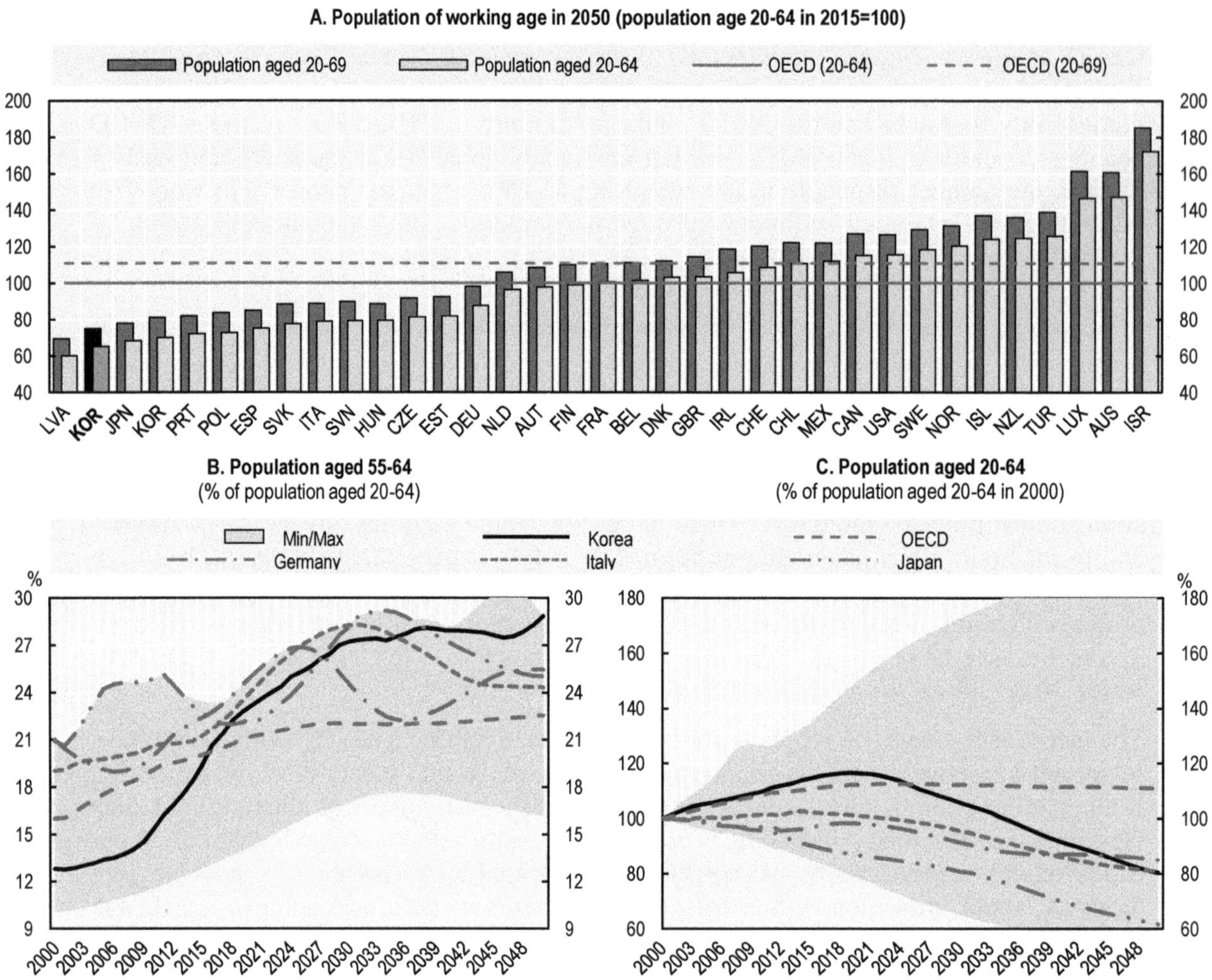

Note: Data in Panel A show the extent to which the decline in the population age 20-64 could be compensated by a shift in the age span of the working population to also include the age group 65-69 (which roughly corresponds to an increase in the retirement age by five years).
Source: OECD Historical population data and projections (1950-2050).

StatLink http://dx.doi.org/10.1787/888933831621

On a more positive note, it is noteworthy that productivity gains remain an important engine of economic growth in Korea (Figure 1.5, Panel B). Labour productivity rose at an annual rate of 3% over 2009-15 – three times the OECD average over the same period.

While the global economic crisis substantially slowed down productivity growth in many OECD countries, demographic pressures could potentially make things worse for Korea, ceteris paribus. Nevertheless, there is room for improvement. First, Korea's absolute gap in productivity with more advanced countries implies that there remains important untapped potential for productivity gains that the government is currently pursuing through a wide range of reforms (see OECD, 2016). Second, Korea's population is becoming rapidly more highly educated (Figure 1.6), which is a key enabling factor for investment in innovation and productivity gains.

Figure 1.5. Economic performance, labour utilisation and labour productivity

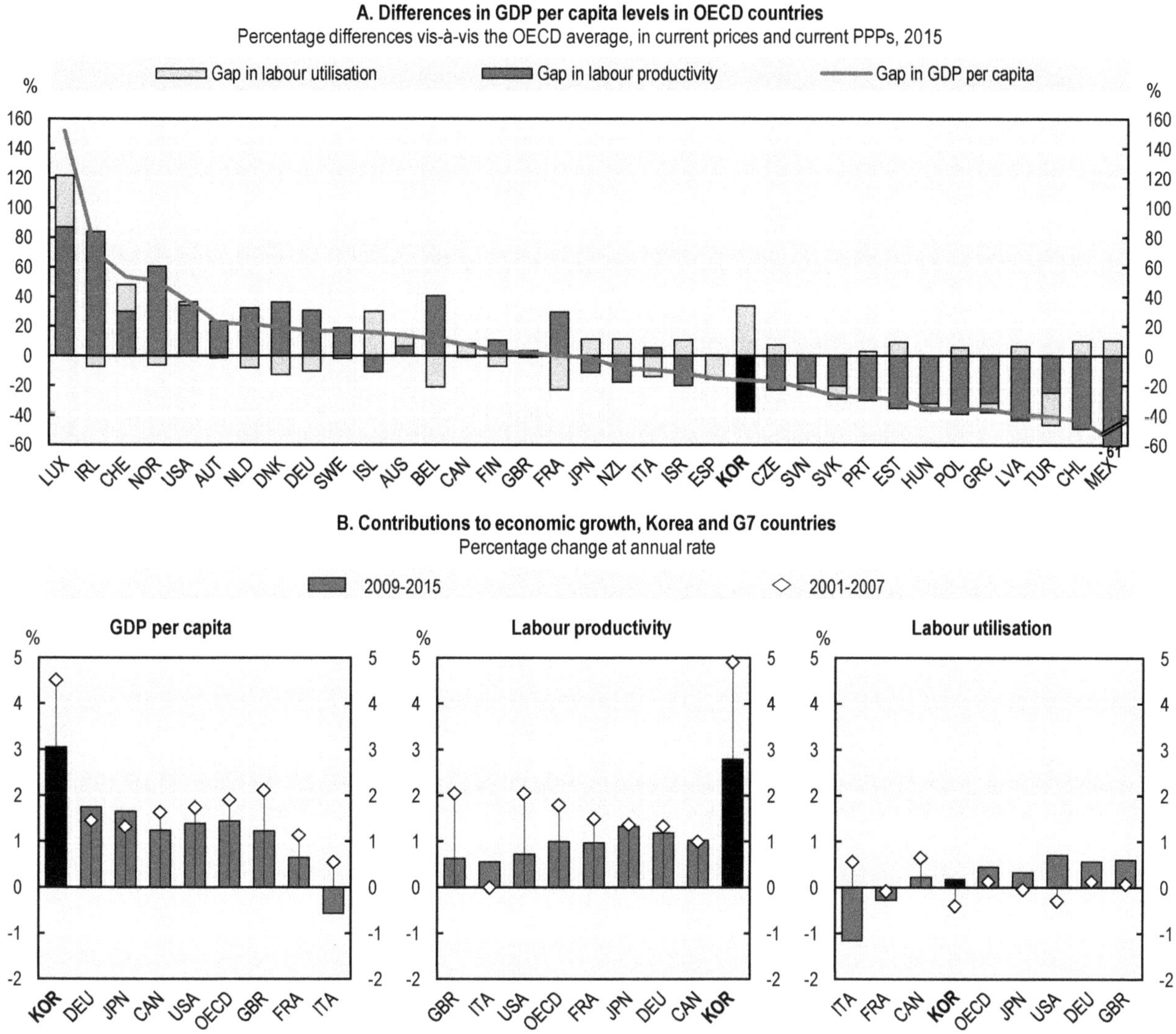

Note: Labour utilisation is measured by the number of hours worked per capita; labour productivity refers to GDP per hour worked.
Source: OECD (2017), *OECD Compendium of Productivity Indicators*.

StatLink http://dx.doi.org/10.1787/888933831640

While only 20% of Koreans aged 55-64 had a tertiary-level qualification in 2016 (compared with 26% on average in OECD countries), a full 70% of those aged 25-34 did – the highest share for that age-group of any other OECD country and well above the OECD average of 43%. The magnitude of this difference in educational attainment between younger and older cohorts is a unique feature of the Korean workforce. Provided that available skills can adequately meet businesses' needs in the coming decades, expanding tertiary education can be a major source of productivity gains.

Figure 1.6. Educational attainment has drastically improved for young Koreans

Persons with tertiary education, share of population in each age group, 2016

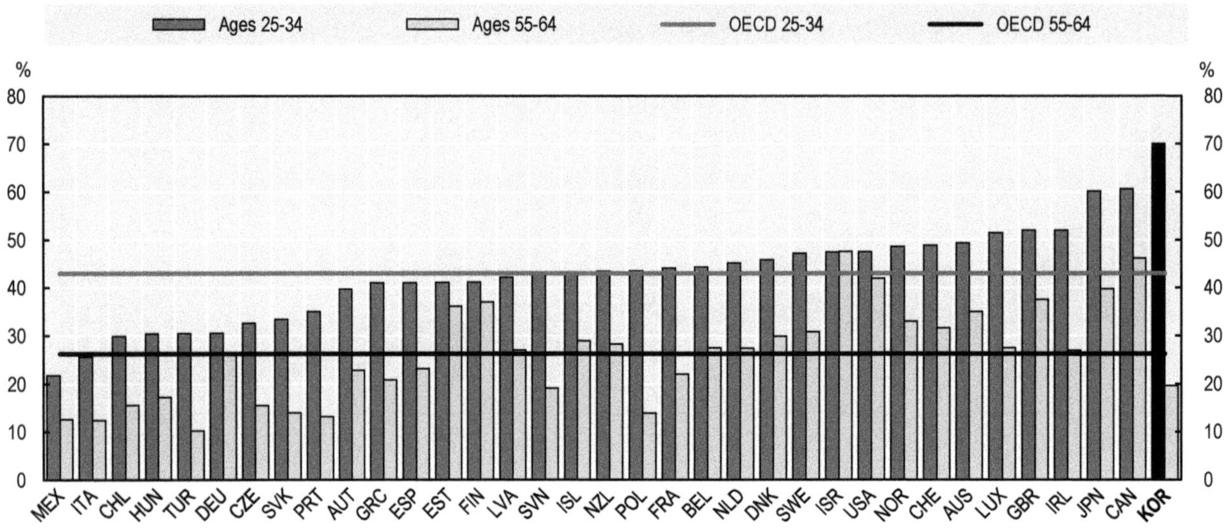

Note: Data for Chile and Ireland refer to 2015.
Source: *OECD Dataset on Educational Attainment and Labour Force Status*, http://stats.oecd.org//Index.aspx?QueryId=79284.

StatLink http://dx.doi.org/10.1787/888933831659

Policies for addressing population ageing should follow a broad perspective covering both short- and longer-term issues. Korea could have the best qualified cohort of older workers in the OECD within one generation if young cohorts are provided with adequate opportunities to upgrade their skills and learn new ones throughout their working lives.

Population ageing could also threaten social cohesion

In 2014, one in every seven Koreans lived in households with a disposable income below 50% of the median – a proportion similar to the OECD average (Figure 1.7, Panel A). But the risk of poverty is unevenly distributed across age in Korea, much more so than in other OECD countries: while poverty rates for young and prime-age Koreans are nearly half the OECD average, they are significantly higher for those in their 50s and above. At almost 15% in 2014, the poverty rate for Koreans aged 51-65 was more than double that of their counterparts aged 41-50. Furthermore, just over two fifths of Koreans aged 66-74 and three fifths of those aged 75 and above were poor – both groups more than three times the relevant OECD average. In part, these outcomes reflect the fact that Korea's pension system is not yet fully mature. More generally, however, these outcomes point towards a need for stronger social protection measures that older people can access.

For Korea's rapidly ageing population, tackling old-age poverty – including among older workers – is essential to maintaining social cohesion. Assuming that the level and age composition of poverty rates would remain unchanged, Korea could face the highest overall poverty rate among OECD countries by 2030 (Figure 1.7, Panel B). While the expected change in the population structure by age – all else being equal – would have almost no impact on poverty among other OECD countries, on average, the incidence of poverty in Korea could increase to 20% of the total population by 2030 and exceed 25% by 2050. Ameliorating this would require bringing the poverty risk faced by Koreans aged 65 and above in line with the OECD average. While these figures are merely illustrative (and must not be regarded as projections), they demonstrate the enormous pressure population ageing is putting on social protection expenditure in Korea.

Figure 1.7. The likelihood to live in a low-income household is very high for older Koreans

Percentage of individuals living in households with disposable income below 50% of the median income

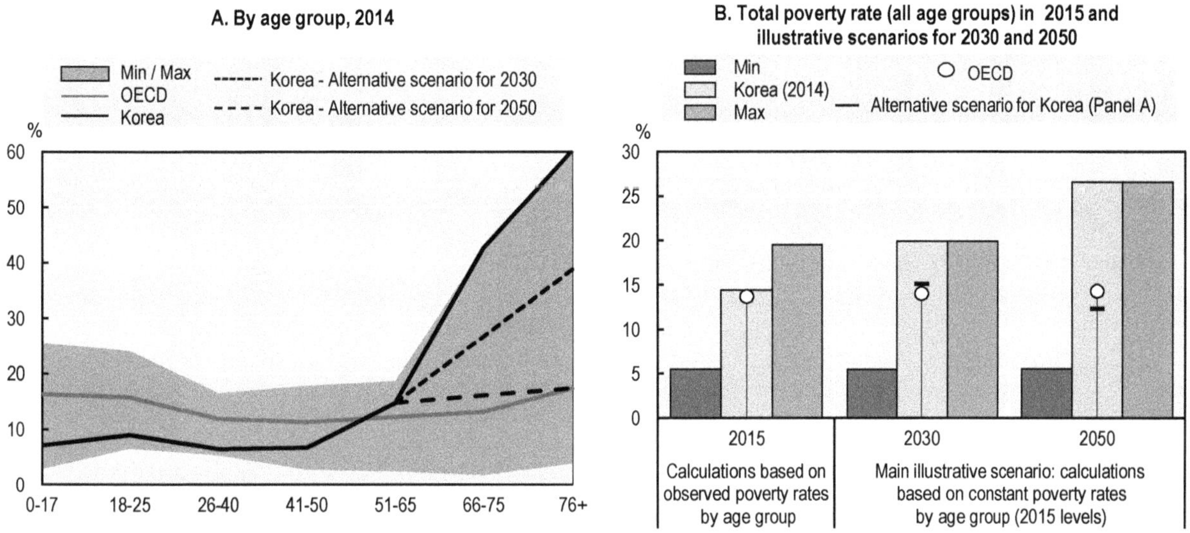

Note: For the Min, Max and OECD average, data refer to 2015, except for Australia, Hungary, Iceland and New Zealand (2014) and Japan (2012).
Source: *OECD Database on Income Distribution and Poverty*, http://stats.oecd.org//Index.aspx?QueryId=66596.

StatLink http://dx.doi.org/10.1787/888933831678

Korea has a number of strengths and opportunities to help it meet the challenge of population ageing. First, higher educational attainment among future cohorts of elderly workers in Korea should help them to sort into more productive and rewarding jobs. Second, more robust old-age pension rights will enable future cohorts of retirees in Korea a higher standard of living. Finally, Korea also has the fiscal space to comprehensively strengthen its social protection institutions while ensuring that public social spending remains cost-effective, employment-friendly and efficiently financed (OECD, 2016).

Meeting these conditions could enable Korea's government to increase both public expenditures and revenues to levels closer to the OECD average without endangering growth prospects (Figure 1.8). Stable growth is further ensured by Korea's strong fiscal position and low government debt. Korea had a budget surplus of 1.4% of GDP in 2015, as compared with a budget deficit averaging 2.8% of GDP across all OECD countries. Korea's general government debt was equal to 45.8% of GDP in 2014 – less than half of the OECD average.

Figure 1.8. Korea's sound public finances provide room for social protection reforms

Selected indicators of public finance (general government) as a percentage of GDP, 2015

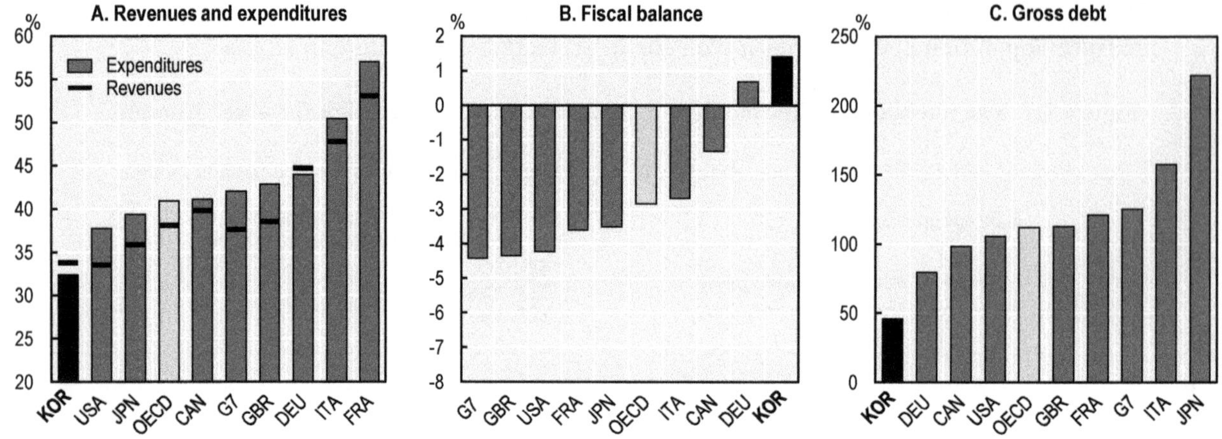

Source: OECD (2017), Government at a Glance 2017, OECD Publishing, Paris.

StatLink http://dx.doi.org/10.1787/888933831697

Conclusion

Korea's population is ageing faster than that of any other OECD country. While many of the key trends are already being felt, the biggest change will occur within the next three or four decades. The number of Koreans aged 65 and above per 1 000 of the working-age population is forecast to quadruple between 2015 and the late-2050s – the highest old-age dependency ratio of any OECD country. Over the same period, the median age of the Korean population is projected to increase from its current 41 years – just one year higher than the OECD average – to nearly 54 – also the highest of any OECD country. Only five decades ago, Korea's median age was 18, one of the lowest in the OECD.

Demographic change on such a significant scale will require concerted policy action on several fronts to safeguard Korea's economy and ensure social cohesion. The following chapters focus, in particular, on what precisely can be done to improve outcomes for Korea's ageing workforce. Three key themes include tackling old-age poverty through more rewarding work; improving opportunities for older workers to find and retain quality work; and boosting individuals' employability throughout their working lives.

Note

[1] Among the G7 economies, only Germany, Japan, and (to a lesser extent) Italy are facing comparable demographic challenges and declining working-age populations. In Germany, the working-age population started to decrease in the mid-1990s (shrinking by 4.1% between 1996 and 2015). In Japan, this happened slightly later but at a higher pace (down 10.4% by 2015 from a peak in 1998). In Italy, the working-age population has continued to grow over the past two decades but at a very low rate. These three countries have experience with population ageing, as also witnessed by their old-age dependency ratios which, at 35% or above in 2015, were high by OECD standards – much higher than Korea's current ratio (see Figure 1.1).

Chapter 2. The exceptional labour market situation of older workers in Korea

This chapter evaluates the leading trends around employment outcomes for older workers in Korea. It focuses on a positive message and a concerning one: while older workers in Korea participate in the labour market more actively than their peers in any other OECD country, they face consistently poor labour market outcomes in terms of job quality – including around the type of work they do, their job security and the remuneration they receive. The analysis lays out some of the main contributing factors.

The statistical date for Israel are supplied by and under the responsibility of the relevant Israeli authorities. The use of such data by the OECD is without prejudice to the status of the Golan Heights, East Jerusalem and Israeli settlements in the West Bank under the terms of international law.

Strong participation for relatively little gain

The labour market situation of older workers in Korea may be summed up in two overarching and contradictory phenomena: older Koreans participate in the labour force more actively than their peers in virtually every other OECD country while the quality of the jobs they hold – in terms of their employment status, job security and remuneration – is incredibly poor. This apparent paradox at the heart of Korea's labour market has no parallel in any other OECD country.

This exceptional situation results, in large part, from the lack of alternative options many among Korea's elderly population encounter. In the lack of a strong social safety net, many find employment to be the only viable means to a livelihood and the only alternative to poverty. Meanwhile, weaknesses around the poor quality of jobs older workers in Korea encounter stem directly from the widespread practice of early retirement from the main job (for most, aged in their early-50s) and the commencement of a "second career" (see Chapter 4). Older workers with adequate savings often launch a second career that involves self-employment or business ownership. While many go down this route, few have the necessary business skills to achieve high productivity and business success. Older workers who frame their second career around a salaried position may be obliged to find work in an altogether alternative economic sector and usually face a low bargaining position. This, all too often, results precisely in poorer working conditions, lower job security and a step down in terms of pay.

With most Koreans effectively retiring only in their 70s, a second career can often extend for up to two decades or more. Renewed policy initiatives to ensure a better deal for older workers – and securing a stable livelihood with decent work conditions – are therefore a priority in Korea.

The OECD's Older Workers Scoreboard gathers a number of indicators to track and elucidate key features of the labour market situation of older workers. Table 2.1 presents these indicators, comparing the findings for Korea with the OECD averages in 2006 and 2016. The main findings for Korea include:

- *Demographic situation*: Korea's old-age dependency ratio is relatively low for now, compared to the OECD average (though it is due to rise rapidly over the coming decades, see Chapter 1). Most Korean workers, nevertheless, remain within the labour force until their early 70s – almost seven years longer than the OECD average for men and around 8½ years longer for women, as of 2016.
- *Employment*: Employment rates among those aged 50-74 are considerably higher in Korea (62.1% in 2016) than the OECD average (50.8%). The gap has also widened slightly over the past decade or so. While more women in Korea are employed in older age than in many other OECD countries, Korea nevertheless has a higher gender gap in employment.
- *Job characteristics*: Older workers in Korea work relatively longer hours than their peers in most other OECD countries, with part-time work accounting for only 11.7% of those aged 55-64 in 2016, compared with an OECD average of 21.1%. Older workers in Korea are also much more likely to be in temporary work (32.7% compared with 7.9% among salaried workers); to be self-employed (38.2% compared with 32.8% among all those employed); and to earn less than their younger counterparts.

Table 2.1. Older workers scoreboard, Korea and the OECD area, 2006 and 2016

	Korea		OECD[a]		Change	
Demographic situation	2006	2016	2006	2016	Korea	OECD
-- Old-age dependency ratio	0.14	0.20	0.23	0.28	0.05	0.05
-- Effective labour force exit age[b] (years) Men	70.9	72.0	63.6	65.1	1.0	1.5
Women	67.6	72.2	62.3	63.6	4.6	1.3
Employment						
-- Employment rate, 50-74 (% of the age group)	56.8	62.1	47.0	50.8	5.3	3.8
of which 50-54	72.6	77.7	73.8	75.7	5.1	1.9
55-64	59.3	66.1	52.7	59.2	6.9	6.5
65-69	42.4	45.0	20.3	25.5	2.6	5.2
70-74	31.9	32.6	12.0	14.6	0.7	2.6
-- Gender gap in employment, 55-64 [(men-women)/men]	0.36	0.32	0.32	0.25	-0.04	-0.07
Job characteristics						
-- Incidence of part-time work, 55-64 (% of total employment)	11.8	11.7	20.3	21.1	-0.1	0.8
Average number of weekly hours worked	18.3	18.6	16.6	16.9	0.3	0.3
-- Incidence of temporary work, 55-64 (% of employees)	39.1	32.7	8.9	7.9	-6.4	-1.0
-- Incidence of self-employment, 55-64 (% of total employment)	53.2	38.2	38.0	32.8	-15.0	-5.2
-- Full-time earnings[c], 55-64 relative to 25-54 (ratio)	0.90	0.91	1.09	1.10	0.01	0.00
Dynamics						
-- Retention rate[d], after 60 (% of employees t-5)	18.2	23.4	40.3	50.3	5.2	10.0
-- Hiring rate[e], 55-64 (% of employees)	44.6	33.9	9.2	9.1	-10.7	-0.1
Joblessness						
-- Unemployment rate, 55-64 (% of the labour force)	2.3	2.8	4.3	4.6	0.4	0.3
-- Incidence of long-term[f] unemployment, 55-64 (% of total unemployment)	(1.1)	(1.0)	26.3	44.3	0.1	17.9
Employability						
-- Share of 55-64 with tertiary education (% of the age group)	10.6	19.7	20.0	26.2	9.1	6.1
-- Participation in training[g], 55-64						
Absolute (% of all employed in the age group)	-	31.2	-	41.2	-	-
Relative to employed persons aged 25-54 (ratio)	-	0.64	-	0.78	-	-

a) Weighted averages for 35 OECD countries with the exception of earnings (27 countries) and education indicators (unweighted).

b) Effective exit age over the five-year periods 2001-06 and 2011-16. The effective exit age (also called the effective age of retirement) is calculated as a weighted average of the exit ages of each five-year age cohort, starting with the cohort aged 40 44 at the first date, using absolute changes in the labour force participation rate of each cohort as weights.

c) Mean gross monthly earnings. Year 2016 refers to 2015.

d) All employees currently aged 60-64 with job tenure of five years or more as a percentage of all employees aged 55-59 5-years previously. Year 2006 refers to 2008.

e) Employees aged 55-64 with job tenure of less than one year as a percentage of total employees. Year 2006 refers to 2007 and 2016 to 2012.

f) Unemployed for more than one year. Data in brackets are based on small sample sizes

g) Job-related training during year prior to the survey in 2012. The OECD average from PIAAC excludes Hungary, Iceland, Latvia, Luxembourg, Mexico, Portugal and Switzerland

Source: OECD estimations from the *OECD Employment Database*, *OECD Earnings Distribution Database*, *OECD Education at a Glance* and the *OECD Survey of Adult Skills* (PIAAC), see: www.oecd.org/els/employment/olderworkers.

StatLink http://dx.doi.org/10.1787/888933831944

- *Dynamics*: Retention of workers past the age of 60 was extremely low in Korea, with only 23.4% of those employed five years earlier keeping the same employer past age 60, compared with an OECD average of 50.3% in 2016. Hiring of older workers, meanwhile, was much higher in Korea than elsewhere, with 33.9% of workers aged 55-64 holding their jobs for less than one year, compared with an OECD average of 9.1% in 2016.
- *Joblessness*: Unemployment and long-term unemployment were extremely low in Korea, compared with most other OECD countries. The unemployment rate in Korea among labour force participants aged 55-64 was just 2.8% in 2016, compared with an OECD average of 4.6%. Meanwhile, the incidence of unemployment lasting longer than one year was just 1.0% among this group in Korea, compared with a significantly higher OECD average of 44.3%.
- *Employability*: Older workers in Korea have relatively low levels of educational attainment, on average, with only 19.7% of those aged 55-64 holding a tertiary-level qualification in 2016, compared with an OECD average of 26.2%. Older workers in Korea also participate less in training compared with both the OECD average and with their younger counterparts within the labour market.

The present chapter elaborates upon some of these leading trends. The following section focuses on Korea's impressive labour force participation among the elderly population. The subsequent section contrasts the initially positive findings with more concerning evidence of ongoing weaknesses around job quality for older workers in Korea – particularly in terms of their status in employment, their job security and their remuneration. A short concluding section brings together the main findings.

Labour force participation and effective retirement

Korea employs more of its elderly population than virtually any other OECD country. In 2017, Korea witnessed employment rates of 72.6% among workers aged 55-59; 60.6% among those aged 60-64; 45.5% among those aged 65-69; and 33.1% among those aged 70-74 (Figure 2.1). These shares compared with respective OECD averages that are much lower at 69.6%, 50.3%, 26.0% and 15.2%. The employment rate in Korea among those aged 70-74 was higher than in any other OECD country.

Other OECD countries that achieve high employment rates among their older populations include Iceland, Israel, Japan, New Zealand and Switzerland. None of them, however, surpass Korea in the very oldest age-brackets. The stand-out trends in Korea hold true among women and men alike. Nevertheless, there is room for improvement in raising employment rates among certain demographics – especially women aged in their 50s.

Korea's employment rate among young people aged 15-29 is slightly lower than the OECD average. This is primarily due to the fact that relatively more young Koreans take part in tertiary education than their peers in other OECD countries. Employment rates among men in Korea converge with the corresponding OECD average around age 30-34 and exceed it among older age brackets (Figure 2.2, Panel A). Among women, Korea's "M-shaped" age-employment distribution shows somewhat depressed rates among the key age brackets associated with childbirth and child care. Nevertheless, the employment rates of Korean women exceed the OECD average around age 60 to become the very highest among those aged in their 70s (Figure 2.2, Panel B).

Figure 2.1. Korea has among the highest elderly employment rates in the OECD

Employment rates in OECD countries for four age groups by sex, 2017

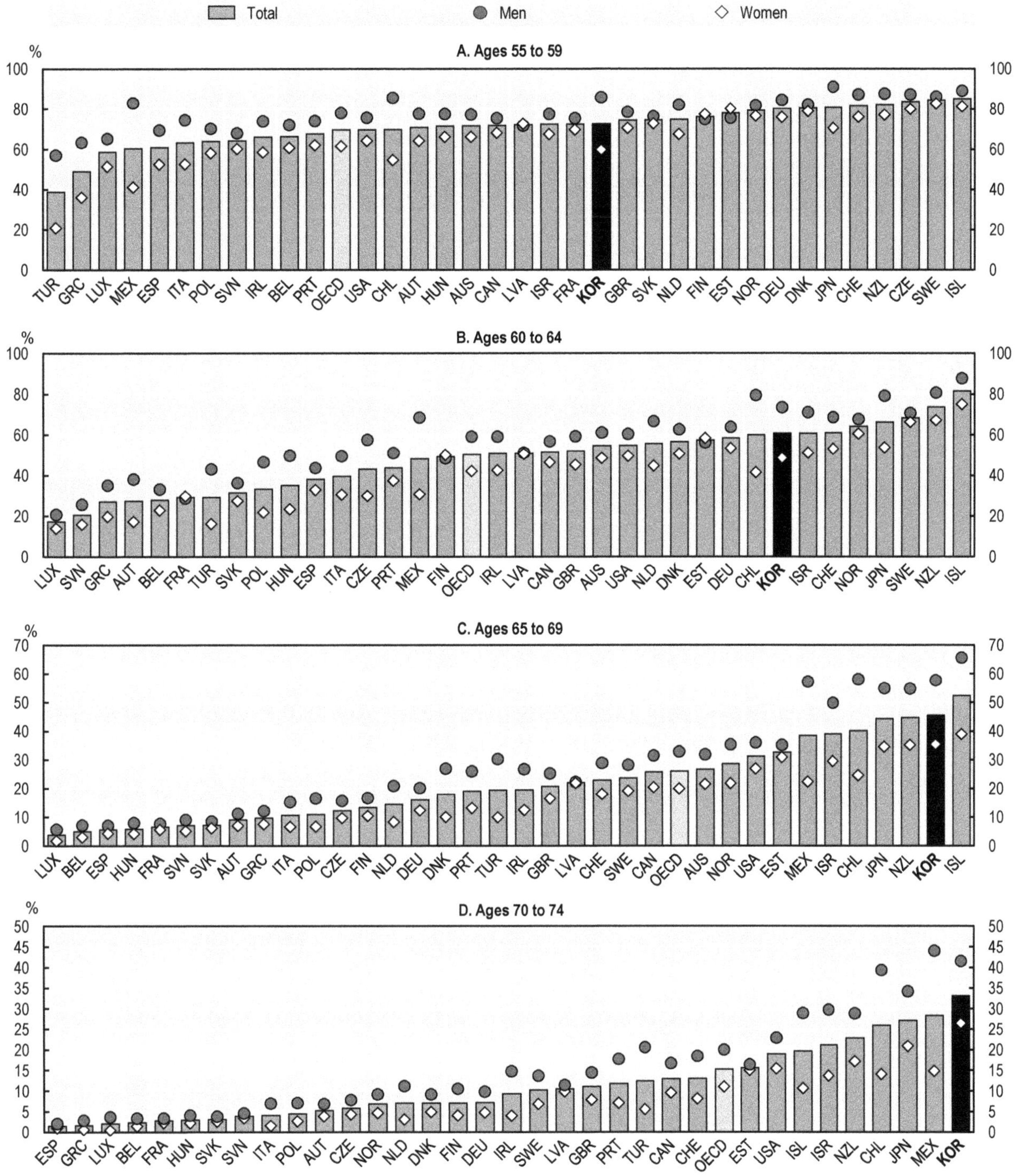

Note: OECD is the weighted average of the 35 OECD countries.
Source: *OECD Dataset LFS by sex and age - Indicators*, http://stats.oecd.org//Index.aspx?QueryId=54218.

StatLink http://dx.doi.org/10.1787/888933831716

Figure 2.2. Korea's employment rates are low among youth but high among the elderly

Employment rates in selected OECD countries by age and sex, 2017

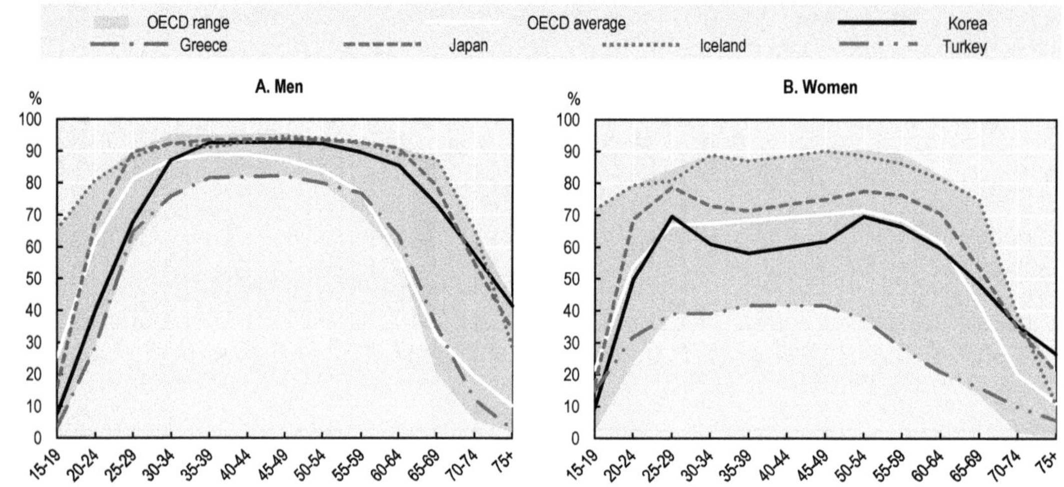

Note: Shaded area highlights the minimum and maximum values of OECD countries (excluding Korea). OECD average refers to the weighted average for all 35 OECD countries.
Source: *OECD Dataset LFS by sex and age - Indicators*, http://stats.oecd.org//Index.aspx?QueryId=54218.

StatLink http://dx.doi.org/10.1787/888933831735

Several OECD countries have observed significant increases in employment rates among older age groups over the past two decades or so. In Korea's case, too, employment rates in those groups have risen somewhat. Employment rates rose steadily among all older age groups from the mid-1980s up to the late-1990s. The Asian Economic Crisis of that time lowered the employment rates in virtually every age group significantly, though all have since regained their pre-crisis levels. In the case of women, today's rates in virtually every age category even exceed the pre-crisis levels (Figure 2.3).

Figure 2.3. Employment rates in Korea have recovered since the Asian Economic Crisis

Employment rates in Korea by age group and sex, 1980-2017

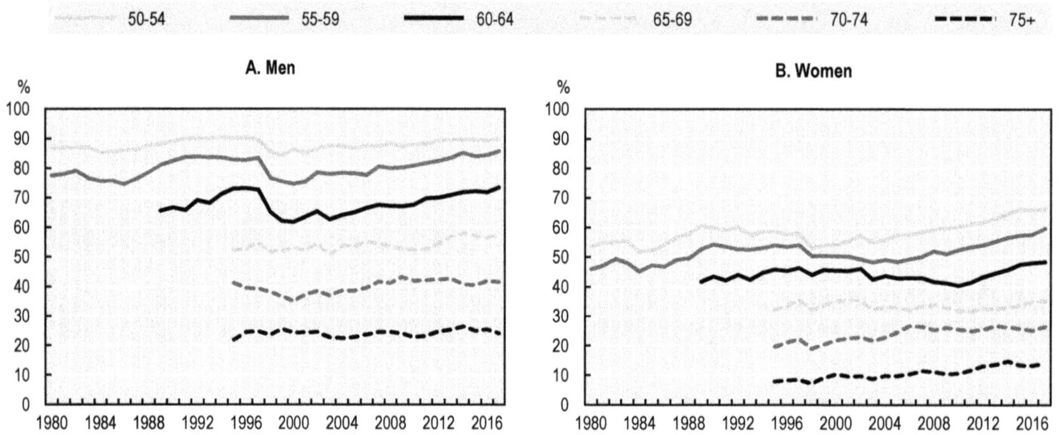

Source: *OECD Dataset LFS by sex and age - Indicators*, http://stats.oecd.org//Index.aspx?QueryId=54218.

StatLink http://dx.doi.org/10.1787/888933831754

Korea's high employment rates among the elderly partly come about through its consistently low unemployment rates among all age groups. Unemployment rates in most OECD countries tend to increase sharply with age, producing a significant bulge in their age-unemployment distributions. In the Korean case, however, unemployment rates remained consistently lower than 3% for all mature age groups in 2017 (though they were somewhat high at around 8.6-10.6% among those aged 15-29).

Korea's employment rate among the elderly has gradually increased since 1980 in line with the increase of the overall employment rate, driven by rapid economic growth. The employment rate for ages 55-64 increased 6.5% percentage points (from 61% to 67.5%) from 1980 to 2017 while the employment rate for ages 15-64 increased 7.5% points (from 59.2% to 66.6%) during the same period. On the contrary, the employment rate of older workers all across the OECD has increased substantially, from 51.5% in 1980 to 60.4% in 2017, much more so than the overall employment rate (which increased from 63.9% in 1980 to 67.8% in 2017). The larger increase in older worker employment in many countries is explained by improved incentives to work, increased pension ages and more generally a closing of early retirement pathways, sometimes including disability benefit.

High employment rates among older workers mean that average workers in Korea will effectively retire at an older age than their peers in other OECD countries. According to OECD estimates based on labour force survey data for the period 2011-16, men in Korea effectively withdraw from the labour market at an age of 72 years and women do so at 72.2 years. Both of these ages are higher than in any other OECD country – where the majority of workers effectively retire before they reach 65 years (Figure 2.4, Panel A).

Estimates based on time series data reveal that Korea's average effective retirement age was only around 66-68 years during much of the 1970s and 1980s. It began to climb significantly only during the late-1980s and currently stands higher than it has ever been (Figure 2.4, Panel B). Korea's time series defies the overall OECD trend, in which the effective retirement age steadily fell during the 1980s and 1990s but has slowly been rising – for men and women alike – since the early-2000s.

All of these trends signal a reassuring message for Korea: for a country undergoing such rapid trend of population ageing and population decline, high employment rates among older workers can nurture a more sustainable future. While many OECD countries experiencing similar demographic changes are struggling to activate their elderly populations, Korea is already there. To this end, part of the solution to Korea's ageing labour market is already in hand. The real challenge now, in terms of going forward, will be to raise the quality of the work older Koreans can access – which currently suffers from significant deficits – and to improve their overall earnings potential.

Figure 2.4. Workers in Korea effectively retire later than in any other OECD country

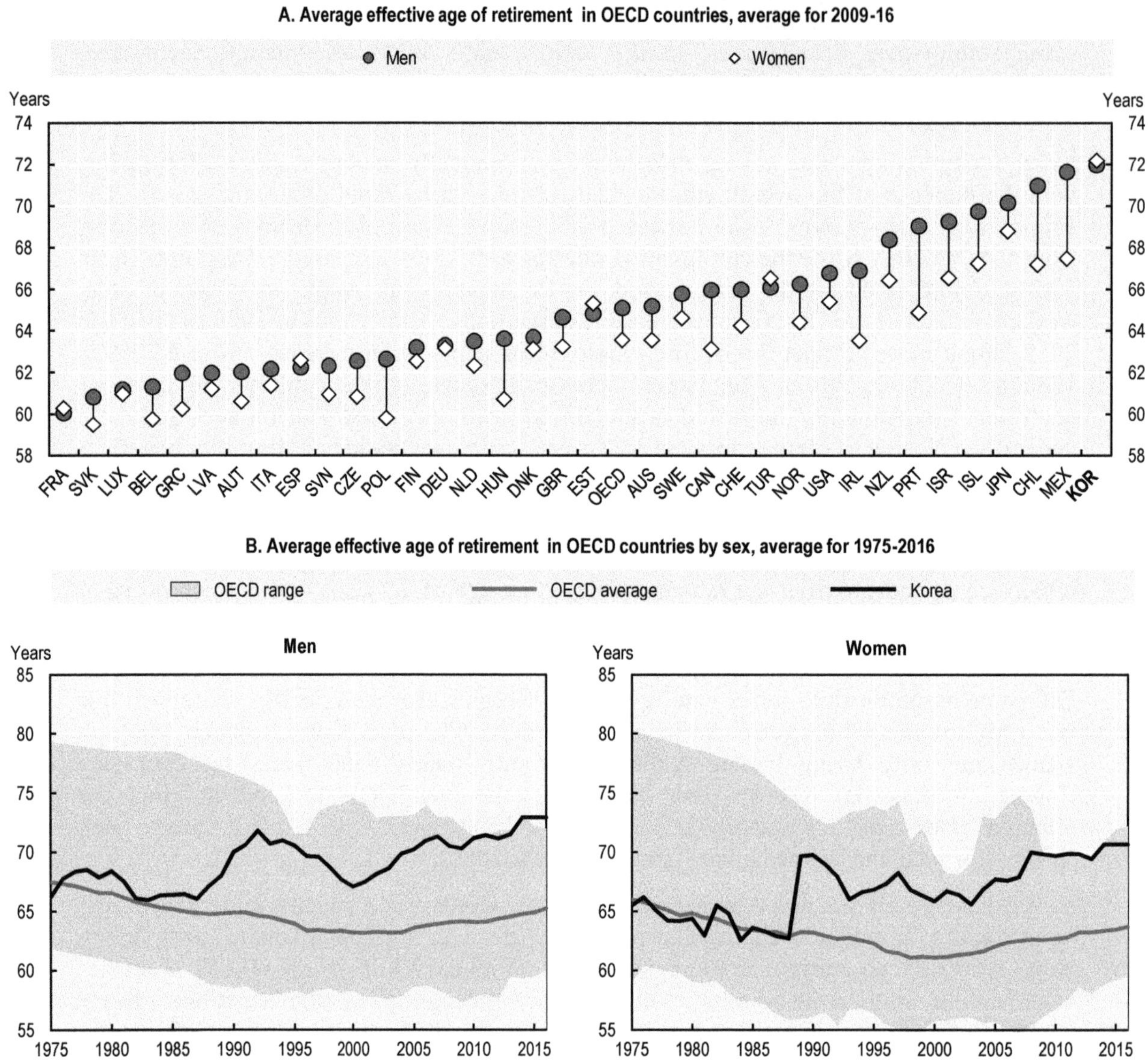

Note: The average effective age of retirement is calculated as a weighted average of (net) withdrawals from the labour market at different ages over a 5-year period for workers initially aged 40 and over. In order to abstract from compositional effects in the age structure of the population, labour force withdrawals are estimated based on changes in labour force participation rates rather than labour force levels. These changes are calculated for each (synthetic) cohort divided into 5 year age groups. The estimates for women in Turkey are based on 3-yearly moving averages of participation rates for each 5-year age group. In panel B, the OECD is the unweighted average of all OECD countries except: Iceland (before 1980); Israel (before 1990); Latvia (before 1994) and the Czech Republic, Germany, the Slovak Republic and Slovenia (before 1996). This also holds true for the range.

Source: *OECD Database on the Average Effective Age of Retirement*, www.oecd.org/els/emp/average-effective-age-of-retirement.htm.

StatLink http://dx.doi.org/10.1787/888933831773

The quality of employment for older workers

For many elderly people in Korea, high employment rates reflect not so much a desire to work as a necessity to do so. Korea's *Additional Economically Active Population Survey for Older Workers* from 2017 reveals that 58% of workers aged 55-79 work primarily to earn or supplement their living costs. Meanwhile, a lower share of only 35% say their primary reason for working is because they enjoy the work itself (Figure 2.5).

Figure 2.5. Elderly Koreans tend to work more out of necessity than by desire

Workers' intention and reasons to work, all workers aged 55-79, 2016

Source: Additional Economically Active Population Survey for Older Workers, 2017.

StatLink http://dx.doi.org/10.1787/888933831792

Ongoing gaps in Korea's social safety net and relatively small family sizes leave many elderly individuals with no alternative livelihood but through work. Even those who gain employment, however, often find that work is not an effective antidote to poverty. Poor working conditions, precarious engagement and low pay feature much more prominently in the jobs of older workers than they do for other segments of the labour market.

Employment status of older workers

One measure of the quality of employment relates to workers' status in employment and, in particular, the prevalence of "non-regular" forms of work. Under a common definition used in Korea, non-regular work encompasses three separate (sometimes overlapping) categories of salaried workers: *non-permanent workers*, who include those engaged on a temporary or fixed-term basis; *part-time workers*, who include those with 35 or fewer regular working hours per week; and *non-typical workers*, who include daily workers, contractors (either engaged for a specific task or paid on commission), temporary work agency workers, domestic workers and other such categories of workers with only loose or spurious ties to the job-giver.

Figure 2.6 shows the prevalence of all three types of non-regular work among salaried workers of different ages in Korea. Beyond age 30, the prevalence of all three types of non-regular work increases gradually with age.

Non-regular work in Korea is especially prevalent among salaried workers over age 60. In 2014, non-permanent work accounted for 42.8% in this age group (compared with 18.7% across all age-groups); part-time work accounted for 33.5% (compared with 10.8%); and non-typical work for 28.9% (compared with 11.2%). Compared to 2004, Korea has seen a significant drop in non-permanent work for workers in their 50s but not those over age 60. Relative to 2004, Korea has also seen comprehensive falls in non-typical work across all age groups, coupled with a significant rise in part-time work among those over age 60 (Figure 2.6).

Figure 2.6. Non-regular work in Korea is concentrated among the elderly

Incidence of non-regular work in Korea by age-group, 2004-14

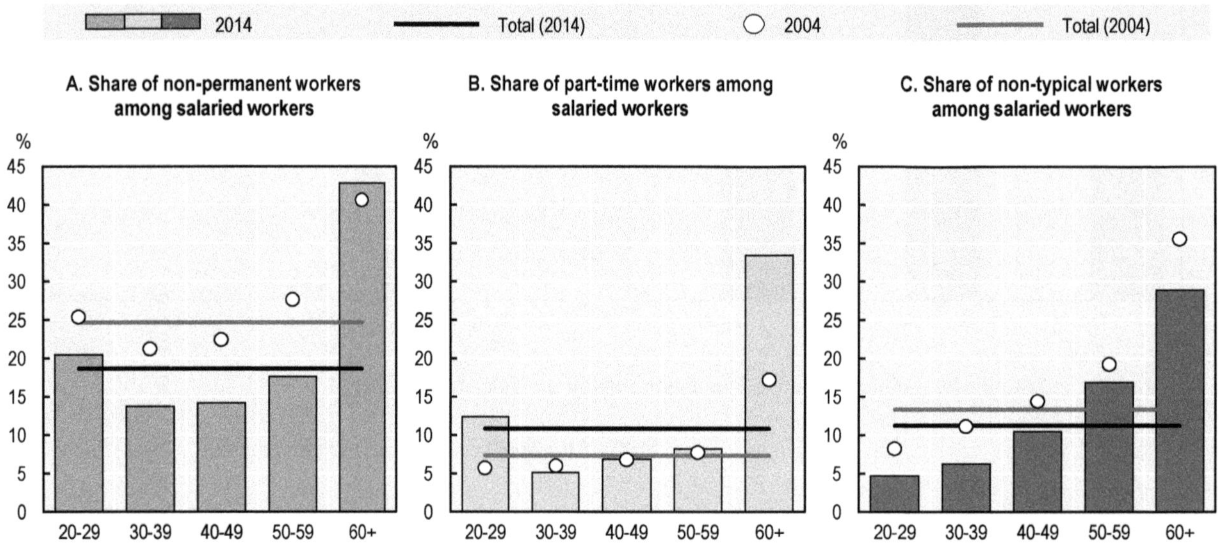

Note: Non-permanent workers comprise of salaried workers with fixed-term employment contracts and other non-permanent contract-holders (such as seconded workers, those working thorough a probationary period at work and others). Part-time work is work comprising of fewer than 36 guaranteed work-hours per week. Non-typical work comprises of daily workers, contractors (both those engaged for a specific task and those paid on commission), temporary agency workers and domestic workers.

Source: Statistics Korea (2017) Economically Active Population Survey: Additional Survey by Employment Type, via Korean Statistical Information Service (KOSIS), http://kosis.kr/eng.

StatLink http://dx.doi.org/10.1787/888933831811

Figure 2.7 compares the share of non-permanent employees in total salaried employment for a range of OECD countries. Korean workers aged 55-64 have the highest incidence of non-permanent work of all OECD countries. While non-permanent workers accounted for 18.3% of all working-age salaried workers in Korea in 2017, they accounted for a significantly higher 30.3% among those aged 55-64 (and as much as 58.4% among those aged 65 and above). In most OECD countries, older workers are *less* likely than the average salaried worker to have a non-permanent position. The converse is true, however, in only three OECD countries: Japan, Korea and Turkey.

Figure 2.7. Older workers in Korea are more likely to be in non-permanent employment than their peers in any other OECD country

Share of non-permanent workers in OECD countries – working-age population (15-64) and those aged 55-64, 2017 (% of total salaried workers)

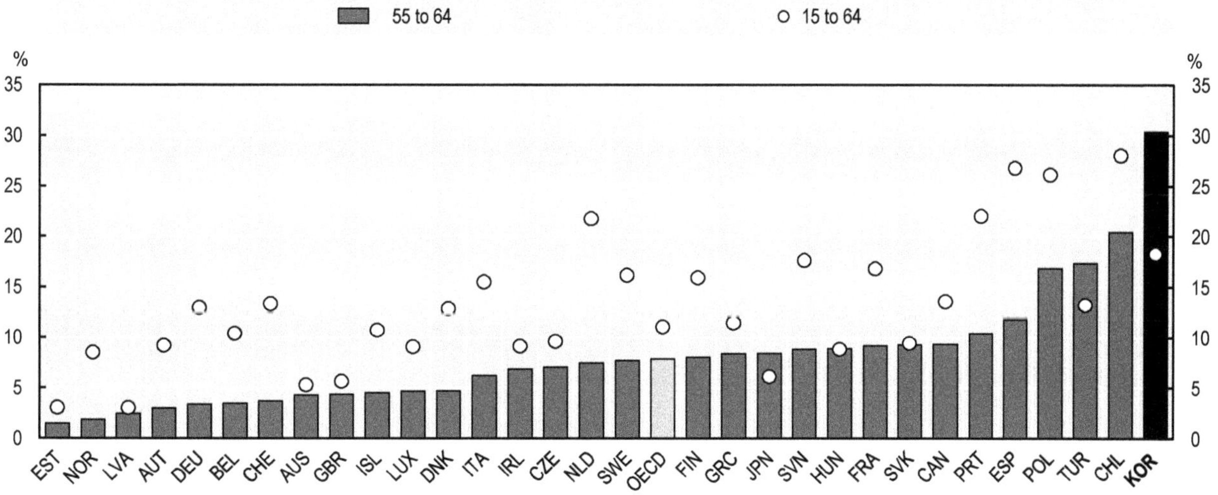

Note: OECD refers to the weighted average of the 31 OECD countries shown in the chart (excluding Israel, Mexico, New Zealand and the United States.

Source: *OECD Dataset on Incidence of Permanent Employment*, http://stats.oecd.org//Index.aspx?QueryId=9589.

StatLink http://dx.doi.org/10.1787/888933831830

Older workers in Korea are also over-represented in "non-salaried" forms of work. Under a common definition used in Korea, non-salaried work encompasses three separate categories of workers: *own-account workers*, who are self-employed but work alone; *employers*, who are self-employed but employ or engage one or more workers; and *contributing family workers*, who primarily assist a family member in an economic activity (either for pay or on an unpaid basis).

Figure 2.8 compares the share of non-salaried workers in total employment for a range of OECD countries. Korean workers aged 55-64 have among the highest shares of non-salaried workers of their peers in most other OECD countries.

Figure 2.8. Older workers in Korea are more likely to be self-employed than their peers in most other OECD countries

Share of self-employed in OECD countries – working age population (15-64) and those aged 55-64, 2017
(% of total employed in each age group)

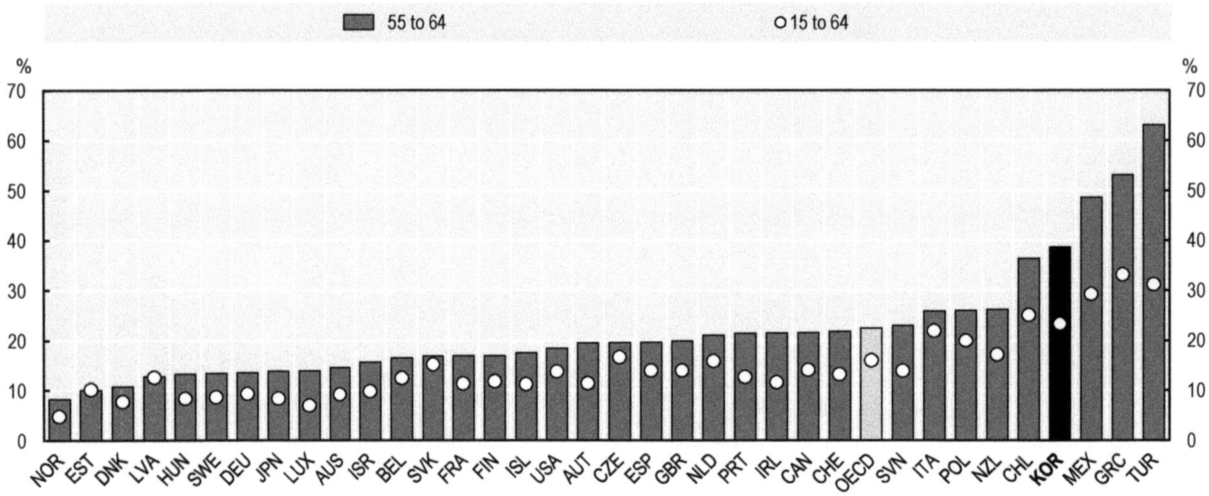

Note: The OECD is a weighted average.
Source: OECD calculations based on the *OECD Employment Database*, www.oecd.org/employment/emp/onlineoecdemploymentdatabase.htm.

StatLink http://dx.doi.org/10.1787/888933831849

Job security for older workers

Korea's common practice of retiring early from the main job is very clearly illustrated through its data on job tenure. Figure 2.9 shows the distribution of job tenure among workers of different ages for Korea and the OECD average in 2016. In Korea's case, longer periods of tenure (of 5-10 years or more) become steadily more common among mid-career workers aged 30-50, before the trend *reverses* among older workers aged in their 50s and over as longer periods of tenure gradually decrease in frequency (Figure 2.9, Panel A). In most other OECD countries, longer job tenure is found more and more commonly among older cohorts of workers without any such reversal in middle age (Figure 2.9, Panel B). In Korea, only 16.3% of workers aged 60-64 years and 9.4% of those aged 65 and above held their jobs for a period of 10 years or longer in 2017. In the OECD as a whole, the equivalent shares were 49.8% and 58.2%, respectively.

Figure 2.9. Average tenure increases with age in most OECD countries, though not in Korea

Salaried workers by age and duration of continuous employment, 2017

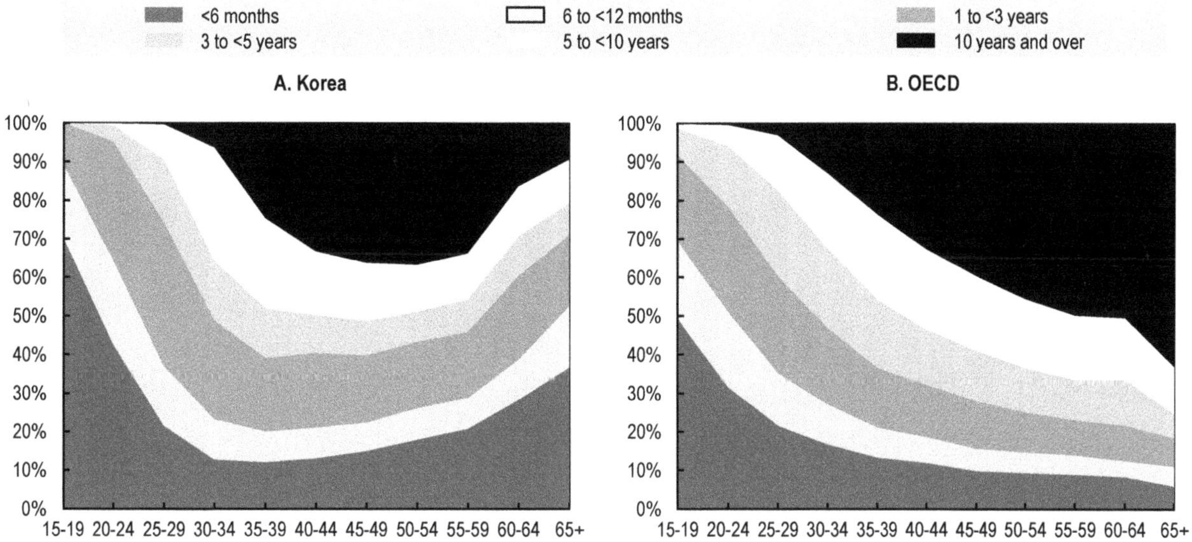

Note: OECD refers to the weighted average of 32 OECD countries (excluding Israel, Japan and New Zealand).

Source: *OECD Dataset Employment by job tenure intervals - frequency*, http://stats.oecd.org//Index.aspx?QueryId=29561.

StatLink http://dx.doi.org/10.1787/888933831868

Figure 2.10 echoes this point by comparing the average durations of continuous employment among salaried workers aged 55-64 years in different OECD countries. Such workers face shorter job tenures in Korea than in any other OECD country for which comparable data are available.

Numerous additional factors affect workers' job tenure in Korea, including gender and educational attainment. Korean men tend to retain their jobs for much longer periods than women do, on the whole; as do more highly educated workers compared with less qualified ones. Gender and education differences in job tenure are largest for older workers: the gender gap amounts to 5.8 years among those aged 50-54 and 5.6 years among those aged 55-59; and the gap between workers with completed tertiary-level education and those with incomplete secondary education amounts to 4.7 years among those aged 50-54, 4.3 years among those aged 55-59, and 5.2 years among those aged 60 and above. This suggests that many older workers in Korea face considerable obstacles around maintaining work that is stable and secure. Many are forced to change jobs a number of times throughout their second career.

Figure 2.10. Older workers in Korea have shorter job tenures than their peers in virtually every other OECD country

Salaried workers aged 55-64 in OECD countries by duration of continuous employment, 2015

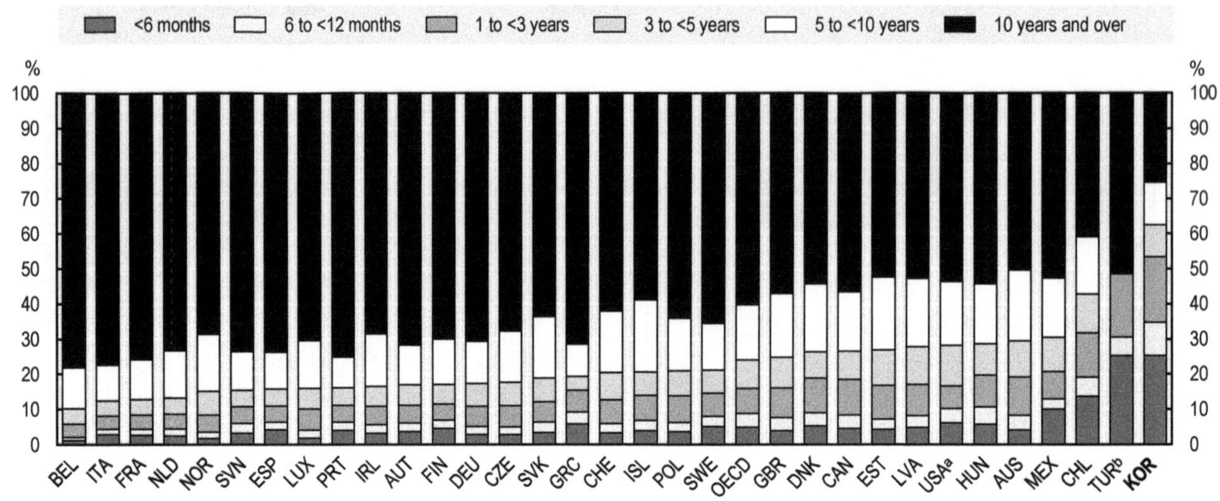

Note: OECD refers to the weighted average of the 32 OECD countries shown in the chart (excluding Israel, Japan and New Zealand).
a) Data refer to 2016.
b) Job tenure 10 years and over refers to tenure three years and over.
Source: *OECD dataset Employment by job tenure intervals - frequency*, http://stats.oecd.org//Index.aspx?QueryId=29561.

StatLink http://dx.doi.org/10.1787/888933831887

Earnings and income of older workers

Given the disadvantages older workers in Korea commonly face around employment status and job stability, many acquiesce to lower earnings in their second career. The average earnings of a salaried worker in Korea in 2016 peaked around the age of 45-49 at KRW 4.0 million on average: KRW 3.1 million of it through regular working time; KRW 0.2 million through over time; and a further KRW 0.6 million in bonus payments (Figure 2.11, Panel A). Workers in the next older age group earned 96.5% of this amount, on average (KRW 3.8 million); those aged 55-59 earned 85.9% (KRW 3.4 million); and those aged 60 and above earned only 61.2% (KRW 2.4 million).

Earnings gaps between different groups within the labour market are exacerbated by age. Men in Korea earn roughly 60% more than women do from their salaried work, on aggregate – among workers aged 45-59, however, the gap amounts to a full 100% (Figure 2.11, Panel B). Graduates of tertiary education earn roughly twice as much as workers with incomplete secondary education on aggregate – among workers aged 60 and above, however, they earn fully three times as much (Figure 2.11, Panel C). Salaried workers employed in enterprises with 100 or more workers earn roughly 70% more than their counterparts in smaller enterprises with only 5-9 workers, on aggregate – among workers aged 40-49, however, the gap is roughly 90% (Figure 2.11, Panel D).

Figure 2.11. Earnings disparities by sex and by educational attainment widen with age

Average monthly earnings of salaried workers in enterprises with five or more workers in Korea by age and type of earnings, 2016 (KRW, millions)

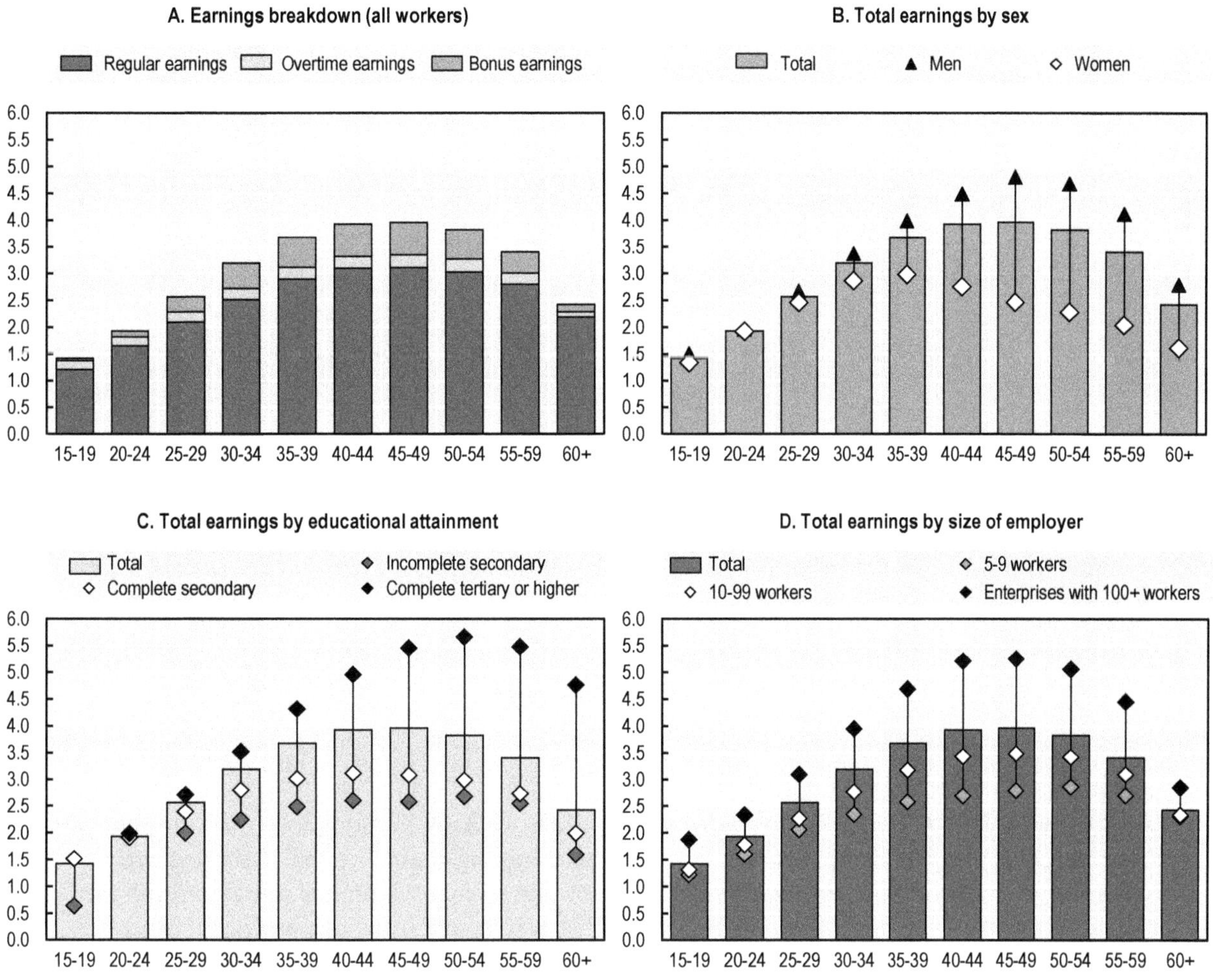

Note: Bonus earnings are calculated based on the previous year's bonus, divided by 12.
Source: MOEL (2016) *Survey on Labour Conditions by Employment Type*, www.moel.go.kr/english/pas/pasMOEL.jsp#.

StatLink http://dx.doi.org/10.1787/888933831906

Households headed by older workers in Korea also tend to have lower incomes than those headed by their younger counterparts. Figure 2.12 illustrates the level and sources of income for two types of households in Korea – households relying mostly on income from salaried work and those relying predominantly on business income – according to the age of the head of the household.

Both types of households have to make ends meet with considerably lower levels of income when the household head is aged 60 or above: household income is about 40% lower for them than it is for households headed by a younger person, irrespective of the main source of household income. Households headed by older workers receive higher social transfers than other households but the extra transfer income cannot compensate the considerable drop in income from salaried work or self-employment.

Figure 2.12. Korean households with an elderly head have lower income – whether or not their primary source of income is salaried work

Average monthly income by age of household head and income source, 2016

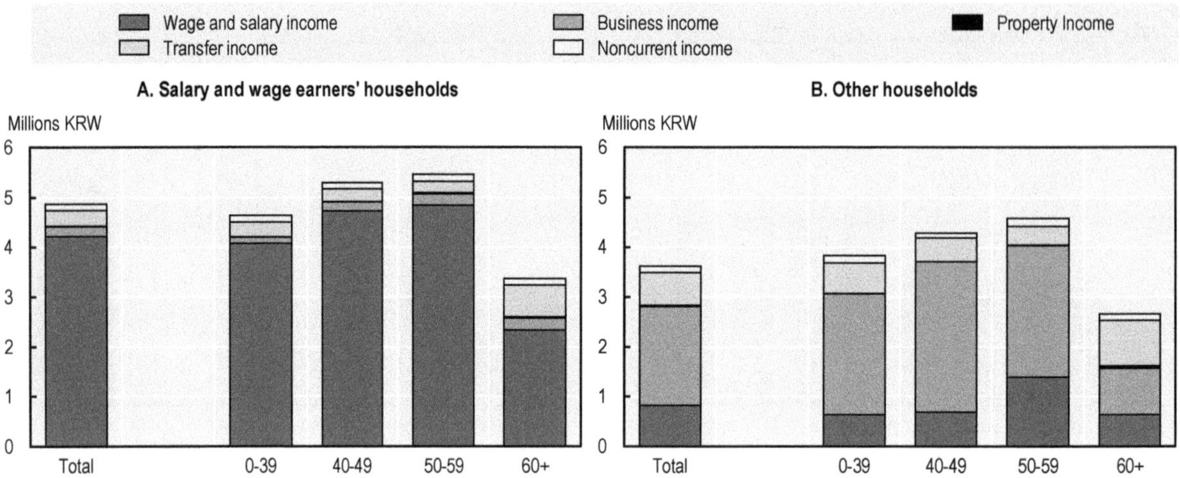

Note: Data exclude single-person households and farms. Salary and wage earners' households include household units where the head of the household is employed by a public or private body and receives wages in return for mental or physical labour.
Source: Statistics Korea (2017) Household Income and Expenditure Survey, via Korean Statistical Information Service (KOSIS), http://kosis.kr/eng.

StatLink http://dx.doi.org/10.1787/888933831925

Conclusion

While many OECD countries struggle to keep older workers in the labour market longer, Korea has already built up a strong work culture among them – even if some have no alternative livelihood but through work. The fact that so many Koreans remain within the labour force well into their 60s and even their 70s may be regarded as a powerful asset for Korea to deal with the demographic trends discussed in Chapter 1 and to make a sustainable transition towards an older society.

While many Koreans remain in work in later years, important obstacles remain around the type of work they have access to; the security this work can offer them; and, ultimately, the remuneration it can generate. On all of these important job-quality aspects, older workers in Korea suffer worse labour market outcomes. Much of this is linked to Korea's prominent culture of early retirement from the main job, followed by a period of years or even decades in a so-called second career. This, in turn, is linked to deeply-rooted recruitment, appraisal and human resources practices among employers in Korea (both public and private) that tend to reward seniority above all other factors – even when it does not translate into higher productivity – and dismiss workers from their main job when they reach their 50s. The rigidities this brings about often result in struggles for older workers and in retirement.

Chapter 3. Improving the employability and working conditions of older workers in Korea

Maintaining the employability of workers throughout their working life is essential to ensure they can stay longer in the core labour market and hold decent jobs until they retire. For Korea, the challenge is threefold. First, as many workers have to start a second career after retiring from their main job, employment services and active labour market policies have an important role to play in helping workers make successful employment transitions. Second, in the medium term building an effective system of continuous vocational training is critical to ensure workers can use and upgrade their competencies and skills throughout their working life, to facilitate ending the practice of mandatory early retirement. Third, efforts to improve working conditions must continue to make working longer with full work capacity possible for older workers.

The statistical date for Israel are supplied by and under the responsibility of the relevant Israeli authorities. The use of such data by the OECD is without prejudice to the status of the Golan Heights, East Jerusalem and Israeli settlements in the West Bank under the terms of international law.

Maintaining and strengthening employability throughout the working life

Job retention rates of Korean workers aged 50 and over are low for a number of reasons which include work and retirement practices discussed in other chapters. Older workers are much less educated than their younger counterparts; this contributes to driving them out of quality career jobs. However, it is not workers' educational attainment only that matters. Providing good opportunities for workers to upgrade their skills and learn new ones throughout their working lives is critical for fostering longer careers in rewarding jobs. In Korea, this is even more important as rapid economic transformation increases the risk of skill obsolescence, in a context where those workers lacking adequate skills are put at a particular disadvantage due to excessive labour market duality.

Many older workers in Korea have been left behind in the technology race

Jobs increasingly involve sophisticated tasks, require analysing and communicating information, and technology pervades all aspects of life. Hence, poor proficiency in information-processing skills not only restrains employment opportunities but also limits access to many services. More than ever, lifelong learning is of key importance, for all workers in all kinds of jobs. Workers in low-technology sectors and those performing low-skilled tasks must learn to be adaptable, because they are at higher risk of losing their job, as routine tasks are increasingly performed by machines, and companies may relocate to countries with lower labour costs. In high-technology sectors, workers need to update their competencies and keep pace with rapidly changing techniques.

Results from the OECD Survey of Adult Skills (PIAAC) suggest that older workers in Korea are not well equipped to deal with skill requirements brought about by technological progress and globalisation. PIAAC provides insights into the availability of skills in 22 OECD countries, by measuring proficiency in several information-processing skills, namely: literacy, numeracy and problem-solving in technology-rich environments (OECD, 2013a). The survey provides two pieces of information on the capacity of adults to manage information in technology-rich environments. One is the proportion of adults having sufficient familiarity with computers to perform information-processing tasks. The other one is the proficiency of adults with at least some ICT skills in solving the types of problems commonly encountered in their roles as workers, citizens and consumers in a technology-rich world. In all countries, skills proficiency reaches its highest levels during young adulthood and then declines with age. In Korea, this decline tends to be more pronounced than elsewhere (Figure 3.1); Korean 55-65 year-olds display low proficiency levels in all skills areas, compared to both their counterparts in other OECD countries and younger adults in their own country:

- Korea displays the fourth-lowest score on literacy among 55-65 year-olds and the third-lowest score on numeracy. Nearly two in three 55-65 year-olds in Korea have no experience with the use of computers or a very low level of familiarity with computer devices and applications – more than twice the OECD average and the highest share among all countries. Conversely, only 4% of older people have a good ability to use computers and solve problems that may arise in their everyday lives, compared to an OECD average of close to 12%.
- In Korea, the generation gap in proficiency is nearly twice as large as the OECD average, in all skill areas, due to 16-24 year-olds scoring high and 55-65 year-olds scoring low by international standards. Accounting for educational attainment and socio-economic background, the disadvantage among older

adults in literacy and numeracy proficiency decreases substantially (by 20%). The adjusted generation gap, however, remains large: in literacy, it is 60% above the average across participating countries, and in numeracy, still double the cross-country average.

Figure 3.1. Korea's older workers have much poorer skills than their younger counterparts or older workers in other OECD countries

Proficiency in literacy, numeracy and problem-solving skills of older workers and comparison with their younger peers, Korea vs. OECD average, 2012

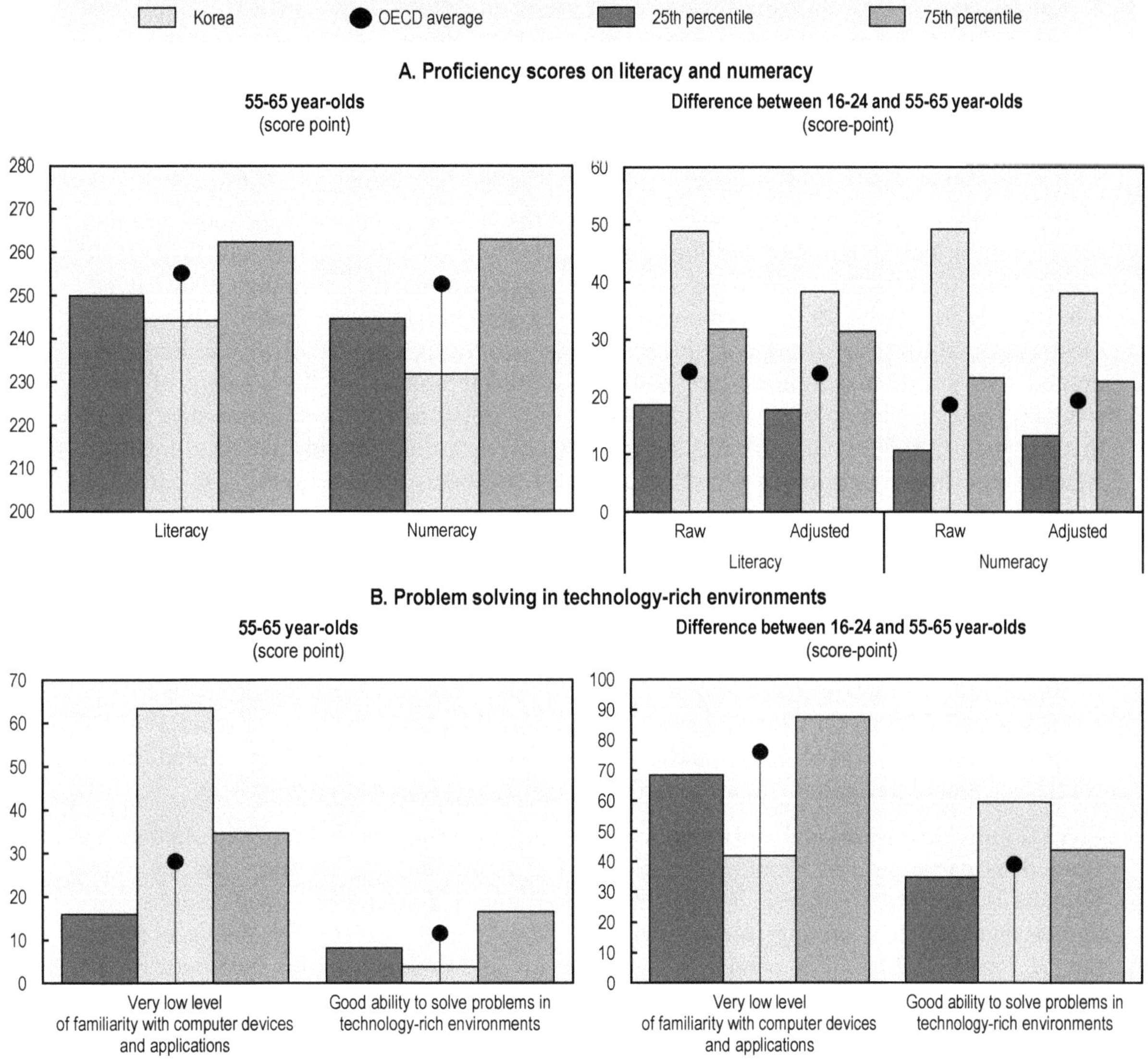

Note: Very low level of familiarity with computer devices and applications: no prior computer experience or failed the ICT core test. Good ability to solve problems in technology-rich environments: proficiency score at level 2 or 3 on problem solving in technology-rich environments. For literacy and numeracy scores, adjusted differences are based on a regression model and take account of differences associated with the following variables: gender, education, immigration and language background, socio-economic background, and type of occupation. OECD is an unweighted average of the 22 countries in PIAAC Round 1.

Source: OECD (2013), *OECD Skills Outlook 2013: First Results from the Survey of Adult Skills*, OECD Publishing, Paris. Tables A3.2 and A3.3

StatLink http://dx.doi.org/10.1787/888933831963

Lower proficiency in foundation skills does not necessarily translate into greater risk of labour market disadvantage since older workers have acquired other skills through longer work experience which are valuable and that younger workers may not hold. However, their job-specific skills may put them at risk of exclusion from the core labour market if they lose their job. In particular, older jobseekers who lack basic skills to use computer devices and applications are likely to encounter strong difficulties in finding a job of high quality all the more so as many of them are in this situation in Korea.[1]

Moreover, the generation gap in both foundation and ICT skills is particularly large, which raises more general concerns about the employability of Korean older workers. For a significant part this skill gap is due to Korea's rapid economic growth, which was accompanied by impressive investments in initial education. But it also suggests that lifelong learning policies have not adapted to the rapid transformation of Korea's economy and society.

Boosting participation in vocational education and training

There is now compelling evidence that the benefits from continuous vocational training can be substantial, in terms of earnings and employment security (OECD, 2013a; OECD, 2006). Empirical studies suggest that overall wage returns to job-related training are relatively high, at 3% or more for one week of training in many cases (Leuven and Oosterbeek, 2008; Brunello et *al.* 2012; Picchio and van Ours, 2013). It can be safely argued that job-related training can have a significant impact on the *income* of older workers (beyond that on wages) if it allows them to delay their retirement or stay longer in their main job. Picchio and van Ours (2013), for example, found that firm-provided training significantly improves future employment prospects, in general but also for older workers: employees aged 50-64 are 4.2 percentage points more likely to retain employment if they have received training on the job in the previous year. This finding implies that continued training opportunities are essential to maintain the employability of workers throughout their working life.

In Korea, only 20% of workers aged 55-64 have received work-related training during the 12 months prior to the OECD Survey of Adult Skills. This participation rate is relatively low compared with an OECD average of 28% and well below the rates of around 35-40% observed in countries such as Denmark, Finland, Norway, Sweden and the United States where vocational education and training (VET) is most widespread (Figure 3.2).

PIAAC provides additional information on *unmet* demand for training (workers who wanted to participate in training but did not). The willingness to learn among older workers is very high in Korea. Slightly more than one in five persons aged 55-64 report unmet demands for training, more than twice the OECD average for this age group (again, Figure 3.2). If all demand was met, Korea would rank among the best-performing countries with respect to education and training for older workers. This suggests older workers in Korea face strong obstacles to access training.

Figure 3.2. Many older workers in Korea want to participate in education or training but fail to do so

Percentage of population aged 55-64 participating in education and training or expressing an interest in training but not actually participating, 2012

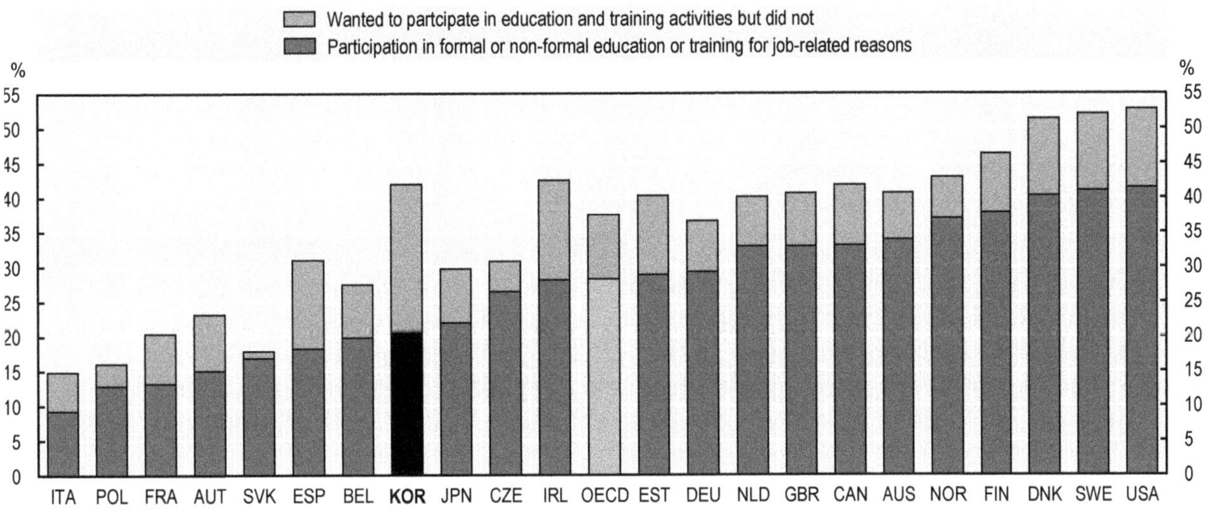

Note: OECD is a weighted average of the countries in the chart. Data for the United Kingdom refer to England and Northern Ireland, data for Belgium to Flanders.
Source: OECD Survey of Adult Skills (PIAAC), 2012, http://www.oecd.org/skills/piaac/.

StatLink http://dx.doi.org/10.1787/888933831982

In virtually all OECD countries, VET is unequally distributed across workforce groups, with women, older workers, low-skilled workers and those in small firms and temporary jobs receiving the least training (OECD 2013; OECD 2006). While employer-sponsored VET is the main channel through which incumbent workers are upgrading their skills in Korea (see Box 3.1), firms' incentives to invest in human capital are low for middle-aged and older workers due to the widespread practice of mandatory early retirement at a relatively young age. Inequalities in access to training have been reduced in recent years, but more should be done. Workers aged 60 and over are still less likely to participate in VET, just as workers with less than middle-school education, workers in firms with 5-9 employees and those not registered to Employment Insurance (Figure 3.4). Workers in firms with less than five employees are least likely to participate in VET among all groups of workers; this group makes up 28% of total employment in Korea.

Box 3.1. Vocational education and training in Korea

MOEL is the main body in charge of vocational education and training (VET), most of which is financed by the Employment Insurance (EI) fund. The EI system is also the main funding source for active labour market programmes, maternity and childcare leave benefits, as well as unemployment benefits. EI was introduced in 1995 and has gradually been expanded over time to cover most Korean employees, at least in theory; effectively, one in four salaried workers are not EI insured, most of them working in micro businesses (OECD, 2018a). However, there is a growing reliance on central funding, particularly for job-search counselling and training for the unemployed, so that workers who are not eligible for EI can also receive support.

As part of the EI system, training is funded by a levy-grant scheme. All firms have to contribute to the EI fund, irrespective of whether their employees undertake training activities. Contribution rates vary from 0.25% to 0.85% of the total taxable wage bill depending on firm size, the lowest rate being applied to firms with fewer than 150 workers while the highest rate applies to firms employing 1 000 or more workers. There are two broad categories of subsidy schemes, depending on whether VET is initiated by an individual worker (employed or unemployed) or by an employer. In both cases, the subsidy amount does not necessarily cover VET expenditure completely, the co-financing element aiming at promoting rational and effective investments into VET. Applicants (individual workers or employers) can find all necessary information about VET courses and providers on a public internet portal (HRD-Net), including curricula, time schedule, available financial supports and eligibility criteria, as well as the assessment of various courses and providers. These assessments, required by the Framework Act on Employment Policy, are conducted on a regular basis by specific agencies under the umbrella of MOEL, with a strong focus on programme relevance to the labour market.

In practice, employer-provided VET is the main channel through which incumbent workers upgrade and develop their skills (Figure 3.3). Employers who provide VET to their employees can receive a subsidy amount of up to 100% of their EI contributions for large companies and up to 240% for SMEs (fewer than 300 workers), conditional on the approval of their training programme (its content, methods and number of hours per worker) by MOEL. They can implement the programme themselves or entrust the task to a private provider accredited by MOEL. SMEs are entitled to additional support to help them improve their organisational capabilities to train their employees. This includes public subsidies for overhead costs and consulting fees for the development of learning activities and on-the-job training. As part of the policy efforts to promote skills development for employees in SMEs, increasing attention is also being paid to collective training provision between large firms and SMEs. Under the National Human Resources Development Consortium (the CHAMP programme, introduced in 2001), large firms, business associations or universities are encouraged through public subsidies to set up a consortium with SMEs in order to share their training facilities and equipment, as well as their experience and knowhow. In 2014, 180 organisations were operating a training consortium under the CHAMP programme, which benefited more than 200 000 SME employees and accounted for 25% of total government expenditure on VET for incumbent workers.

Figure 3.3. Main categories of VET programmes for employees, 2014

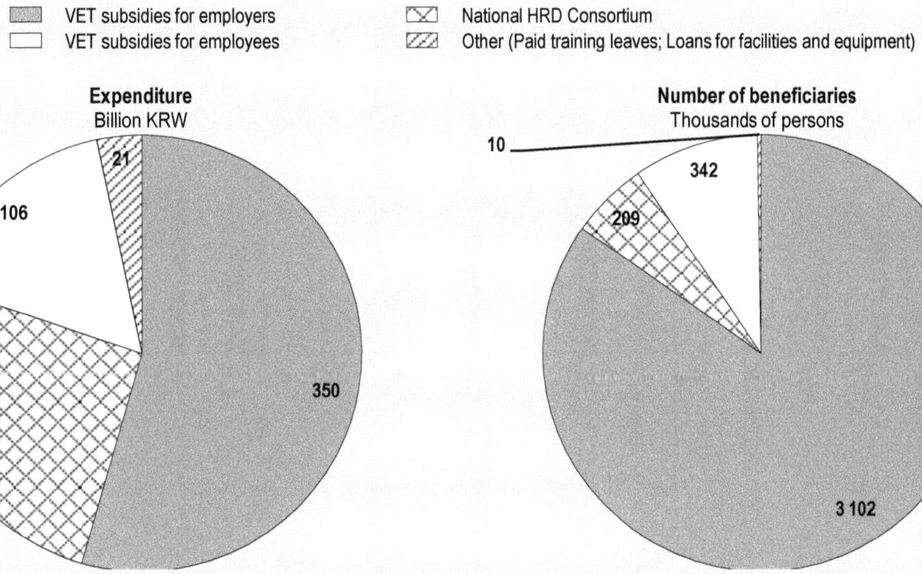

Source: KRIVET (2016), Human Resources Development Indicators in Korea (p.83).

StatLink http://dx.doi.org/10.1787/888933832001

For the unemployed and those workers who are not provided with adequate training opportunities by their employer, a system of Individual Training Accounts (ITA) has been implemented in 2010 (after a pilot phase launched in 2008). This scheme provides financial support in the form of vouchers for individual employees willing to undertake training on their own initiative ("My Work Learning Card System for Workers") and to jobseekers ("My Work Learning Card System for Jobseekers"). All jobseekers can apply, but only incumbent workers aged 40 and over, SME employees, and non-regular workers (as well as self-employed with employment insurance on a voluntary basis) are eligible. The training card is issued by the Public Employment Service, after a screening process aimed at evaluating the applicant's training needs and aspirations. Card holders can select any courses within the list of programmes approved by MOEL, up to an amount of KRW two millions over one year (three million for jobseekers with low income). Information on the employment rate of each course and training provider is provided on the HRD-Net website so that potential trainees can see which courses are most effective. They should complete at least 80% of the programme in order to receive the grant and they have to pay 30-50% of the training costs out of their pocket, depending on whether the selected courses are closely related to work activities. Jobseekers who find a job can get a refund, and those from low-income households are exempted from the upfront payment. Since the introduction of ITAs in 2010, the screening process and the conditions for receiving training grants have been strengthened in order to increase their effectiveness in bringing people back into work.

Source: OECD (2014), *Skills beyond School: Synthesis Report*, https://doi.org/10.1787/9789264214682-en.

Figure 3.4. Inequalities in access to training are considerable in Korea

VET participation rates for selected groups of the Korean population, relative to the average for all groups, 2007 and 2015

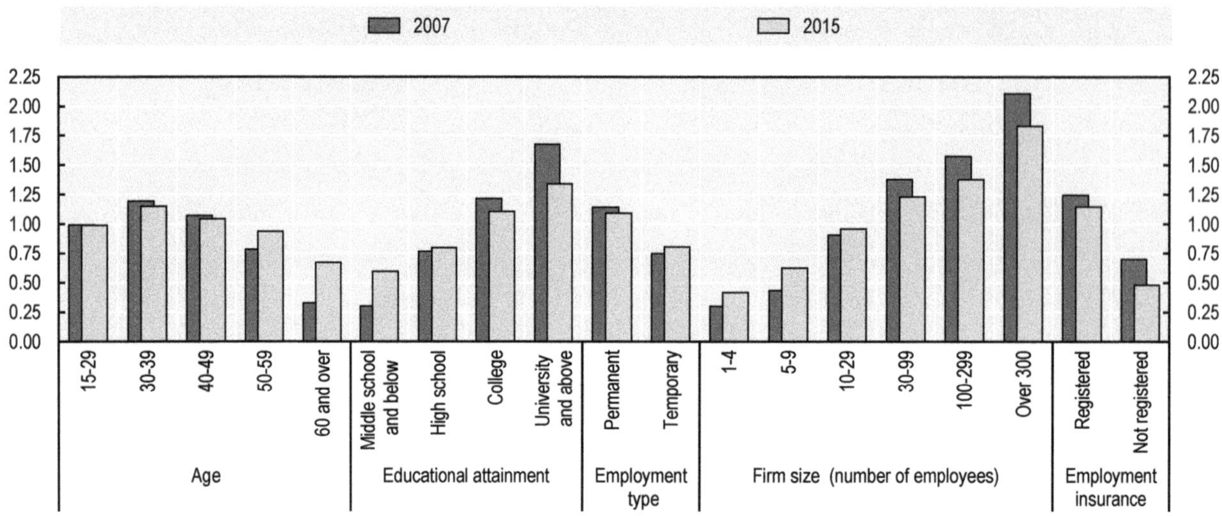

Source: KRIVET (2016), Human Resources Development Indicators in Korea (p.73).

StatLink http://dx.doi.org/10.1787/888933832020

Supports for and obstacles against the take-up of training

Additional financial supports are provided to vulnerable groups in order to enhance their training opportunities and curb inequalities (see Box 3.1). Workers aged 40 and over, non-regular workers and those employed in SMEs who want to undertake VET on their own initiative can apply to a voucher programme in order to buy training courses approved by MOEL. In addition, the subsidy scheme for firm-sponsored VET is favourable to SMEs, which are also entitled to specific supports aimed at improving their organisational capabilities to train their employees. However, this various financial supports could be more effective if a centralised body with expertise in VET and adequate equipment was in charge of organising VET programmes for SMEs. Because they often lack experience and training facilities, it remains difficult for them to provide sufficient VET opportunities for their workforce.

The National Human Resources Development Consortium (CHAMP programme) addresses a number of organisational and technical constraints faced by SMEs, as it provides financial incentives for large companies, business associations or universities to set up a consortium and to share their know-how, equipment and training facilities with SMEs through this consortium. Based on a win-win approach, this programme has expanded remarkably over time. The CHAMP programme offers good opportunities for building or strengthening partnerships between large firms and their subcontractors, firms in the same industry or region, or universities and businesses, which in turn can give rise to positive externalities. Because training sessions are organised in the context of these partnerships, they can be better focused and more relevant to business needs, with an immediate payoff in terms of increased productivity for both the beneficiaries (SME employees) and the organizers (in particular, large firms).

Time-related constraints are a major obstacle to training participation in Korea, for all age groups (Figure 3.5). Being too busy at work is the most prevalent reason reported by workers to explain why they did not participate in any VET programmes albeit they would have wanted to do so. This reason represents almost 40% of all answers in the age group 55-64, the highest proportion among the OECD countries for which information is available and nearly twice the average for these countries. When accounting for childcare and family responsibilities, time-related constraints represent 56% of all answers, 20 percentage points more than the cross-country average for this group. Conversely, financial constraints do not appear to constitute a major obstacle to training participation for older workers, accounting for only 9% of all answers in Korea. This is well below the OECD average for this age group.

Figure 3.5. Lack of time is the main obstacle in Korea to participate in vocational education and training

Percentage of persons reporting that they wanted to participate in VET but did not, by age group, Korea vs. OECD average, 2012

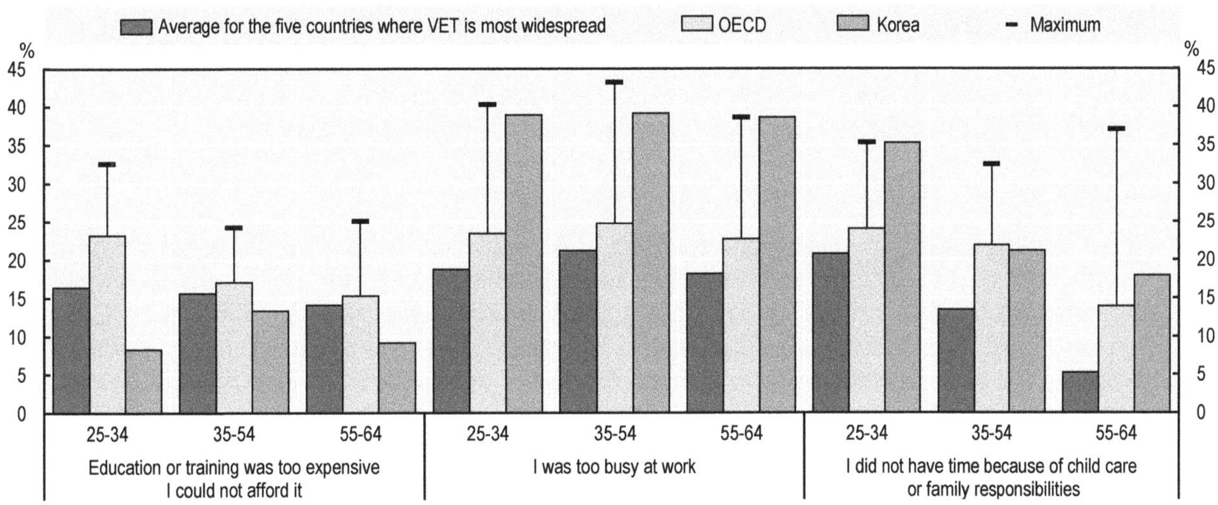

Note: The five countries are: Denmark, Finland, Norway, Sweden and the United States. OECD is a weighted average of the 22 countries in PIAAC Round 1.
Source: OECD Survey of Adult Skills (PIAAC), 2012, http://www.oecd.org/skills/piaac/.

StatLink http://dx.doi.org/10.1787/888933832039

Policy priority should be placed on easing the time constraints Koreans face to participate in training. The new guidelines on working time are an important step forward as they should help reduce the incidence of very long working hours. However, additional measures should be taken, notably for SMEs that often face labour shortages and therefore may experience strong difficulties in freeing up time for their employees to take training. This situation creates a vicious circle whereby poor working conditions and career prospects render it difficult for SMEs to attract skilled workers, which in turn deteriorates working conditions by imposing long working hours on incumbent workers, thereby limiting their training opportunities. Breaking this vicious circle would require measures helping SMEs to find and hire replacement workers quickly, in addition to financial supports such as hiring subsidies and/or subsidised training leaves for employees. These support measures could be combined with job placement services provided by the Public Employment Service (PES).

The Danish *Job-rotation* scheme is a good example of an integrated approach, combining up-skilling of incumbent workers with work practice and network building for unemployed persons. Under this scheme, employers can set up a training plan for their employees in cooperation with the municipal job centre, benefit from assistance in recruiting replacement workers and receive a public subsidy for hiring a long-term unemployed to replace the employee on training. The replacement worker can also receive a short training before starting work.

A similar scheme could be implemented in Korea, for example in cooperation with the Job Hope Centres for middle-aged and elderly people (see further below). Such a system could provide networking opportunities and on-the-job training to workers who have to start a second career after retirement from their main job, while ensuring better access to VET for middle-aged and older workers to upgrade their skills and stay longer in their main job. Such scheme could also be combined with the CHAMP programme to encourage temporary transfers of employees from large firms to SMEs and allow workers in SMEs to take time off work in order to receive training. To ensure a successful implementation, an integrated approach involving the PES and the VET consortiums established under the CHAMP programme could be an effective way to provide more and better training opportunities in Korea, notably for disadvantaged workers.

Enhancing the ability of the VET system to deliver the right skills for jobs

VET serves two main purposes: providing job-related skills with a direct return on productivity, employability and earnings, and providing foundation skills, which have less immediate returns but are essential to support lifelong employability. Effective VET systems must find the right mix, targeted to industries, firms and occupations, as well as workers. The appropriate skills mix tends to evolve throughout the working life, with foundation skills becoming less important as people grow older. Programmes designed on the basis of an apprenticeship concept – combining short classroom sessions with a firm-based approach – could be effective for older workers, as could be informal and self-determined training with a clear focus on practical and relevant work problems.

Results from PIAAC suggest there is scope for improvement in this respect. Only one in three older workers in Korea rate the relevance of their recent training activities as "very useful" for their current job, as compared with 54% on average in the 22 OECD countries for which information is available (Figure 3.6). Some 27% of these training activities were reported "somewhat useful" or "not useful at all"; this is well above the cross-country average of 17% for this age group. With on-the-job training accounting for only one-third of all training activities, the Korean VET system focuses less on helping workers to deal with practical issues they may encounter in performing their current job duties than is the case in other OECD countries, where on average half of all training activities are on the job. By contrast, open or distance learning is relatively widespread in Korea, accounting for 24% of all training activities (7% on average in OECD countries). A common pitfall of these training methods is to follow a too theoretical approach that is not sufficiently attuned to real work activity, notably for older workers.

Figure 3.6. Fewer older workers in Korea than in other OECD countries consider their training activities as very useful

Main types of training activities (all workers) and their practical usefulness for jobs (older workers only), Korea vs. OECD average, 2012

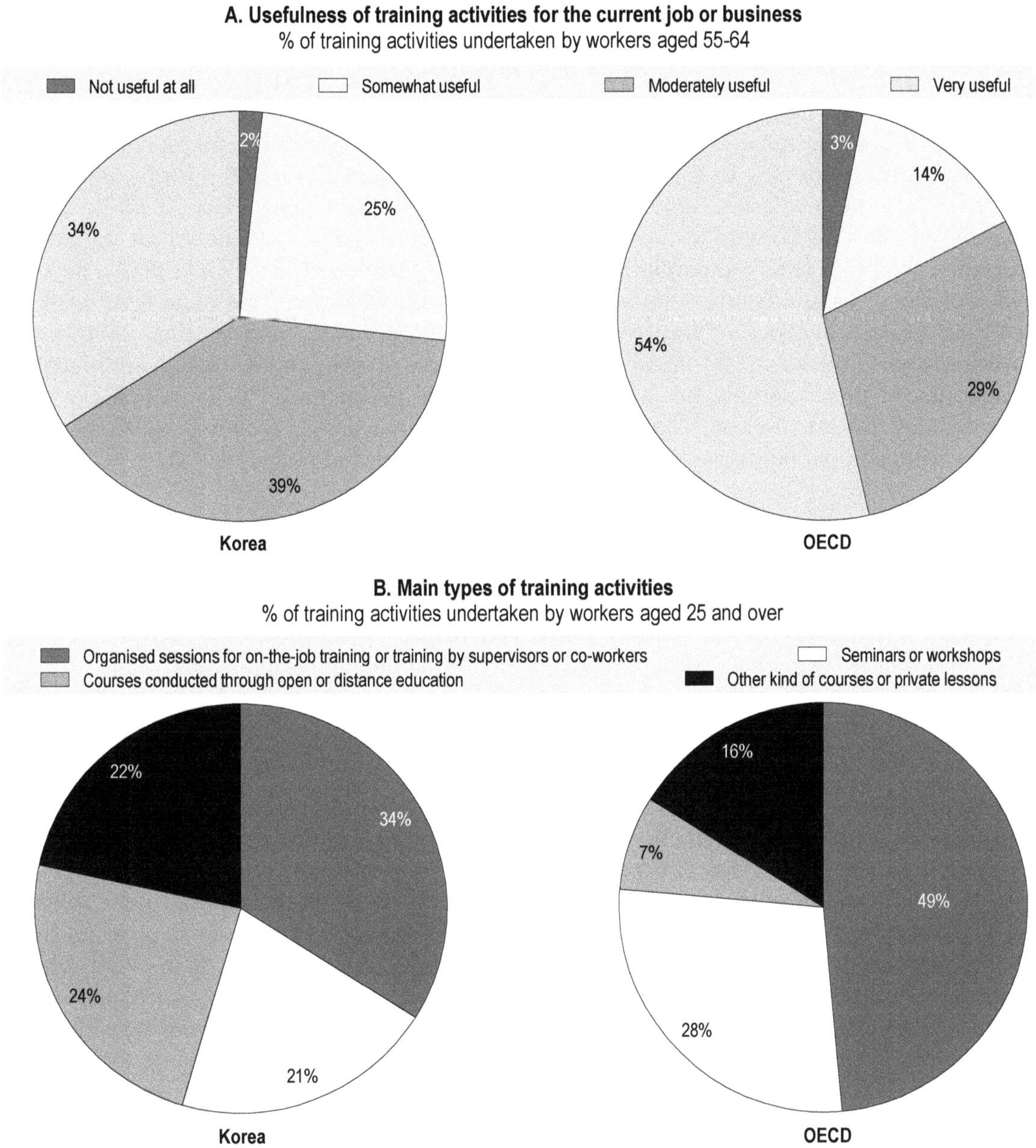

Note: **Open or distance courses** are similar to face-to-face courses, but take place via postal correspondence or electronic media, linking instructors/teachers/tutors or students who are not together in a classroom. **Organised sessions for on-the-job training or training by supervisors or co-workers** is characterised by planned periods of training, instruction or practical experience, using normal tools of work. **Courses** are typically subject oriented and taught by persons specialised in the field(s) concerned. They can take the form of classroom instruction (sometimes in combination with practice in real or simulated situations) or lectures. OECD is a weighted average of the 22 countries in PIAAC Round 1.

Source: OECD Survey of Adult Skills (PIAAC), 2012, http://www.oecd.org/skills/piaac/.

StatLink http://dx.doi.org/10.1787/888933832058

Open or distance learning and on-the-job training can be useful to reach out to SMEs. These training methods are very flexible, making it possible to take better account of SMEs organisational problems and barriers for training. Sessions can be adapted to a daily work schedule as they can take place at the worksite and be scheduled according to the workload. To be effective, they require a properly designed assessment whereby training needs and objectives are identified precisely. Open or distance learning will best suit workers who prefer to learn alone at their own pace.

Open or distance learning programmes require high-quality service providers to be effective. While the same holds true for all employment and training measures, this is especially true in this case as a number of specific implementation issues must be handled by efficient intermediaries, able to identify specific needs and offer flexible and innovative solutions tailored to those needs. Regular and rigorous evaluation of training activities and providers is important in this regard. As mentioned in OECD (2014), these types of exercises are mostly done at the national level, whereas at the local level there tends to be less analysis of the overall impact of programmes and whether they are meeting their objectives. As local governments have a role in designing additional programmes, there should be a greater focus on evaluating local policies and programmes. Information on what works could be shared across localities in Korea as well as with national ministries to inform future programme and policy design.

Making skills and competencies acquired throughout working lives visible

Having a clear picture of existing skills and qualifications and a better understanding of future skill needs, is a requirement for rational and efficient investments in vocational education and training by individuals, firms and society as a whole. This requires two tools: *relevant qualification systems*, adequately reflecting the supply and demand of skills and competencies; and *reliable procedures to assess and validate* skills and competencies that people acquire during their careers. Formal validation is necessary in order to be able to recognise skills adequately and render them transparent to employers.

In case of involuntary job loss, the recognition of prior learning and acquired experience can play a crucial role in helping workers find a quality job that matches their actual competences and skills. This is especially important for mid-career and older workers, whose initial qualifications may be outdated. Many of them have acquired new skills through their work experiences, but most often they do not have certificates to prove it. In Korea, providing workers with opportunities to assess and validate their skills and competencies against a national qualification standard before or, at the very least, as soon as they have to leave their main job for mandatory early retirement, would help them build a second career that better matches their expectations and abilities. While there are some early-intervention measures designed to help workers approaching the age of mandatory retirement to prepare their employment transition, these measures mainly consist in outplacement services. As part of these initiatives, greater attention should be paid to formal validation of acquired experiences.

From a longer-term perspective, the main challenge faced by Korea is to better link education, including vocational education and training, with labour market needs. While the education level of young cohorts and business needs have changed dramatically in the last few decades, the VET system has not been responsive enough to this fast-changing environment. In particular, the national qualification system has remained focused on technical skills and does not constitute anymore an adequate screening device for employers, a proper signalling device for employees, and a relevant policy tool for public authorities to evaluate skill developments and anticipate skill needs (OECD, 2014).

The development of new National Competency Standards (NCS) is an important step forward as it provides a picture of the skills required for various jobs, in line with the competencies needed in the labour market. But the big remaining challenge for the government is to operationalise and promote the use of the NCS. This requires a comprehensive package of measures to reflect the NCS in both VET provision and qualification frameworks. The reform process is underway (MOEL, 2015), but more should be done to mobilise all relevant stakeholders, including VET providers, employer associations and trade unions, as ultimately they will be the main channel for disseminating and implementing successfully the NCS (OECD, 2014).

Labour market reforms could contribute to foster the interest of social partners in the NCS. From the perspective of trade unions, the benefits from having effective instruments for increasing, assessing and recognising the value of lifelong learning are currently limited due to the deeply-rooted seniority-based system for setting wages and granting promotions, which weakens the link between competencies and earnings. From the perspective of employers, the widespread practices of long working hours and mandatory early retirements reduce the value of investing in the skills of their workforce: long hours can compensate for reduced productivity, and early retirements can be used when the gap between earnings and productivity becomes too large. The policy measures taken recently in those areas can bring about some changes in the status quo as an effective VET system, acknowledged by business associations and approved by trade unions, would constitute the best guarantee for ensuring a *fair* transition towards a competency-based labour market.

Helping older jobseekers back into quality jobs

Improvements in vocational education and training are critical for Korea to keep older workers employable and make it possible for them to stay in their jobs longer. But it will take time until the current wage and employment practices, including seniority wages and honorary retirement, will be overcome and even then, not all older workers will be able to retain their jobs. Providing older jobseekers with effective support to move back into rewarding and productive jobs, is essential to foster a more inclusive labour market. In the context of Korea's rapidly ageing population, combined with a high degree of labour mobility of older workers, it is important that middle-aged and older jobseekers have access to good employment services and effective active labour market programmes (ALMPs) to help them make job transitions and to minimise the costs of those transitions.

Strengthening the capacity of the Public Employment Service

MOEL Job Centres are the primary point of contact for jobseekers in Korea which can be characterised by a labyrinth of employment services that exist alongside each other (see Box 3.2). MOEL Job Centres are responsible for administering unemployment benefits as well as providing job counselling, job training, job matching, placement, career guidance and vocational psychology testing. MOEL Job Centres also provide job-matching services for firms which have vacancies; administer wage and training subsidy programmes aimed at firms and workers; and visit firms to identify problems they face with recruitment and labour regulations. They also work with local governments and communities to encourage job creation at the regional level.

Box 3.2. The structure of employment service provision in Korea

Korea's employment services are regulated through three Acts: the Framework Act on Employment Policy, the Employment Security Act, and the Employment Insurance Act (KEIS, 2012a). The Framework Act provides strategic orientation for labour market policies and sets out the governance structure for programme implementation and evaluation, while the other two acts contain practical provisions for implementing employment services and unemployment insurance benefits, respectively. In addition, the Framework Act sets up the Korean Employment Information Service (KEIS), responsible for collecting information and monitoring and assessing programmes and service providers on a regular basis.

For older workers, there are two broad categories of employment services in Korea: those available to all jobseekers and specific services for workers aged 40 and over. In both cases, publicly funded employment services can be classified into those directly managed by public agencies and those commissioned to non-governmental organisations or employment agencies in the private or not-for-profit sector. The service structure in Korea is rather complex, with many providers of employment services (see Table 3.1).

Table 3.1. Employment services for middle-aged and older workers (2014)

	Job Centers (% change since 2007)	Employment Support Centers	Job Hope Centers	Senior Citizen Talent Banks (% change since 2007)
Managing body	Central government (MOEL)	Local governments	Tripartite organisation (KLF)	Non-profit organisations
Main services	Unemployment benefits administration, job-matching services and ALMPs (including training)	Job-matching services	Job-matching and vocational guidance	Job-matching services
Beneficiaries	All jobseekers	All jobseekers	Workers aged 40+	Jobseekers aged 50+
N° of centers	86	243	25	53 *(+6)*
N° of staff	4 563 *(+56)*	1 364	174	106 *(+6)*
N° of registered job vacancies	1 695 711 *(+68)*	n.a	46 242	195 916 *(+146)*
N° of registered jobseekers				
All age groups	2 933 866 *(+49)*	n.a	-	
... among which EI recipients (%)	33%	n.a	-	
Persons aged 40 and over	1 306 362 *(+82)*	n.a	85 100	167 199 *(+118)*
... among which EI recipients (%)	45%	n.a	23%	n.a
Jobseekers per staff	643 *(-4)*	n.a	489	1 577 *(+106)*
Jobseekers per job vacancy	1.73 *(-11)*	n.a	1.84	0.85 *(-11)*

Source: Work-Net, Middle-aged Job Hope-Net, Employment Insurance.

StatLink http://dx.doi.org/10.1787/888933832191

The Job Centres run by the MOEL are the primary providers of employment services. Job Centres have seen a significant increase recently in the number of staff, jobseekers served and job vacancies handled. Middle-aged and older workers have greatly benefited from this improvement: the number of jobseekers aged 40 and over served by Job Centres increased by 82% (2007-14), compared with a 49% increase for all age groups over the same period. The number of vacancies handled by Job Centres also increased, by 68%, resulting in a slight decrease of the number of jobseekers per vacancy which in turn may facilitate their placement. However, with on average more than 600 registered jobseekers per staff, the caseload of a Job Centre counsellor remains extraordinarily high.

Local governments also provide employment services through a network of regional or municipal agencies, the Employment Support Centres, partly financed by the central government. The latter has primary responsibility for the design and implementation of national employment policies, while local governments develop specific programmes tailored to local labour market needs. Local governments have a more extensive network of agencies than the MOEL (243 Employment Support Centres in 2014 in comparison with 86 Job Centres nationwide), but their agencies tend to be small (5-6 employees) and merely play a supporting role in the service delivery chain, with a focus on job-placement services in connection with direct job creation programmes offered by local governments. They are also responsible for activating recipients of social assistance.

To assist late career workers in their employment transitions, in 2013 the government integrated outplacement support centres and job centres for older professionals into Job Hope Centres for middle-aged and older workers. They are managed by the Korea Labour Foundation, a tripartite body under the umbrella of the MOEL, and provide services similar to those provided by MOEL Job Centres but they are better resourced as they tend to serve more vulnerable jobseekers, on a more individual basis. Only 23% of jobseekers registered with Job Hope Centres in 2014 were receiving EI benefits, while the proportion of EI recipients was nearly double for jobseekers (aged 40 and over) registered with a Job Centre. Job Hope Centres also provide vocational guidance and outplacement services to employees approaching the age of mandatory early retirement and willing to prepare for their second career. Considering the broad range of activities, the number of jobseekers per Job Hope Centres staff are high (albeit lower than that in Job Centres), all the more so as their customers need more intensive assistance and are harder to place.

To ease pressure on Job Centres, MOEL has been active in promoting the development of employment agencies in the private and not-for-profit sector. As a result, these play an increasingly important role in facilitating job matching for the most employable on the one hand and delivering the Employment Success Package Programme (ESPP) on the other. ESPP is directed towards specific groups facing difficulties in the labour market and at high risk of poverty – a significant number of whom middle-aged and older jobseekers – and provide these groups with customised assistance and enhanced services to help them back into work (OECD, 2013b; OECD, 2018a).

For job-matching services, a network of private employment agencies and training institutions, the so-called "Senior Citizen Talent Bank" designated by the MOEL, is directed especially at helping jobseekers aged 50 and over find a new job. This network has expanded markedly over the last decade, with the number of jobseekers served and job vacancies handled more than doubling since 2007. However, the majority of Talent Banks are micro businesses with one or two employees, offering placement service for rather precarious jobs in most cases (part-time jobs and jobs of short duration).

Finally, the increased use of the internet as a job-search tool is also contributing to the expansion and development of employment services in Korea. MOEL's Work-Net website is an important tool for connecting jobseekers with available vacancies. Work-Net was launched in 1998 and its functions have expanded over time. From 2011, users have been able to search for jobs listed on other privately operated websites and from local governments. Users can also view their job application history, take vocational aptitude tests and manage their relationship with the Job Centre online, including updating their jobseeker registration and applying for courses or counselling sessions. Employers can list vacancies and search for new staff. The system also provides information for counsellors and local governments providing employment services.

Source: KEIS (2012a), Public Employment Information System, Korea Employment Information Service, Eumseong, OECD (2013), *Korea: Improving the Re-employment Prospects of Displaced Workers*, https://doi.org/10.1787/9789264189225-en, OECD (2018), *Towards Better Social and Employment Security in Korea*, https://doi.org/10.1787/9789264288256-en.

In view of their extensive responsibilities and central importance in the delivery of employment services, MOEL Job Centres are *under-resourced*. At 0.04% of GDP, public expenditures on delivering services, administering benefits and dealing with clients are the fourth-lowest in the OECD area; less than a quarter than the OECD average of 0.13% of GDP and only about a tenth of the spending in some high-spending countries like Germany and Denmark (Figure 3.7). Even taking into account the low level of unemployment in Korea, public spending on employment service operations remains low: The ratio of PES spending (as a share of GDP) to the unemployment rate is nearly half the average ratio for OECD countries, and four to eight times lower than in the countries with the highest spending-to-unemployment ratios.

Figure 3.7. Employment services in Korea are highly under-resourced

Expenditure on administering employment services and benefits administration as share of GDP (left scale) and relative to a country's rate of unemployment (right scale), 2016

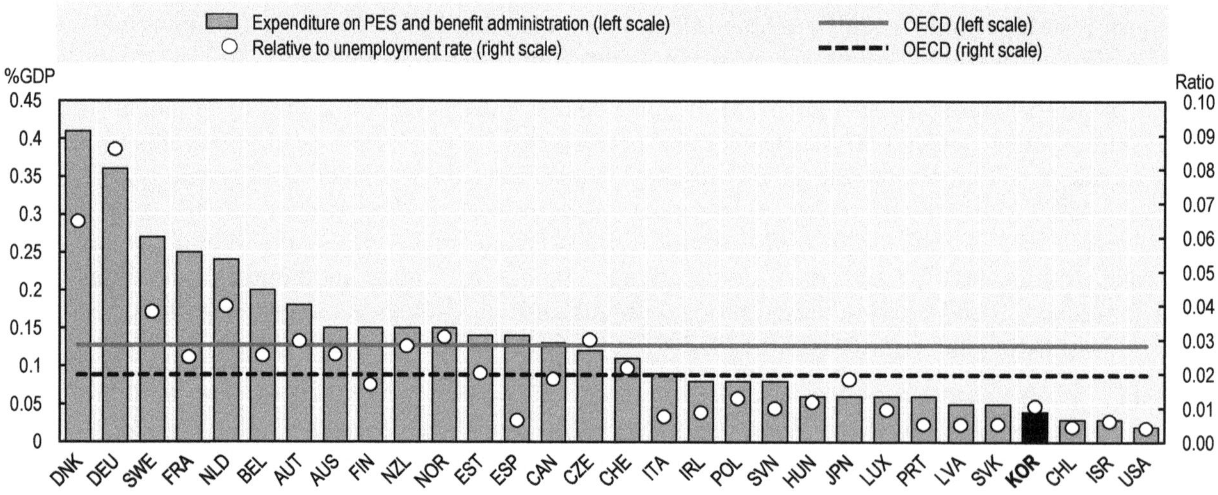

Note: Data for France, Italy and Spain refer to 2015.
Source: *OECD Dataset on Public Expenditure and Participant Stocks on LMP*, https://stats.oecd.org//Index.aspx?QueryId=8540.

StatLink http://dx.doi.org/10.1787/888933832077

Consequently, although the number of jobseekers who register with MOEL Job Centres has increased markedly over the past decade, there are still relatively few people in Korea who use the PES to find a new job. Only one in four prime-age jobseekers in Korea report they have been in contact with the PES in the past month to find work, the lowest proportion in the 22 OECD countries for which information is available, and 30 percentage points below the cross-country average. Among jobseekers aged 55 to 64 years, at close to 40%, the share using the PES in their job search is somewhat higher – though still 15 percentage points below the corresponding OECD average (Figure 3.8).

Figure 3.8. Employment services are used less often in Korea than elsewhere by people looking for a job

Use of public and private employment services as a tool to find work, as a share of all jobseekers in the country, by age group, 2012

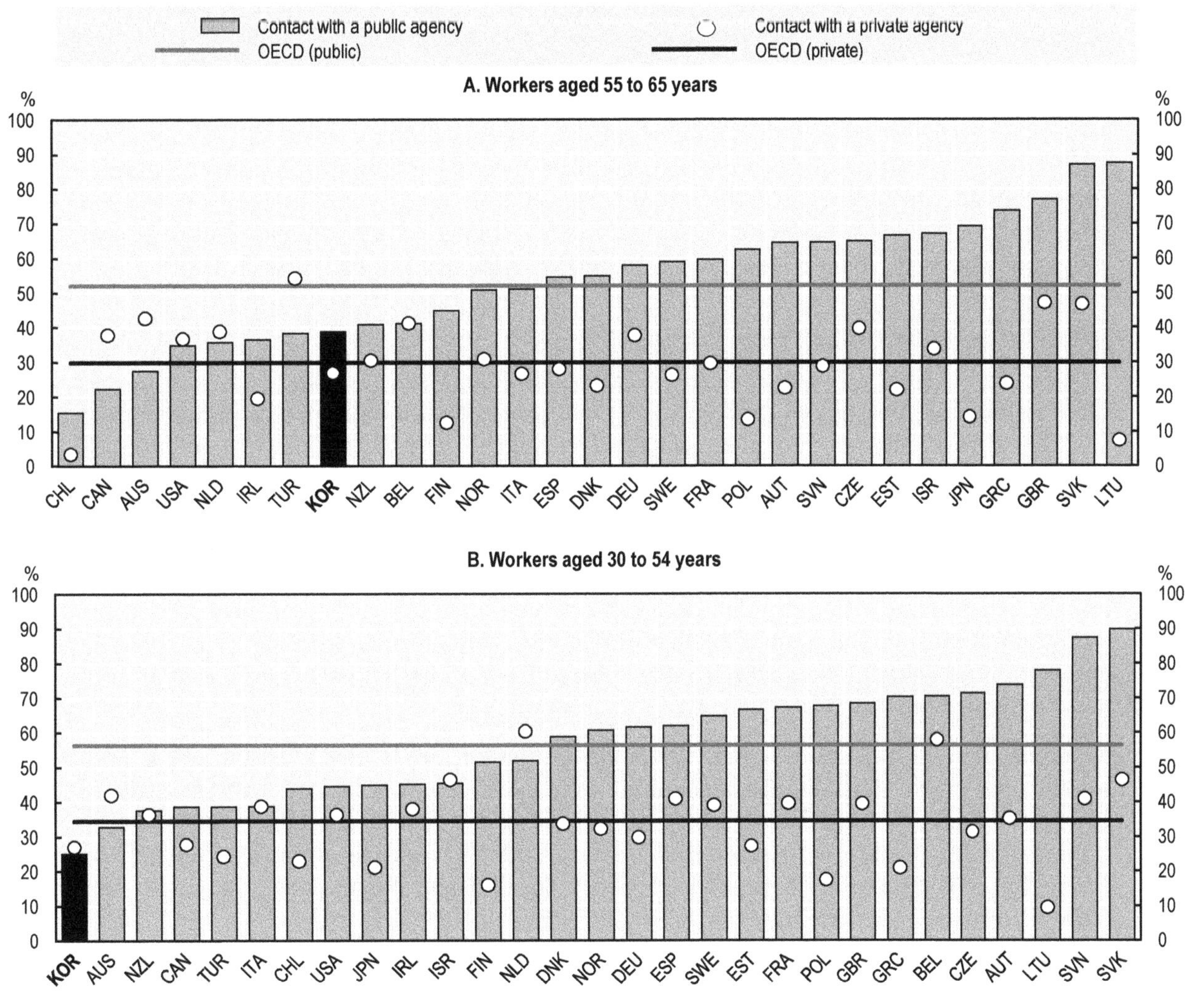

Source: OECD Survey of Adult Skills (PIAAC), 2012, http://www.oecd.org/skills/piaac/.

StatLink http://dx.doi.org/10.1787/888933832096

Important steps have been taken in recent years to ease pressure on the under-resourced MOEL Job Centres, with a significant increase in the number of Job Centre staff as well as an increased use of external providers to contract out more employment services, in particular for middle-aged and older workers. In addition, the MOEL's Work-Net website has become an important tool for connecting jobseekers with available vacancies, which should allow staff to spend more time providing face-to-face counselling to jobseekers. Yet, older people, notably the most vulnerable among them, seldom use the internet as a job-search tool because they often lack the basic ICT skills needed to use online services. For jobseekers aged 50 and over, a recent study by Choi (2016) shows that personal contacts through family, friends, former colleagues or business contacts remain the primary way of finding work. This tends to lengthen unemployment spells as employment agencies are more effective than personal contacts in providing older jobseekers with adequate employment opportunities.

In order to secure successful employment transitions, additional public resources should be devoted to employment service provision in Korea. Despite recent improvements, Job Centre staff remains overloaded and has no choice other than concentrating on the provision of job-matching services, with limited attention to reaching out to older jobseekers, monitoring job-search activities and assuring the quality of job matches. Older jobseekers in particular benefit from face-to-face help by professionals to find a decent job after they retire from their main job. As long as early and honorary retirement practices force older workers out of employment, even if on a "voluntary" basis, every effort must be made to help them back into good salaried jobs or self-employment.

Improving the quality of employment services

A pressing concern is to improve the *quality* of job matches for older jobseekers, who often move into low-paid and insecure jobs that in practice do not provide entitlement to social insurance. Many non-regular workers are trapped in a vicious circle whereby they are more difficult for the public authorities to reach because they are not eligible for EI benefits, which in turn puts them under pressure to take up any job in order to make ends meet, no matter what kind of job it is. When the pension system will be fully mature, there is a distinct risk that the employment rate of older workers could decline as for many of them there will be a real trade-off between continuing to work in a job of low quality and retiring. It is important that public service providers are given incentives to pay greater attention to the quality of jobs offered, beyond helping older jobseekers return to employment quickly.

In Korea, there is a legal requirement for public authorities to evaluate and assess on a regular basis the performance of public employment agencies, as well as that of contracted agencies in the for-profit or non-profit sector. The evaluation results have an impact for Job Centre staff, in terms of pay, and for external private providers, on conditions of the renewal of their contract with the PES and the amount of payment they receive from the government.

The incentives for private providers have been changed several times in the past few years, moving the system from paying for services to paying for employment results and further to rewarding more sustainable employment and, in the most recent step, in 2017, employment of better quality (measured by the person's wage in the new job). This is the right strategy although an evaluation of the system is lacking and the frequent changes, sometimes from one contract to the next, make it difficult for providers to adjust to any new setup. Added to this, the duration of provider contracts is very short – just one year –

making it difficult for providers to invest into longer-term competencies of their staff. A quality assurance framework is also in place in Korea to ensure only good service providers stay in the market. However, the framework could be strengthened and better enacted, as it has proven difficult to eliminate underperforming providers in a period of rapidly growing outsourcing and service demand (OECD, 2018a).

Incentives for MOEL Job Centres could be strengthened along these lines, to reflect the recent shift to a stronger focus on finding good-quality employment also for older jobseekers. The current performance evaluation of Job Centres is predominantly based on outputs such as the number of jobseekers served, job vacancies handled and successful placements. Such approach could encourage the PES to place older jobseekers quickly into low-paid and highly insecure jobs, although a new performance management system was introduced in 2011 that includes job quality indicators such as the earnings level, actual social insurance coverage and employment stability of new hires (KEIS, 2012b). Job quality aspects should be given greater attention and Job Centre staff should have incentives to examine basic working conditions, including the safety of the working environment, before matching jobseekers with employers.

Measuring and monitoring the quality of services should also include a thorough evaluation of active labour market programmes, as required under the Framework Act on Employment Policy, with the aim to abolish ineffective and to promote the most effective and efficient programmes. It is important that rigorous programme evaluation includes a variety of outcomes including post-programme employment rates but also a number of job quality indicators such as career progression, employment stability, employment security and the level of wages.

Providing effective employment service at an early stage

In a strongly segmented labour market like in Korea, the *first* job after mandatory early retirement can have important consequences for the remaining working life. Early intervention measures can be particularly effective in helping workers keep a firmer foothold in the core labour market as they age. Early intervention in this case would mean to assist workers before they reach the age of mandatory early retirement. The situation here is similar to that of workers who were made redundant for economic reasons who, as recent OECD analysis shows, are helped best and most effectively through measures that start before their actual dismissal (OECD, 2018b).

Starting a second career is challenging and needs to be well prepared so that it can be achieved successfully, in a productive and rewarding job. As the age for mandatory early retirement is known well in advance by both parties and without uncertainty, early intervention should be relatively easy to organise. Information about existing employment services and support measures should be provided on a systematic basis to all workers who are approaching the age of mandatory early retirement in order to encourage and enable them to prepare for their second career and to make the best use of their acquired skills and competencies.

There are different ways to provide early intervention or outplacement services for (potential) early retirees. Such services can be provided by firms themselves, either publicly subsidised or not, or by the PES, or by specialised employment services. A number of large companies in Korea provide in-house outplacement services to smooth the dismissal and retirement process, to maintain good community relations and to help workers approaching mandatory retirement with the transition into their "second career". In this regard a forthcoming reform, which was long debated before actually implemented

(MOEL, 2014), is very welcome: The government plans to revise the law to make the provision of outplacement services to early retirees mandatory for larger companies. The initial plan was to include all companies with 300 or more employees but this number is still under discussion. Consideration should be given to expanding this regulation to also include mid-sized companies with 50-299 employees. Evidence suggests that initiatives by companies can have good outcomes in terms of the quantity and quality of job opportunities for their early retirees. In part these positive outcomes may reflect the good reputation these large companies have among prospective employers as well as their large network of subcontractors which often face labour shortages (because they pay a much lower wage) and may constitute a source of potential employers for those retiring early from a large firm.[2]

Between 2001 and 2013, a special programme was in place in Korea – the Job Transfer Support Programme – to encourage more firms to provide outplacement services. It was financed from the EI scheme and applied to contributing firms and employees. The number of workers benefitting from the programme, however, was small – some 1 400 workers per year (MOEL, 2012) – because the take-up in small companies was very low and deadweight costs were massive (KLI and KRIVET, 2007) as the subsidy was used mostly by large companies, which would have offered such services themselves anyway, as part of their normal management practices. The recent abolition of the programme was, therefore, reasonable. However, early intervention services for small and medium-sized companies, matching the mandatory outplacement services of large companies, are critical. Such services must be provided by the existing employment service infrastructure and include active outreach to workers approaching the age of retirement from their main job. Active outreach is also important because older jobseekers entitled to EI and severance payments may not be aware initially of how precarious their situation is, and will tend to turn to the employment service much later than they should have done.

Much can be learned in this regard from policies targeting displaced workers, i.e. workers who have lost their jobs for economic reasons (e.g. due to plant closure or downsizing). The most vulnerable among them are also older workers with long tenure and workers who worked in small companies. Sweden and Canada have effective policies in place to secure prompt support for this group, which offer good benchmarks for mandatory retirees in Korea. Displaced workers in Sweden will be supported very quickly through the Job Security Councils. These Councils, which are funded by employer contributions and regulated in collective agreements, provide services to all workers in a sector or an occupational field. Services are provided even before a worker is actually dismissed and irrespective of the size of a company or a dismissal thus also including all supply-chain workers (OECD, 2015a). Workers in Canada who are displaced from a firm in the course of a dismissal that affects less than 50 people can enrol in an outplacement plan run by the countries' public employment service. In this way, workers from small enterprises can receive the same kind of support as those dismissed from big enterprises which, similar to Korea, are obliged to set-up their own outplacement programme (OECD, 2015b).

Acknowledging the importance of (re-) employment support for the many early retirees, Job Hope Centres were created in Korea in 2013 as employment agencies specialised in the challenges of middle-aged and older workers (those over age 40). The centres, most of which operated by the tripartite Korea Labour Foundation (KLF), originated from the previous outplacement support centres which existed since 2005. Job Hope Centres offer outplacement programmes and counselling services to businesses which plan to provide outplacement services to their employees close to retirement as well as retirees. Services are tailored to individual needs and can include training or retraining before starting job search, as vulnerable older workers often lack basic ICT skills needed to use online job services. Job Hope Centre services are commonly processed in three stages, including diagnosis through one-on-one consultation with a professional to determine the direction of service; actual service execution based upon the employment activity plan prepared in stage one; and post-service management (KLF, 2016).

In 2016, there were 31 Job Hope Centres operating around the country. Their success has not been evaluated yet but the large caseload of almost 500 jobseekers per counsellor working in those centres (see Table 3.1 in Box 3.2) makes it difficult to provide services tailored to individual needs and to achieve the stated objectives. Funding for Job Hope Centres will have to be beefed up considerably to ensure all early retirees needing help – whether EI insured or not and including those retiring from companies with fewer than 300 employees – can be supported quickly and effectively. Effective employment services in other OECD countries typically operate with caseloads of around 100 clients, and caseloads much smaller than this to deal with disadvantaged jobseekers.

Streamlining and coordinating employment services

The plethora of employment services provided in Korea can make it difficult for jobseekers to know what services are available; how to access them; and which services to approach in which situation. There is also considerable room in the current structure for unnecessary duplication of services. There is scope in Korea for better coordinating the various employment services as well as streamlining and, possibly, merging some of them, to make the provision of services more efficient and more effective.

Korea is well aware of the complexity of its service landscape and has taken steps towards a more integrated delivery of employment and welfare services, through the creation of Employment and Welfare Plus Centres which will gradually replace the current network of close to 100 MOEL Job Centres. These new Plus Centres operate as a one-stop service which includes all MOEL and EI employment services but also welfare services provided by the local government and other outsourced services to address financial and family problems – the aim being to be able to offer the right service to the right people faster and more efficiently. The planned integration of the Job Hope Centres for middle-aged and elderly people into the Employment and Welfare Plus Centres could contribute to providing more integrated labour market services for older workers and enhancing their access to services. However, care must be taken in this process that the integration of services is not used to reduce total spending further as each and every service is under-resourced, as discussed above.

The biggest continuing segmentation in Korea is that between MOEL-funded services – which are gradually integrated – and the employment services funded and provided by local governments. There is potentially considerable overlap and duplication of services although there may be a role for both sides. For instance, local government services can be better tailored to local needs and take advantage of closer links with local businesses. That said, in other countries local links would typically be exploited by local offices of an otherwise nationally or regionally structured service with a national supervisory authority. In Korea, the two services exist alongside each other, with limited links between them.

In this regard an initiative in one larger Korean city is a promising step to help jobseekers understand the services available and get in contact with the most appropriate provider to help them find new work: In Busan City, all employment service providers meet on a regular (quarterly) basis to share information and develop joint programmes. Bringing this idea to a structural level, recent efforts to give MOEL a broader role in coordinating services on a regional level are highly welcome. Sufficient resources need to be provided to ensure this role is taken serious and sufficient power be given to the coordinator to ensure the avoidance of duplication and to improve service efficiency.

Streamlining of services would also come with efficiency gains because, contrary to MOEL, local governments seldom devote sufficient resources to properly evaluate their programmes, even in well-resourced areas such as Seoul City. This limits opportunities for local governments to learn from each other's (and from their own) experiences and for the most effective local programmes to be rolled out more widely. Future efforts to increase the role of local governments in providing active labour market programmes, in the context of an ongoing decentralisation process, should include a requirement for mandatory evaluation of all programmes, at least the larger ones, and devoting adequate resources for evaluation and sharing of results and experiences between regions.

In this regard, the approach in Denmark is worth mentioning where municipalities are in charge of delivering social and employment policy. Three steps are taken to ensure strong and coherent outcomes across the country: First, performance of every municipality is monitored rigorously by a regional supervisory body which can also provide support to poor performers. Secondly, the results of every single municipality (such as employment outcomes of single programmes for various groups of jobseekers) are made transparent and published instantly on a public website that can be accessed by every Danish citizen. Thirdly, regular exchange of good practices stimulates cross-municipality learning. In addition, Denmark has a system of financial incentives for municipalities to ensure that funding provided to them by the national government is used in an "active" way, to minimise people's dependence on social benefits and maximise employment.

Finding the right mix of services for older jobseekers

In 2016, following a continuous increase over a period of about a decade, Korea spent 0.37% of its GDP on active labour market programmes (ALMP), which is lower than the OECD average of around 0.5% of GDP (Figure 3.9, Panel A). The mix of programmes is very different from the mix provided in other OECD countries. Half of Korea's ALMP spending is on direct job creation while spending on training and service operations – the biggest components in most other OECD countries – is rather low (Figure 3.9, Panel B).

Direct job creation

Direct job creation programmes have gradually been abolished in the past one or two decades in most OECD countries because they were shown to be ineffective, trapping people into low quality, public local service jobs rather than helping them into regular, non-subsidised employment. To that extent, Korea should phase out some of its spending on such programmes especially for younger jobseekers in exchange for increased spending for measures that help them into higher-quality work.

Figure 3.9. Active labour market programmes in Korea are in most cases delivered as direct job creation schemes

Spending on active labour market programmes as share of GDP (left scale) and relative to the unemployment rate (right scale) and composition of total spending by type of programme, Korea vs. OECD countries, 2016

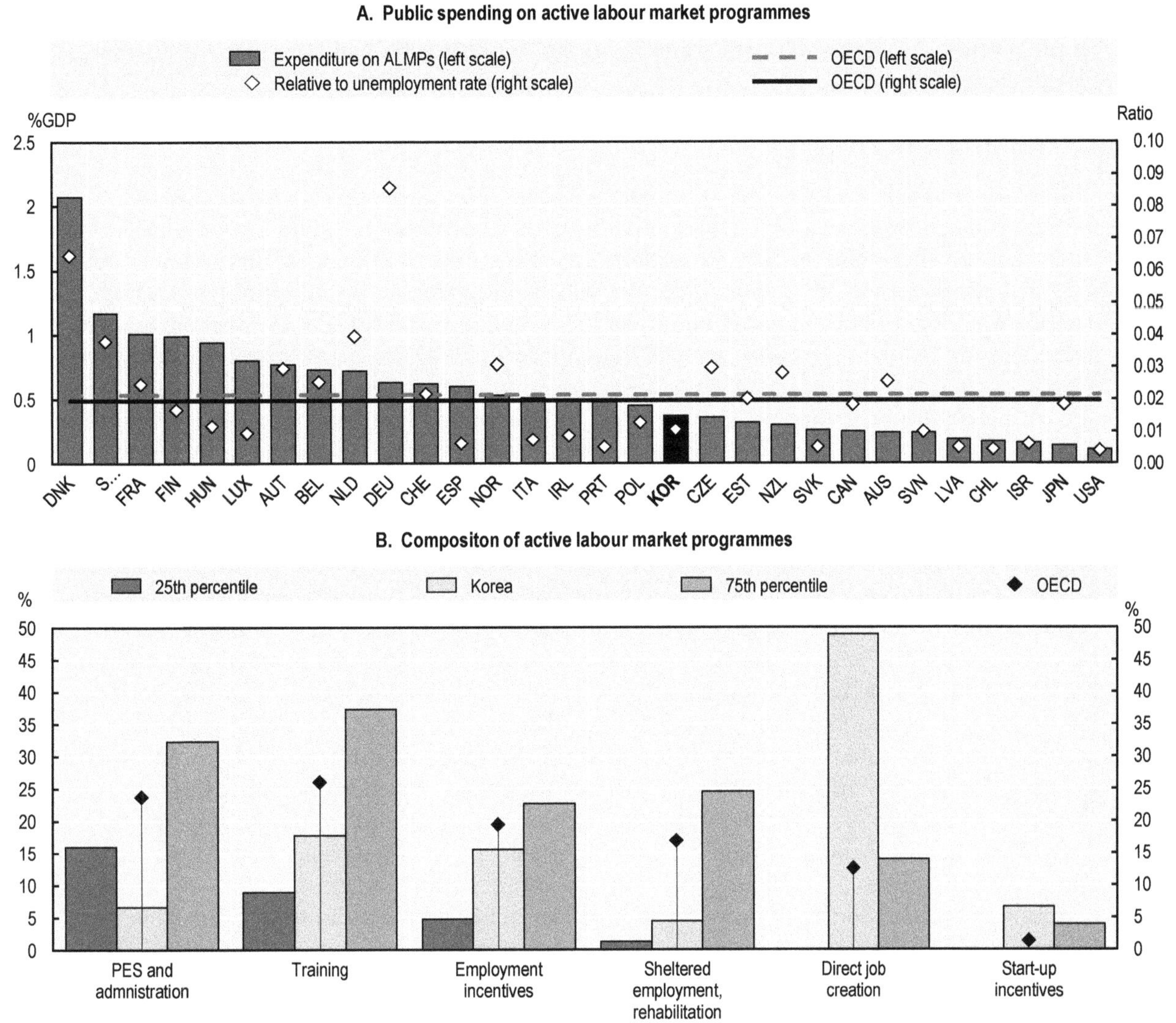

Note: Data refer to 2015 for France, Italy and Spain.

Source: OECD Database on Labour Market Policies, https://stats.oecd.org/Index.aspx?DataSetCode=LMPEXP.

StatLink http://dx.doi.org/10.1787/888933832115

However, direct job creation in Korea also has another important role as a programme to tackle the enormously high levels of poverty of older people, both in the age group 50-64 and 65 and over. Very different from other OECD countries, more than half of the total spending on direct job creation in Korea is for people over the age of 65 i.e. above the legal retirement age. This situation hints towards an important issue which characterises the policy challenge in Korea in many areas: the system must support those currently in troubles while being made fit for the future, when the structure and problems of the population will look different. The many very poor older people today, with low skills and low employability, need direct help which these job creation programmes provide. But in the medium term, direct job creation of this kind – which is to a large extent provided by local employment services – must be phased out as it is ineffective in helping people into well-paid jobs of good quality. Meanwhile, as direct job creation traps older people in precarious employment, it should be coupled with efforts to improve their employability through vocational training so that more people can step into the regular, private labour market.

Employment incentives

Employment subsidies will also help older workers and jobseekers to access the labour market. Such subsidies can be useful in two forms: Incentives to retain workers in their main job and incentives to help jobseekers into new jobs of decent quality. Remaining longer in the main job is the most effective way to keep the quality of employment high. The main policy tool encouraging employers in Korea to retain their older workers longer is the subsidy for the wage peak system, introduced in 2006 and given to employees who accept a wage cut which is partially compensated. In view of the gradual increase in the age of mandatory retirement, the wage peak system should be introduced by firms more widely. Trade unions also need to cooperate on introducing the system to improve employment prospects. Otherwise, firms facing a loss in competitiveness would be prompted to continue pushing out older workers before the mandatory retirement age.

The most important hiring subsidy for older jobseekers in Korea is the Internship Programme of the Middle and Older-aged, introduced in 2013, which provides internship opportunities for unemployed people aged 50 and over to connect to regular jobs. Firms that hire an eligible worker can receive a subsidy equal to 50% of the wage paid (up to KRW 800 000 per month) during an internship period of three months. After this period, KRW 650 000 per month can be paid for another six months if the employer offers a regular job to the intern. Take-up of the scheme, however, is low: In 2014, 7 734 older workers had been hired as interns and 4 795 of them had then been converted to regular workers. More can be done to promote the scheme, especially also among smaller companies. Changes could include: i) reducing red tape to make it easier for companies to apply for the subsidy; ii) making the subsidy more flexible in time as the six-month period may be too short for employers to consider applying for it; and iii) integrating the hiring subsidy with targeted training schemes to improve the employability of eligible jobseekers to make them more attractive for potential employers.

Individualised services for individual needs

The most innovative labour market programme in Korea in recent years is the Employment Success Package Programme (ESPP). ESPP is a comprehensive intervention which can last up to one year and is tailored to individual needs and targeted on three groups: jobseekers with very low income of less than 60% of the median wage, irrespective of age; youth and other disadvantaged groups such as disabled jobseekers or lone parents, irrespective of their income; and other vulnerable groups with incomes below the median, including middle-aged and older jobseekers.

The strength of the programme is that it combines: 1) intensive *counselling*, including psychological testing, group counselling and the establishment of an individual action plan; 2) targeted *training* in line with individual needs, including vocational training and business start-up training; 3) *job placement* support, including the provision of job-search skills; and 4) *financial incentives* for jobseekers to participate in the programme and in training and to stay in employment afterwards. Such, it combines all those elements that have been shown to make activation successful.

ESPP was first introduced in 2009. The number of participants increased rapidly and continuously, from 20 000 in 2010 to 300 000 in 2016. The increase concerned young people mostly, who initially were not included in the target group, but also affected all other groups. In 2015, one in four ESPP participants were over age 40, most of them belonging to the low-income group, 12% were over age 50 and 3% over age 60.

A recent performance evaluation has shown that ESPP is effective in bringing programme participants into employment, including middle-aged and older jobseekers as well as the low-income group of which 20% are over age 50 and 44% over age 40 (Figure 3.10).

Figure 3.10. ESSP participation improves employment outcomes for all participants, including older jobseekers

Employment rates 0.5/1/2/3 years after application for participation in ESPP, programme participants versus non-participants, by type of participant, 2014

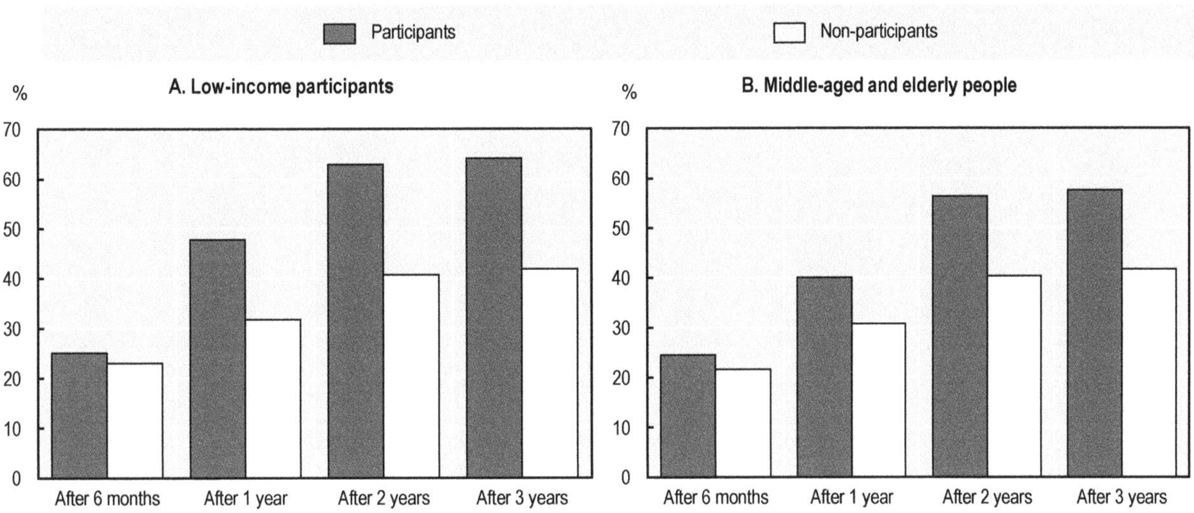

Note: ESPP: Employment Success Package Programme. Non-participants are people who have applied for ESPP but were not selected for the programme.
Source: Lee, B. (2016), "An evaluation of the employment impact of the Employment Success Package Program", Korea Labour Institute, Seoul.

StatLink http://dx.doi.org/10.1787/888933832134

ESPP participation should be expanded further to include a larger share of older jobseekers which benefit from the more individualised support. Administrative data also suggest that in the future more emphasis should be put on securing employment of better quality for those using ESPP: while most participants complete the programme, many of those initially moving into employment are jobless again six months later and half of those finding employment are in low-paid, non-regular jobs (OECD, 2018a).

Improving the working conditions for older workers

Good working conditions can play a significant role in an era of rapidly ageing societies as a means to keep older workers in the labor market longer. Korea has seen significant progress on working conditions over the past decade through declining working hours and the establishment of occupational health and safety systems. However, the situation still needs to be improved especially for older workers. They face relatively poor working conditions including long working hours and more frequent occupational accidents.

Reducing long working hours

Korea has had among the longest working hours in the OECD area for many decades. The average number of hours actually worked per workers in 2017 was 2 024, well above the OECD average of 1 759 hours. Long working hours are widespread regardless of age, gender, company size, industry, and region, and older workers are no exception: usual weekly working hours for Koreans aged 55-64 years are among the longest in the OECD for men and the longest for women (Figure 3.11, Panel A). While accustomed to long working hours, they also choose to work longer to complement their low hourly wages.

Figure 3.11. Older workers in Korea work longer than in almost any other OECD country

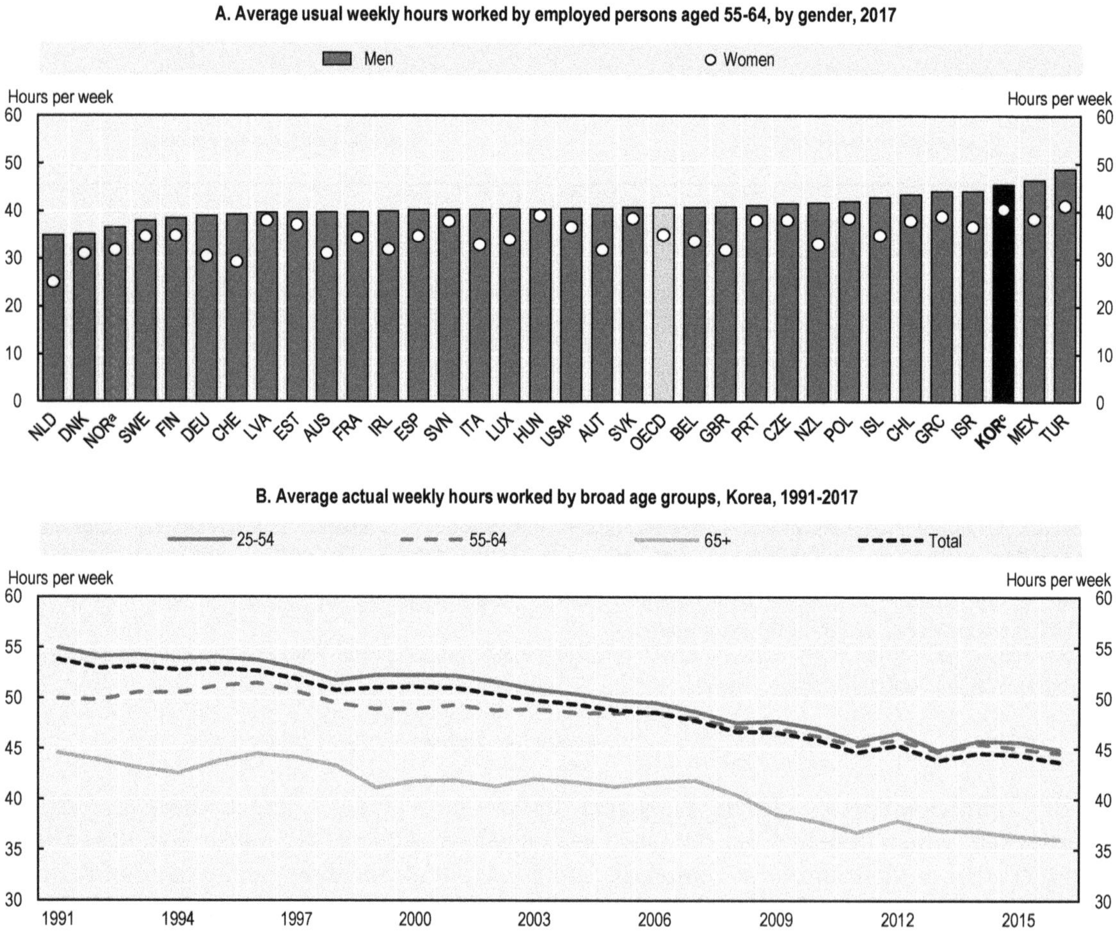

Note: The OECD is an unweighted average of the countries shown.

a) Data refer to 2016.

b) Data refer to employees only.

c) Data refer to actual hours worked.

Source: *OECD Dataset on Average usual weekly hours worked on the main job* https://stats.oecd.org/Index.aspx?DataSetCode=AVE_HRS.

StatLink http://dx.doi.org/10.1787/888933832153

Long working hours can have particularly harmful consequences for older workers, in terms of both their health and their skill development, as this has adverse impacts on their participation in education and vocational training (see above) which in turn perpetuates the high incidence of low-quality jobs. Older workers in Korea, on average, work just as much as their younger peers. However, recent efforts by the Korean government to reduce working hours have borne fruit: average monthly hours of work across all age groups have declined from 217 hours in 1993 to 198 hours in 2006 and 180 hours in 2017, according to the Survey on Labour Conditions. The downward trend in average hours worked has affected all age groups to a similar extent (Figure 3.11, Panel B). A further reduction in working hours for all workers in Korea is essential.

The decline in Korea in average hours worked is a direct consequence of the recent reduction in statutory working hours. Since 2004, the legal work week in Korea is 40 hours (previously 44 hours and before 1990, 48 hours) plus up to 12 hours of overtime work. Like in previous instances, the 40-hour week in Korea was introduced gradually over time, according to enterprise size, in a first step, in 2004, affecting companies with 1 000 or more employees only and in a last step, in 2008, those with 5-19 employees.

In practice long working hours remain widespread, however. Firms prefer to meet increased demand by lengthening working time rather than expanding the number of workers, in view of high fixed hiring and firing costs. Workers also choose to work overtime to cover their expenses for housing and private education for their children. The legal framework still has a number of significant loopholes that allow overly long overtime work. First, in practice the maximum work week is often 68 hours, instead of 52 hours, because the Labour Standards Act does not specify whether weekend working hours should be included in the maximum. Secondly, 26 businesses[3] currently have no upper limit on overtime work since they are exempted from the provisions on working hours, because they are regarded necessary for the convenience of the public or in consideration of their business characteristics. Around 3.3 million people are employed in these businesses. Finally, provisions on working hours, recess and holidays do not apply to workers engaged in companies with less than five employees or in certain industries such as agriculture, forestry, and fishery.

There have been long and intense debates on the reduction of working hours among trade unions, employers and the government for several years. In September 2015, the tripartite partners had reached an agreement which was included in a package on structural labour market reform but the agreement became invalid when the social partners split up soon afterwards. In autumn 2017, Korea's new government is putting forward a new proposal which includes most of the previous agreements, including the following:

- Weekend work should be considered as overtime; to be implemented gradually, depending on the size of the company. Special overtime work shall be allowed for justifiable reasons (e.g. a rise in orders) and with a written agreement between representatives of the employer and the workers, with an upper limit of 8 hours per week.
- The number of businesses that are excluded from the provisions on working hours shall be reduced from the current 26 to 10, and measures to address the long-hour work practice in the 10 excluded occupations shall be identified.

The biggest remaining loophole after acceptance of this reform would be the lacking regulations for micro-businesses. This is critical as almost 40% of all older workers are employed in companies with less than five employees. It will therefore be very important for the tripartite partners to find measures that better regulate work and working time in this part of the labour market.

Lower working hours, however, will also lead to lower incomes. This is problematic for older workers, in view of their low incomes and high levels of poverty. To address this issue, the Korean government introduced a new allowance system for older workers over age 50 beginning in 2016, which compensates 50% of their income loss if they work 32 hours or less per week. This system could be a significant channel not only to promote the reduction of working hours, but also to retain older worker longer at their main job with the wage peak system. It may also give older workers more time for vocational training, which is needed to enhance their productivity. In addition to providing financial support on the reduction of work hours, the government needs to introduce a system which provides older workers with a right to request a reduction in working hours if necessary for health reasons. The combination of a legal right and financial support could lay a solid foundation on facilitating the reduction of working hours for older workers.

Addressing occupational accidents

High standards of occupational health and safety can help workers remain productive for longer and promote higher labour force participation among older workers. Korea has made progress in reducing occupational accidents and establishing safety regulations and policies through legislation, financial support, education and awareness campaigns. Consequently, the total industrial accident rate has declined substantially from around 4% in the 1970s to around 0.5% in 2013. In 2013, a total of approximately 90 000 workers had an occupational accident.

Three factors strongly determine the rate of occupational accidents: job tenure, gender and age. The majority of occupational accidents happen to older male workers with limited experience on their job. Among men age 50 and over with job tenure of less than one month, the risk of an occupational accident is as high as 4.16% in 2013 whereas for female workers of all ages and for male workers with job tenure over two years, the rate is below 0.5%. With job tenure of more than 20 years, the risk goes down to 0.2% (Figure 3.12). Hence, while employees aged 50 and over are only about one-third of the workforce, they account for more than half of all occupational accidents. Data also indicate that occupational accidents often occur in the transition from the main job to the new job in an unfamiliar environment, which will often be a job that is highly insecure, low paid and more dangerous to work in. Thus, during their second career, older workers often face several different working environments and are exposed to a range of new hazardous work factors. This is further proof of how important it would be to ensure older workers can stay in their core jobs longer, ideally until effective retirement, and – if that is not possible – to help them proactively into better second-career jobs.

Figure 3.12. Occupational accidents are still frequent in Korea in precarious jobs

Share of Korean workers aged 50 and over and below age 50 experiencing an occupational accident, by gender and job tenure, 2013

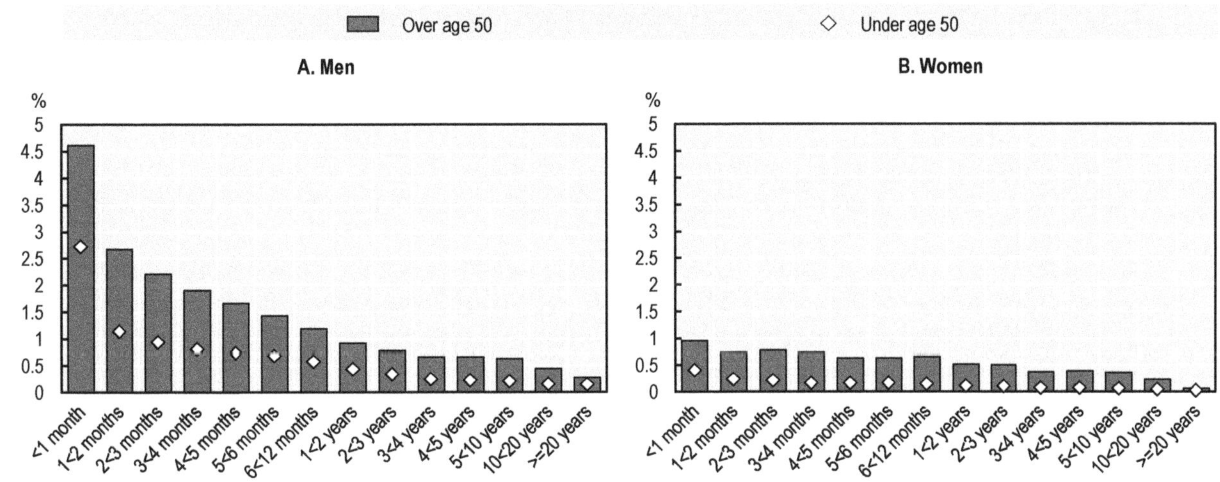

Source: OSHRI (2014), Issue Report, Occupational Safety and Health Research Institute, Ulsan.

StatLink http://dx.doi.org/10.1787/888933832172

More can be done by the government to improve the working and health conditions of older workers in a rapidly ageing society, going beyond reducing the risk of occupational accidents. Older workers must be made aware of the risk factors in their new jobs and about how to deal with them. Employers must have strong responsibilities and incentives to provide working conditions conducive to their (older) workers' health and to prevent job strain, occupational diseases and work accidents. They should take workers' physical and mental health into account when designing overall working environments, including the machinery, working tools, work methods and working hours. The government could establish a system to monitor the health status of (older) workers regularly, in cooperation with local health institutions, especially for those moving in and out of unemployment and insecure employment. In addition, steps should be taken to introduce employer-paid sick leave and a cash sickness benefit, as discussed in detail in OECD (2018a); like the United States but contrary to almost all other OECD countries, Korea lacks statutory or collectively-agreed regulations that address sickness as a major labour market issue.

Conclusion

The high employment rates of older workers in Korea seem to suggest that the country is well prepared for the rapid ageing of its population in the years ahead but this is only partly true. Older workers in Korea often work in jobs of very poor quality and because they have to work to make ends meet. Much has to be done to ensure employability of workers throughout their life and to retain workers in high-quality jobs or bring them back into such jobs in their second career. The challenge in Korea is threefold: to ensure that workers have the skills needed in a fast-changing labour market, throughout life; that those losing a job are helped back quickly into jobs of equal quality; and that working conditions allow workers to work productively for longer.

An effective system of continuous vocational training is critical to ensure workers can upgrade their competencies and skills throughout life, to facilitate ending the practice of mandatory early retirement. Older workers in Korea tend to have poor skills and are underrepresented in vocational training, often because of time constraints. Promising steps to improve this situation include strengthened efforts to deliver training to workers working in SMEs; training that is adapted to workers' as well as workplace needs, in terms of both the contents of training and the way in which training is delivered; tools to hire replacement workers to free people up during their working hours; and tools that validate acquired skills to deliver training that is adapted to the skill level.

As many workers have to start a second career after retiring from their main job, effective employment services are essential to help them transition into new jobs of similar quality. The challenge for a more effective system of employment services is to ensure sufficient capacity, high service quality, early intervention, well-coordinated services, and the right mix of services. Korea has moved on in all five aspects. Most important for the years to come will be to increase the capacity of the employment service to deliver individually targeted services, including those offered through ESPP, as well as outplacement services delivered to workers who are retiring or expected to be retiring soon. While such services are generally provided by big companies, often with considerable success, such services are largely lacking for those retiring from smaller enterprises. Increasing resources for effective services can partly be achieved by a gradual shift in the focus of policies away from direct job creation, in line with the maturing of the pension system which will make the poverty-reducing element of these job creation programmes less pertinent. Higher effectiveness of services can be promoted through continued efforts to coordinate and streamline the services offered by different stakeholders, and by rigorous evaluation of all employment programmes, including those offered by local governments.

Finally, efforts to improve working conditions must continue to make working longer with full work capacity possible for older workers. Among the most important aspects of work in this context are working hours and workplace health. Korea has made successful efforts in the past two decades to reduce its overly long working hours but hours remain among the longest in the OECD, for all age groups and women and men alike. Current efforts to reduce and clarify statutory hours are therefore welcome. However, it will be important in this context to also include workplaces with less than five employees as 40% of all older workers work in such micro businesses. Similarly, it will be important to improve health and safety in those micro businesses as they are responsible for the largest number of occupational accidents. Achieving this will require concerted actions by the social partners and the government, stronger responsibilities and incentives for employers and a better-regulated safety net for sickness matters.

Notes

[1] For France, Behaghel, Caroli and Roger (2011) show that new technologies and innovative working practices tend to be tilted against older workers. The adoption of the internet and of network-interconnected computers as well and increased responsibilities conferred upon the operators tend to boost the wage bill share of workers in their 30s and reduce that of older workers. The less-educated among them are worse off because they are less well placed to learn new technologies (Behaghel and Greenan, 2010).

[2] Samsung Electronics, for example, employs 11 professionals who provide services to 300-400 employees per year approaching the firm's mandatory retirement age of 55. Service outcomes are

stunning: Around 92% find new jobs and another 5% successfully set up their own businesses. Around 94% of re-employed programme participants receive the same or higher wages in their new jobs and some 70% hold more senior positions than in the jobs they left (OECD, 2013b).

[3] The 26 businesses include the following: transport; goods sales and storage; finance and insurance; movie production and entertainment; communications; educational study and research; advertisement; medical and sanitation; hotel and restaurant; incineration and cleaning; barber and beauty parlour; and social welfare.

References

Behaghel, L., E. Caroli and M. Roger (2011), "Age Biased Technical and Organisational Change, Training and Employment Prospects of Older Workers," IZA Discussion Papers 5544, Institute for the Study of Labor (IZA), Bonn.

Behaghel, L. and N. Greenan (2010), "Training and Age-Biased Technical Change," *Annals of Economics and Statistics*, GENES, issue 99-100, pages 317-342.

Brunello, G., G. Weber and C.T. Weiss (2012), "Books Are Forever: Early Life Conditions, Education and Lifetime Income," IZA Discussion Papers 6386, Institute for the Study of Labor (IZA), Bonn.

Choi, E. (2016), "Older Workers and Federal Work Programs: The Korean Senior Employment Program (KSEP)", *Journal of Aging & Social Policy*, 28:4, 308-324.

KEIS (2012a), Public Employment Information System, Korea Employment Information Service, Eumseong.

KEIS (2012b), Employment Effects Evaluation, Korea Employment Information Service, Eumseong.

KLI and KRIVET (2007), An In-Depth Evaluation of the Employment Insurance Programmes, Korea Labor Institute and Korea Research Institute for Vocational Education and Training, Seoul.

KLF (2016), "Korean society concentrating on re-employment of the middle and prime-aged", Korea Labor Review, vol. 60 (autumn), Korea Labor Foundation, Seoul.

KRIVET (2016), Human Resources Development Indicators in Korea, Korea Research Institute for Vocational Education and Training, Seoul.

Lee, B. (2016), "An evaluation of the employment impact of the Employment Success Package Program, Korea Labour Institute (KLI), Sejong.

Leuven, E. and H. Oosterbeck (2008), "An alternative approach to estimate the wage returns to private-sector training", *Journal of Applied Econometrics*, vol. 23, issue 4, 423-434.

MOEL (2012), Current Policy Issues, Ministry of Employment and Labour, Sejong.

MOEL (2014), "MOEL unveils comprehensive employment measures for older people", 24 September 2014.

MOEL (2015), 2014 Employment and Labour Policy, Ministry of Employment and Labour, Sejong.

OECD (2006), *Skills Upgrading: New Policy Perspectives*, Local Economic and Employment Development (LEED), OECD Publishing, Paris, https://doi.org/10.1787/9789264012516-en.

OECD (2013a), *OECD Skills Outlook 2013: First Results from the Survey of Adult Skills*, OECD Publishing, Paris, https://doi.org/10.1787/9789264204256-en.

OECD (2013b), *Korea: Improving the Re-employment Prospects of Displaced Workers*, Back to Work, OECD Publishing, Paris, https://doi.org/10.1787/9789264189225-en.

OECD (2014), *Skills beyond School: Synthesis Report*, OECD Reviews of Vocational Education and Training, OECD Publishing, Paris, https://doi.org/10.1787/9789264214682-en.

OECD (2015a), *Back to Work: Sweden: Improving the Re-employment Prospects of Displaced Workers*, Back to Work, OECD Publishing, Paris, https://doi.org/10.1787/9789264246812-en.

OECD (2015b), *Back to Work: Canada: Improving the Re-employment Prospects of Displaced Workers*, Back to Work, OECD Publishing, Paris, https://doi.org/10.1787/9789264233454-en.

OECD (2018a), *Towards Better Social and Employment Security in Korea*, Connecting People with Jobs, OECD Publishing, Paris, https://doi.org/10.1787/9789264288256-en.

OECD (2018b), *OECD Employment Outlook 2018*, OECD Publishing, Paris, https://doi.org/10.1787/empl_outlook-2018-en.

OSHRI (2014), Issue Report, Occupational Safety and Health Research Institute, Ulsan.

Picchio, M. and J. van Ours (2013), "Retaining through training even for older workers", *Economics of Education Review*, vol. 32, issue C, 29-48.

Chapter 4. Improving hiring and job retention for older workers in Korea

This chapter looks at how current policies and practices around hiring and firing affect older workers in Korea. The discussion focuses on potential rigidities introduced by Korea's seniority-centred professional appraisal culture and the impact of its employment protection legislation for older workers. The discussion evaluates recent policy initiatives to address some of these issues and looks at how they might contribute to better outcomes. The conclusion outlines some concise recommendations for policy makers to consider.

The statistical date for Israel are supplied by and under the responsibility of the relevant Israeli authorities. The use of such data by the OECD is without prejudice to the status of the Golan Heights, East Jerusalem and Israeli settlements in the West Bank under the terms of international law.

A labour market dismissive of its oldest participants

Korea's labour market will have to improve the opportunities for older people to continue working in good jobs. An important issue for more inclusive ageing and employment policies in Korea is to encourage employers to place older workers into better jobs, including by retaining them longer in their main job. Not only would older people benefit from more fulfilling work and age-friendly workplaces but employers would also benefit in terms of improved staff engagement, reduced staff turnover, institutional memory and opportunities for knowledge transfer (Marvell and Cox, 2017).

Job retention among older workers in Korea remains very low compared with most other OECD countries. In 2016, only 23% of all Korean workers aged 55-59 were working with the same employer they had five years before – less than half the equivalent figure of 50% for the OECD as a whole (Figure 4.1). Meanwhile, hiring rates of jobseekers aged 55-64 were high in Korea, almost four times higher in 2016 than the OECD average (34% compared with only 9%).

Figure 4.1. Older workers in Korea have short job tenure but finding a new job is fairly easy

Hiring[a] and retention[b] rates in OECD countries, 2016

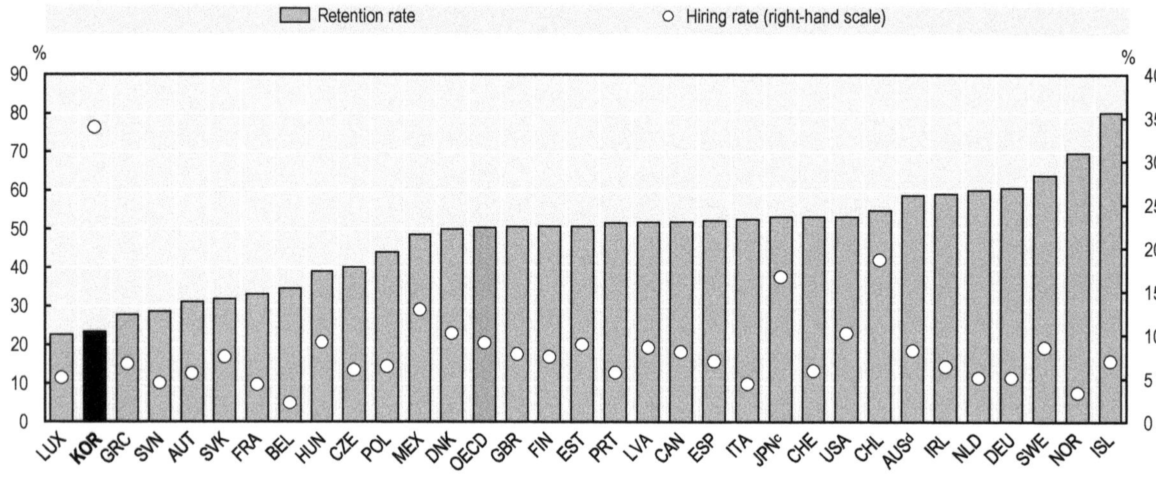

a) Employees aged 55-64 with job tenure of less than one year as a percentage of total employees.
b) All employees currently aged 60-64 with job tenure of five years or more as a percentage of all employees aged 55-59 5-years previously (4-years for the United States).
c) Data for the retention rate refers to 2015 and to 2012 for the hiring rate.
d) Data refer to 2015.
Source: *OECD Older Worker Scoreboard, 2016*, http://www.oecd.org/els/emp/ageingandemploymentpolicies.htm.

StatLink http://dx.doi.org/10.1787/888933832210

Employment practices towards older workers

It is common in Korea for employers to enforce a strict mandatory retirement policy. Some employers decide such rules unilaterally while others deliberate them through collective bargaining. Such self-imposed rules automatically terminate the employment relationship of any worker reaching a specified age-limit. Such rules also constrain hiring at or close to the given age-limit. Job termination of this kind is lawful in Korea unless the rules are stipulated in a discriminatory or arbitrary way. Beyond formal mandatory retirement, it is also common for employers in Korea to petition their older employees to voluntarily separate from their job before reaching the mandatory retirement age through certain incentives. This widespread practice is known as "honorary retirement" (Box 4.1).

According to Korea's Additional Economically Active Population Survey for the Elderly, the average age of separation from the main job (i.e. the job a given worker has held for the longest duration) for workers aged 55-64 (including the self-employed) was as low as 51.6 among men and 47.0 among women in 2016 (Table 4.1). More than half of such separations occurred among workers aged 50-59. The average age of separation from the main job has remained consistently low since the indicator was first calculated in 2005.

Table 4.1. Workers in Korea separate from their main job at a relatively young age

Age of separation from the main job for workers aged 55-64 in Korea by gender, 2016 (years)

	Share of workers (%)					Average age of separation (years)
	Below age 30	Ages 30-39	Ages 40-49	Ages 50-59	Ages 60-64	
Men	0.4	5.5	24.5	58.4	11.2	51.6
Women	14.3	6.8	21.8	51.0	6.2	47.0

Source: Statistics Korea, Additional Economically Active Population Survey for the Elderly.

StatLink http://dx.doi.org/10.1787/888933832324

For men, the most important reason for separation from the main job was the business situation such as business closure or bankruptcy (38%), followed by honorary retirement and layoffs (16%) and mandatory retirement (15%) (Figure 4.2). By contrast, for women, illness came first (28%), followed by business closure or bankruptcy (25%) and family care (21%). The high share of job separations accounted for by the business situation is probably related to the fact that many older workers are self-employed.

Figure 4.2. Older workers in Korea tend to leave their jobs involuntarily

Main reason for separating from the main job among workers aged 55-64 in Korea by sex, 2016

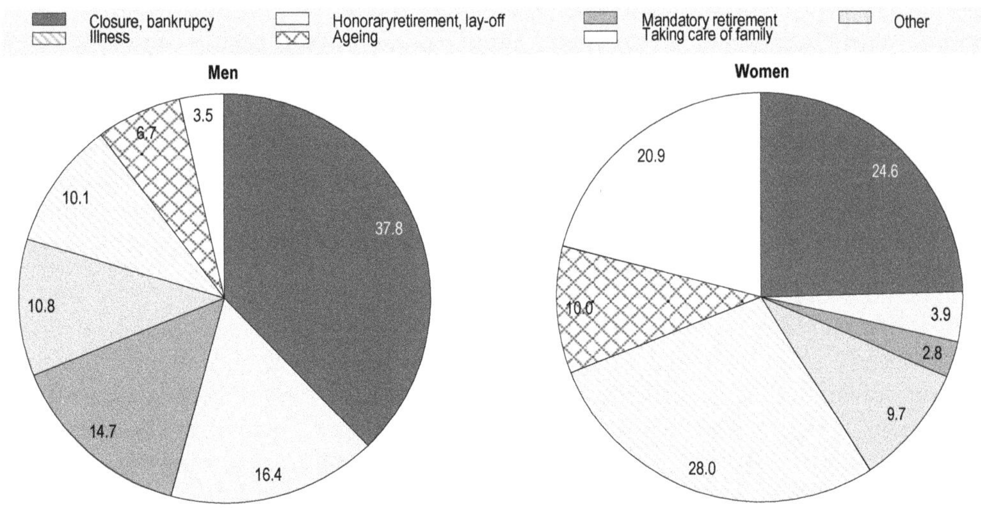

Note: Includes self-employed persons.
Source: Statistics Korea, Additional Economically Active Population Survey for the Elderly.

StatLink http://dx.doi.org/10.1787/888933832229

Box 4.1. The phenomenon of "honorary retirement" in Korea

The term "honorary retirement" refers to voluntary retirement before the mandatory retirement age. Usually, an honorary retirement plan is initiated by employers by notifying employees about the plan and its eligibility criteria and conditions. In most cases, such a plan entails considerable compensation in return for retirement, although there is no rule governing the compensation level, which may be freely set.

Employers can unilaterally establish such a scheme which is not regarded as a dismissal and not subject to dismissal rules. However, in practice, employers try to reach an agreement with trade unions or limit the category of honorary retirement to non-trade union members such as white collars or high-level employees so as to avoid resistances from trade unions. Honorary retirement is thus a kind of voluntary termination of the employment contract under a mutual agreement between the employer and the employee, this practice being sometimes related to traditional Confucian values of honour and respect for older people.

Honorary retirement is often used by employers who need to reduce their workforce. These redundancies are not subject to dismissal rules in principle and, thus, employers may avoid legal uncertainty that could result from collective dismissals. Although Korea's labour law stipulates dismissal rules for redundancy (dismissal for managerial reasons), honorary retirement is widely used for smooth implementation of adjustments of the workforce. It is also directly related to the procedure of a collective dismissal. Under the labour law, honorary retirement is accepted by the court as a measure to avoid or minimise lay-off (i.e. a collective dismissal).

Honorary retirement is also frequently implemented independently of a reduction of the workforce. Many (large) firms systematically implement this plan to reduce the share of older workers, without intending to reduce the overall workforce. This is done for two main reasons. First, it is used to reduce the number of older workers who are being paid above their productive value because of a seniority-based wage schedule. Second, in doing so, it can create more room for promotion of less costly and more productive younger workers, which could elicit more commitment from them.

Honorary retirement plans are prevalent mainly in large firms and in the public sector. In SMEs, individual agreements to terminate the employment relationship are more prevalent, with or without compensation for termination. Even if compensation is paid, the amount is usually small. Greater acquiescence by employees facing redundancies in SMEs partly reflects an acknowledgement of the difficult business situation that SMEs often experience and the greater opportunities they have to find similar jobs in other SMEs. Of course, the existence of stronger trade unions in large firms and in the public sector is also a key reason for this difference.

Employers argue that they have to adopt a costly honorary retirement plan to overcome Korea's overly strict dismissal rules. According to them, even in the case of a lawful collective dismissal, it is difficult to take actions faced with severe resistance from trade unions. Trade unions argue that honorary retirement plans are, in many cases, actually involuntary in that targeted workers are pressured to apply for the plan by the threat of being disadvantaged if they refuse.

Source: Phang et al. (2012), "Practices of the Mandatory Retirement Ages and Retirement Management in Enterprises", Korea Labour Institute, Sejong.

Despite relatively early retirement from the main job, most of Korea's older workers remain within the labour market. Most of those exiting their main jobs around this age begin a so-called "second career". This second career might be in an altogether different economic sector and typically entails a sharp reduction in earnings, job quality and job security. For many, a second career may entail self-employment and business-ownership – though without necessarily having the skills or networks necessary for success. This very unique and long-standing situation in Korea has contributed, in large part, to the high poverty rates observed among the elderly population. Some of the ways in which this pressing issue can be addressed are discussed throughout this chapter.

Factors driving age-based employment practices

Seniority-based professional appraisal

Workers who stay longer with a firm typically have considerably higher wages than workers who joined more recently. This holds true for many OECD countries, and may arise for a number of different reasons. First, older workers may be more productive as they have longer work experience, which in turn may result in broader competencies and greater complexity of tasks and duties. Second, tenure effects may reflect positive assortative matching between firms and workers, whereby higher wages would be a result of employers' selecting better workers to stay in their firm while, similarly, workers would be less prone to leave better-paying firms. Third, firms may incentivise workers to remain in the firm and exert effort in exchange for higher wages in the future. Unlike the two first explanations, this motivation effect may encourage firms to incite workers with longer tenure to take early retirement or lay them off, if possible, if these workers do not have correspondingly higher levels of productivity. Concerns have thus been raised about potential negative employment effects for older workers of pay scales that increase with tenure, regardless of job duties and/or work performance.

Comparing wages in the manufacturing industry, Kim et al. (2015) found that in Korea the average wage of employees with tenure of 20-30 years was 2.7 times the average wage of employees with tenure of less than one year – a ratio much higher than in other OECD countries, except Japan. While the importance of seniority in wage-setting has diminished over time in many OECD countries, seniority-based wage-setting practices are still dominant in Korea. According to the Additional Survey on Labour Force at Establishments, a seniority wage system was in place in 2017 in 60.3% of establishments with 100 or more employees. This is perhaps the single most important factor driving negative employment outcomes for older workers in Korea.

However, there are large differences in wage-setting practices between large firms and SMEs, and between regular and non-regular workers. Large firms still maintain a strong seniority-based wage system while in SMEs seniority wages have become less evident. Average job tenure tends to increase with firm size, ranging from 2.5 years in firms with less than five employees to 3.1 years in firms with 5-9 employees and 10.4 years in firms with 300 or more employees, according to the Economically Active Population Survey in 2012. Moreover, Hwang et al. (2005) found a very weak seniority effect on wages among non-regular workers using the Korea Labour Income Panel Survey data in 2002: the gap in wages between regular and non-regular workers is larger among prime-age workers and narrower among younger and older workers. This implies that a significant number of older workers move from seniority-based wage jobs in large firms to low-paid jobs without a seniority premium, mostly in SMEs.

Why does the seniority wage system persist in Korea?

Seniority-based wage-setting has a long history in Korea. It first came about during Korea's early period of industrialisation as a means to recruiting (and retaining) higher skilled workers who were in very short supply at the time. Seniority-based wage-setting was enforced through strong support from incumbent workers – who have much to gain from its rewards – and employers satisfied by the simplicity of its approach. Arguably, seniority-based wage-setting mechanisms have also found fertile ground in Korea's Confucian social norms that have long enforced strong age-based hierarchies within society. In theory, seniority is not the same as age but in many cases, the two elements go hand in hand in Korea. Seniority-based wage-setting saw average job tenure in Korea rise substantially over time: from 3.6 years to 6.2 years between 1985 and 2010 among establishments with five or more employees and from four years to nine years among those with 500 or more employees (Jeong et al., 2011).

Understandably, the seniority wage system is strongly supported by employees and trade unions because it works in favour of regular employment and strengthens solidarity among union members. The lifetime expenditure pattern of typical Korean households has also contributed to the persistence of the seniority wage system. This pattern can be characterised by the practice of providing continuous financial family support for older parents and children, especially for private education, tertiary education and marriage.[1] This means that expenditures tend to peak for households as the breadwinners reach their late 40s and early 50s.

How does the seniority wage system affect employment of older workers?

The basic link between early retirement from the main job and the seniority-based wage system lies in the gap between the wage level and productivity. If wages rise steeply with seniority, employers will have a disincentive to retain older workers since it becomes too costly to hold onto these workers relative to their productivity. Many empirical studies find a negative effect of Korea's seniority-based wage system on employment of older workers (Phang et al., 2012; Hwang, 2005; Hwang, 2012; Korea Development Institute, 2011; Kim et al., 2007). International comparisons also point out that this wage system could impair career prospects for older workers (Box 4.2). In Korea, wages are estimated to increase by 13.4% as tenure (with the same employer) increases from 10 to 20 years, even after controlling for observable skills, skill use at work, job complexity dimensions and the accumulation of skills associated with more experience (Figure 4.3).[2] This is the highest expected wage growth among OECD countries for which data is available, more than double the cross-country average of 6.1%. These estimation results thus confirm that older workers are at greater risk of job separation in Korea than in other OECD countries.

Figure 4.3. Tenure has a more significant effect on wages in Korea than elsewhere

Expected wage growth as tenure increases from 10 to 20 years, 2012

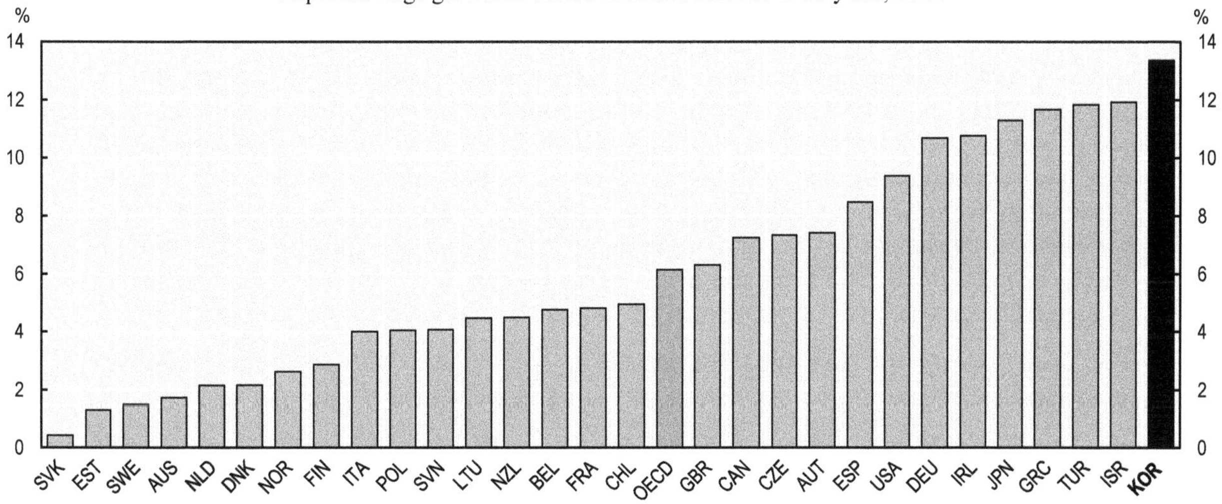

Note: See Box 4.2.
Source: Authors' own compilation based on data from OECD's Survey of Adult Skills (PIAAC).

StatLink http://dx.doi.org/10.1787/888933832248

Another factor is linked to promotion. As higher positions are limited, older workers who had not been promoted are likely to retire. Basically, firms would prefer that such older workers retire voluntary to make more room for promoting younger workers. Together, under the workplace culture based on seniority and age, such older workers may want to retire because it is uncomfortable to work under the supervision of younger colleagues with shorter seniority. The practice of honorary retirement (see Box 4.1) could be seen as a compromise to reconcile the different interests between employers and older workers. In any case, the strong influence of seniority in Korea's firms adversely affects job security of older workers and is a main cause for early retirement from the main job.

How to transition towards job-based professional appraisal?

The Korean government fully recognises the adverse effect of the seniority-based wage system on the employment of older workers. It has given impetus to transition towards a job-based system. While wage policy is primarily determined by the social partners, public authorities can help impulse positive changes in at least three ways:

- By working with social partners to develop new criteria, such as well-designed qualification frameworks, for anchoring wage-setting practices and ensuring fair pay for workers, in connection with their job requirements and skills;
- By raising awareness and understanding of these new criteria and the benefits from using them instead of seniority criteria, for both workers and employers.
- By ensuring a smooth transition period, including through the provision of transitory compensating measures to minimise the potential loss of lifetime earnings that the current cohort of workers may incur.

Box 4.2. The relationship between wages, tenure and skills

The internationally comparable data on individuals' skills collected by PIAAC enables a new perspective on the relationship between wages, tenure and skills/productivity (OECD, 2016). As the survey contains information on many aspects of skills and job tasks, it allows for a better estimate of productivity at the individual level. To the extent that longer tenure coincides with higher levels of human capital and productivity, the association between tenure and wages should become relatively weak when controlling for various measures of skills and work tasks. Any remaining influence of tenure on wages of individuals with the same levels of observable skills and job complexity may indicate an increased risk of negative employment outcomes for older workers.

For each country, the expected wage growth – as tenure with the same employer increases – is derived from the estimation of a standard Mincer wage equation:

$$\text{Ln } W_i = \beta_0 + \beta_1 S_i + \beta_2 X_i + \beta_3 X_i^2 + \beta_4 T_i + \beta_5 T_i^2 + \beta_6 G_i + \varepsilon_i \quad (1).$$

The dependent variable is logged hourly wages (trimmed of the highest and lowest percentiles to control for outliers, and reported in 2012 USD); S is defined as years of education; X as potential labour market experience (equal to age minus years of schooling minus age when school typically starts); and T as tenure with current employer. G is a vector of controls, which includes in particular: three indices of skill proficiency (literacy, numeracy, and ability to use computer), four indices of skills use at work (ICT, reading, writing, and numeracy); four indices of task complexity (autonomy, influence, supervision and planning); and training participation in the past 12 months. Each regression includes controls for gender, immigrant status, parental educational attainment, marital status, number of children, and controls for missing values. Results are weighted by the complex sampling weight in PIAAC.

Since the estimation framework allows for the effect of an additional year of continuous tenure on wages to vary (quadratic specification of tenure in the wage equation), the estimated coefficients on tenure (β_4 and β_5) are not easy to interpret directly. Therefore, a summary indicator of the slope of earnings profiles is calculated, which corresponds to the expected wage growth when tenure with the same employer increases from 10 to 20 years: $\Delta = \ln W_{T=20} - \ln W_{T=10} = 10\beta_4 + 300\beta_5$.

OECD (2016), *Skills Matter: Further Results from the Survey of Adult Skills*, https://doi.org/10.1787/9789264258051-en.

The new National Competency Standards (NCS) and the progressive implementation of Qualification Frameworks based on the NCS constitute an important step in the right direction. For each industry, the NCS provide a classification of jobs into various categories, and for each category, they set out specific competencies – in terms of skills, knowledge and attitude – workers should possess to achieve their job duties successfully (OECD, 2015a). NCS-based criteria are progressively being used for hiring individuals in the private and public sectors. The right foundations for a job-based system of industrial relations are in place, and the transition is underway.[3] As a matter of fact, there has been a decreasing trend in the prevalence of seniority-based systems for setting wages in recent years: while seniority-based wages were applied in 71.9% of firms with 100 or more employees in 2013, this proportion had fallen to 60.3% by 2017.

In addition, public authorities aim to foster the transition towards a job- and skills-based system by providing information, guidelines and other relevant services. In this respect, the Korea Labour Foundation provides briefing sessions, consulting services and free counselling to help companies engage in a dialogue with employees and/or their representatives. The government releases information on best practices, based on a selection of firms that have successfully reformed their practices through improvements to the wage-setting system. But there is still a lack of knowledge among key stakeholders concerning the market wage for a given job that requires specific skills. Government efforts to reduce this knowledge gap should be pursued and strengthened.

To speed up the transition process and overcome resistance from workers and their representatives, some compensation measures may be necessary for the current cohort of workers who have been hired before the transition and have been paid according to a seniority-based system for a number of years. To the extent such pay systems encompass a lifecycle dimension whereby younger workers tend to receive wages lower than their productivity levels in exchange of higher pay – above productivity levels – at older ages, the current cohort of workers may suffer a loss in lifetime earnings.

As sketched out in Figure 4.4, this potential loss would reach a maximum level for middle-age workers: by switching from a seniority-based to a job-based wage system, they will lose their deferred wages almost entirely (Figure 4.4, Panel A). A simple way for firms to redistribute the accrued amount of deferred wages is to postpone the age of mandatory early retirement. Symmetrically, postponing that age without a corresponding change in the wage-setting system would impose large costs on employers (Figure 4.4, Panel B). Therefore, there is scope for social partners to agree on changes in both wage and early retirement practices, for the benefit of workers and employers alike. To strengthen incentives for social partners to engage in such a dialogue, public subsidies can be provided on a temporary basis. In this respect, efforts have been made to introduce a wage peak system, whereby the employer commits to maintain older workers in their job in exchange for a wage cut that is partly compensated by government subsidies granted to employees (see further below).

The experience of Japan indicates that seniority-based systems for setting wages are not set in stone and that the transition towards a job-based system may not occur without some kind of initial impulses (OECD, 2018). In Japan, the main driver was a decade of economic stagnation following the collapse of the Japanese asset price bubble in the early 1990s. Back then, many Japanese companies replaced a large part of their workforce with temporary workers with little job security and much poorer benefits. In turn, fears of job loss led regular workers to accept lower wages in order to maintain their jobs. Job-based systems for setting wages have gained momentum in this context of difficult labour market conditions. In 2016, about three in four Japanese companies applied a job-based system for managerial positions, as compared with one in five in 1999. And even for non-managerial positions, this proportion was 56.4% in 2016 compared with 17.7% in 1999. Symmetrically, the percentage of firms that reflect age and tenure in their pay scales has declined in Japan from 32.2% to 24.8% for managerial positions, and more steeply, from 78.2% to 49.6% for non-managerial positions.

Figure 4.4. Illustrating the theoretical link between wages and mandatory retirement

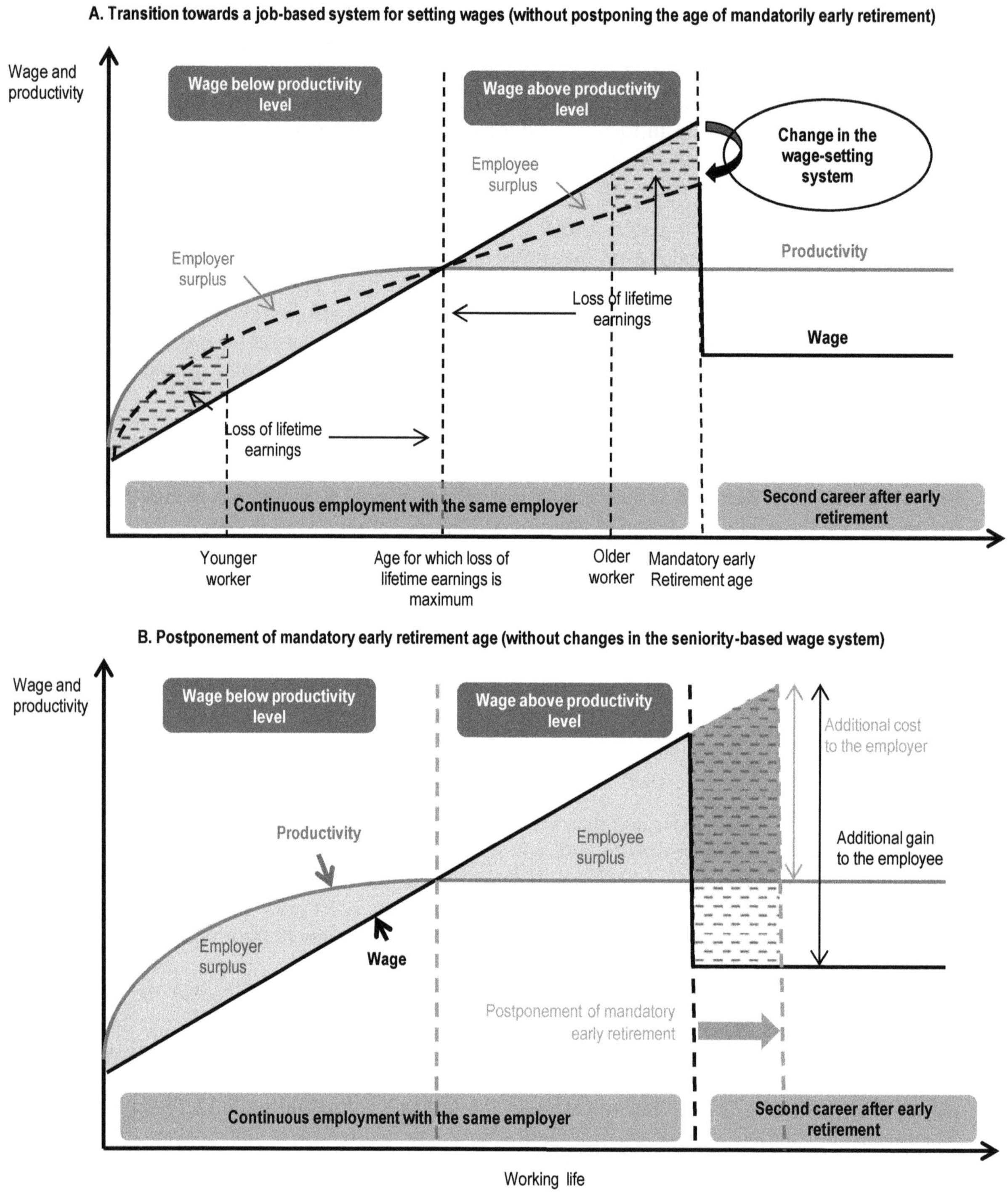

Source: OECD Secretariat.

Employment protection laws

Employment protection laws can play an important role in increasing the stability and quality of employment. Overly rigid employment protection laws, however, can diminish employment opportunities especially for vulnerable social groups, thus compounding existing labour market disadvantages and dualities between younger and older workers; women and men; low- and high-skilled workers; and regular and non-regular employees (OECD, 2013b). Employment protection laws can thereby have an important influence over employers' decisions around hiring and retaining of older workers.

Stricter regulation on individual dismissals of permanent workers

Protection of permanent workers against individual dismissal is stronger in Korea than on average across OECD countries based on OECD's employment protection index, mainly due to procedural inconveniences and protection against unfair dismissal (Figure 4.5).[4]

Figure 4.5. Korea has relatively strong employment protection for permanent workers

Index of protection of permanent workers against individual dismissals: difficulty of dismissal in OECD countries, 2013 (0=no regulation; 6=detailed regulation)

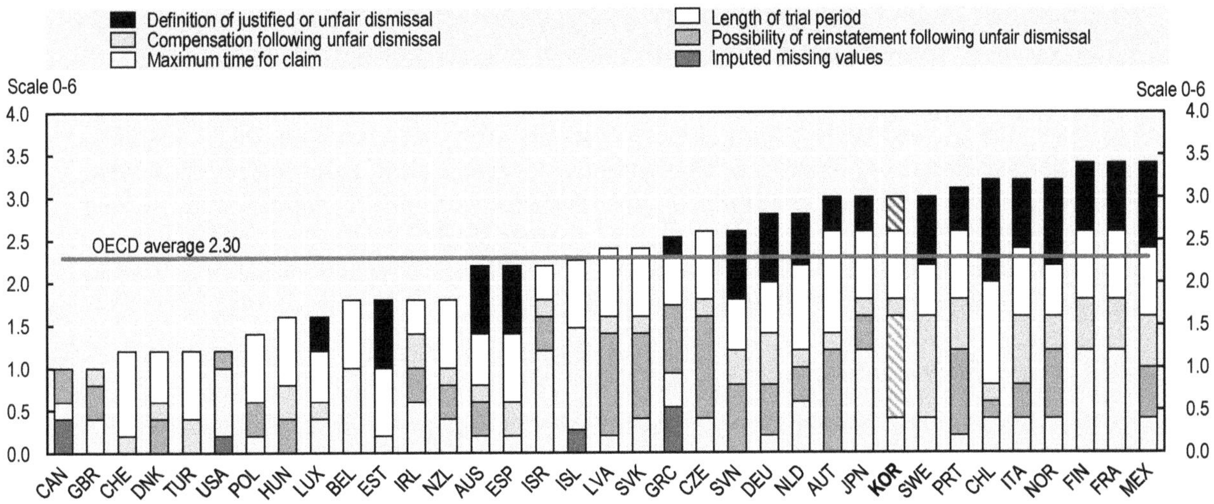

Note: The figure presents the contribution of different subcomponents to the indicator for difficulty of dismissal. The height of the bar represents the value of the indicator for difficulty of dismissal. For the sole purpose of calculating the indicator of difficulty of dismissal, missing values of specific subcomponents are set equal to the average of other non-missing subcomponents for the same country, excluding the maximum time for claim.
Source: *OECD Employment Protection Database*, http://dx.doi.org/10.1787/lfs-epl-data-en.

StatLink http://dx.doi.org/10.1787/888933832267

In particular, Korean rules are stronger in regard to the possibility of reinstatement following unfair dismissal. In Korea, Austria and the Czech Republic, if dismissal is recognised as unfair, reinstatement is almost always granted or offered to the worker. This is likely to create strong disincentives and uncertainties not only to firing, but also to hiring (OECD, 2013b). By contrast, except in the case of dismissal based on explicitly prohibited grounds such as discrimination, reinstatement is for example never offered to workers (or employers can choose compensation instead of reinstatement) in countries like Belgium, Estonia, France, Luxembourg, Spain, Switzerland and Turkey.

A clear tendency towards reducing the strictness of employment protection for permanent workers is observable over the past decade in OECD countries. One of the main policy interventions since 2008 has been a limitation of the possibility of reinstatement in the case of unfair dismissal (OECD, 2013b). Korea needs to take into account the possibility of limiting reinstatement in the case of unfair dismissal in order to reduce uncertainties on dismissal and enhance job mobility of vulnerable groups, including older workers. Such change should go hand-in-hand with a significant reinforcement of social protection for non-regular workers (OECD, 2013b; OECD, 2015a).

Uncertainty in collective dismissals

Another peculiarity in employment protection in Korea is uncertainty in the case of mass workforce adjustments or collective dismissals. With regard to the dismissal rule for redundancy, one of the most critical issues has been the interpretation of the requirement of "urgent managerial reasons". For example, the Ssangyong Automobile case was finally decided in the Supreme Court after five years of contention with different rulings and interpretations at different litigation levels. In the past, dismissals for managerial reasons were possible only if a firm was faced with a high and imminent risk of bankruptcy, but later the court began to allow dismissals also when a reasonable cause for improvement of the business situation or the competitiveness exists, even in the absence of imminent possibility of bankruptcy.

However, the judicial review on this requirement is still a key issue and hotly disputed, and determinations are not sufficiently consistent to give a clear guidance for employers. The bottom line should be to minimise uncertainty arising out of interpretation of legal requirements, notably of "urgent managerial reasons". Clarification on this issue must give sufficiently accurate guidance to employers, which could be done through legislation or a tripartite agreement, or both, as appropriate.

Impact on labour market duality

Korea's labour market duality is very marked with a high share of all workers found in non-regular employment. Strict regulation on individual dismissals of permanent workers combined with lenient regulation on fixed-term contracts has led employers to use more widely non-regular workers for flexibility reasons. In addition, there is also comparatively strict regulation for Temporary Work Agency (TWA) employment in Korea (Figure 4.6). TWA is not allowed for some industries such as construction and is permitted for only 32 occupations for a maximum period of two years. For the rest, TWA is allowed only in the case of a temporary and intermittent need not exceeding the maximum of six months. Furthermore, a person who intends to carry out a TWA business has to obtain permission from the Ministry for Employment and Labour (MOEL), and must report regularly to the ministry. Regulations according to the Act on the Protection of Dispatched Workers also determine that a sending employer and a using employer shall not treat a TWA worker in any discriminatory way in comparison with a worker who performs the same work in the business of the using employer.

Figure 4.6. Korea has relatively strong regulations on temporary work agencies

Index of regulation on temporary contracts in OECD countries, 2013
(0=no regulation; 6=detailed regulation).

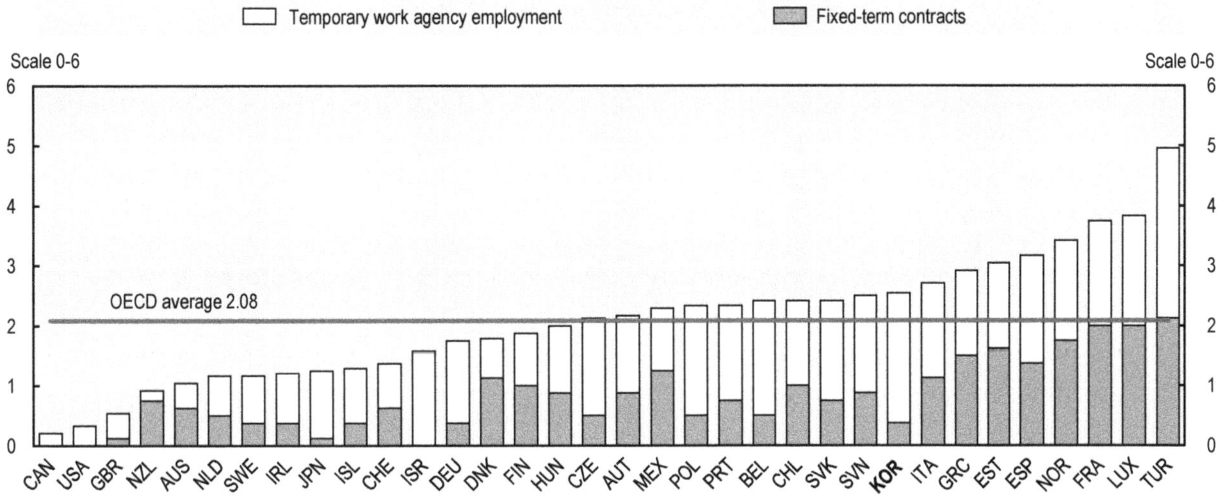

Note: Data refer to 2013 for OECD countries and Latvia, 2012 for other countries. The figure presents the contribution of the indicator of regulation for standard fixed-term contracts (EPFTC) and the indicator of regulation for TWA employment (EPTWA) to the indicator of regulation on temporary contracts (EPT). The height of the bar represents the value of the EPT indicator.
Source: OECD (2013), *Employment Outlook*, Figure 2.9, http://dx.doi.org/10.1787/888932852675.

StatLink http://dx.doi.org/10.1787/888933832286

Stringent TWA regulation, in particular the narrow scope of permitted occupations, encourages employers to prefer fixed-term contracts over TWA employment. The share of fixed-term workers in total employment was 15% in 2014 while the share of TWA workers was only 1%. However, fixed-term contracts and TWA employment are not the only forms of precarious, non-regular employment in Korea. Employment by in-house subcontractors who work for a single firm in the firm's own premises is also widespread, particularly in the manufacturing industry because jobs for direct production are not included in the list of permitted TWA occupations. This form of employment is largely unregulated (Box 4.3).

Future change will need to regulate such unlawful in-house subcontracting practices. The scope of lawful in-house subcontracting needs to be more strictly interpreted, as appears to be happening in court decisions recently, and supplementary measures should be taken to improve TWA regulation. Experience from the Netherlands suggests that TWA employment can open opportunities to improve the quality of non-standard forms of work, provided legal provisions are carefully designed and backed up with collective agreements (Bovenberg et al., 2008). Since the adoption of the so-called Flexibility and Security Act in 1998, TWA workers in the Netherlands have, depending on tenure, a right to a fixed-term or permanent contract with the agency, training facilities (individual budget) and pension entitlements. After 26 weeks of working for the same company, they are entitled to the same wage as employees of that company. The user company saves on hiring and firing costs, but pays more for a temporary worker than for their own employees as the costs for the agency are added to the wage costs of the agency worker.

On the other hand, Dutch legislation facilitates recourse to TWA workers for firms, while abolishing a permit system for TWAs with respect to their placement activities.

Box 4.3. In-house subcontracts in Korea

In Korea, many prominent large firms use in-house subcontracts to reduce labour costs. In-house subcontracts refer to a work pattern in which subcontractors work for principal firms (usually large firms) in the premises of the principal firm. Usually, the subcontractors hire their own employees who work in the principal firms' premises. Although Korea has very strong regulations on TWA, there is no regulation under labour law on such subcontract work, except for some restrictions in relation to occupational health and safety; thus, civil or commercial laws govern the relationship of in-house subcontracts.

This work pattern has been controversial in Korea for many years because the working conditions of employees of subcontractors are much lower, compared with employees of principal firms, even in the case of similar and comparable jobs. The more disputed issue is that the border between TWA and in-house subcontracting is unclear. In some cases, the court decided that the in-house subcontract in dispute is actually a TWA contract. Notably, the Supreme Court has decided in this way in the Hyundai Automobile case; Hyundai Automobile (the principal user) was thus obliged to directly hire most of the employees of its in-house subcontractors.

There are no official statistics on the size of in-house subcontracts in Korea. According to a MOEL survey in 2010 on establishments with 300 or more employees, 41% of the surveyed establishments used in-house subcontracts, with the number of employees of in-house subcontractors (326 000) being much higher than the total number of TWA workers (211 000). Lee (2012) also finds, using the Workplace Panel Survey data in 2007 and 2009 that the most important reason for using in-house subcontracts is to reduce labour costs and that large firms tend to use more in-house subcontracts than SMEs. He also finds a substitution effect between in-house subcontracts and regular jobs and a negative effect of use of in-house subcontracts on total job creation, although they could contribute to firms' profitability.

Source: Lee, B.H. (2012), "Reason for Using In-house Subcontract and its Impacts on Employment", Korea Labour Institute, Sejong.

The social partners also played a key role in the Dutch reform process. Employer organisations and trade unions reached an agreement on regulating the legal position of TWA workers, in complement to legal provisions under the Flexibility and Security Act. The Collective Labour Agreement (CLA) for temporary agency workers provides for matters such as conditions for hiring and separation, but also wages, training and education, holidays and leaves, as well as pensions. In particular, it sets minimum standards that apply to all temporary agency workers. The main employer representative in the TWA sector, ABU, and trade unions renegotiate the CLA every five years, in line with labour market developments (ABU, 2012). Social partners, in particular the ABU, also play an important role with respect to compliance issues. For instance, to become and remain an ABU member, a private TWA must satisfy a number of membership criteria and rules of conduct. ABU membership is seen as quality mark for user companies, but also for temporary workers. ABU members are expected to meet quality standards regarding employment conditions, payment of social security levies, and safety in the workplace. To ensure the quality of ABU membership, the ABU has a comprehensive system of quality checks, including audits which are carried out by special auditing institutions.

The Dutch reform is an example how a balanced reform of TWA regulations, providing additional rights to TWA workers while opening up new business opportunities for TWAs, can constitute a win-win strategy. But achieving this requires collective and well-coordinated efforts, by public authorities, employer representatives and trade unions. In the Netherlands, this was made possible not only thanks to the conducive industrial relations landscape, but also because the TWA sector was large enough to be well structured and organised, led by large firms that were unionised. Korea is far away from such a situation because it has significantly poorer working conditions for temporary agency workers, mirrored in shorter employment duration (35 months compared to almost 90 months for regular workers) and lower wages (KRW 11 500 vs. KRW 18 000).

Special employment protection rules for older workers

An appropriate balance needs to be found between protecting jobs of older workers and enhancing their labour mobility in terms of improved hiring rates and job-to-job moves. Special employment protection rules for older workers can be counterproductive. Policies that penalise firms for laying-off older workers can have a negative impact on reducing their hiring or may lead to substitution between workers of different ages. Firms may also seek to avoid these penalties through various early retirement arrangements and schemes. For example, in Poland, older workers are protected against dismissal during the last four years before reaching the retirement age, but in practice they are likely to lose their job just before reaching the protected age period, facing a high risk of becoming long-term unemployed as employers are reluctant to hire highly protected workers (OECD, 2015b).

In Korea, there is no special employment protection rule targeted at older workers. The court sometimes rules that it is not unfair or unreasonable to better consider older workers with longer tenure in the selection criteria for a dismissal for managerial reasons. But this is not an absolute norm and the court tends to interpret this requirement in a more flexible way, giving more focus on faithful consultation with trade unions. However, to dismiss older workers first could be unlawful because it violates the age-discrimination legislation unless there is a reasonable cause.

By contrast, regulation on temporary contracts permits exceptions for older workers. Employers may use workers aged 55 or more as temporary workers beyond two years, with no time limitation. Similarly, user firms may use a TWA assignment beyond two years with no limitation if TWA workers are aged 55 or more. These special rules for older workers in regulations on non-regular employment are supposed to provide more employment opportunities to older workers who otherwise may be less employable than their younger counterparts. This could help older workers find employment in relatively low-quality jobs, but also potentially with a substitution effect against younger workers in regular jobs. Such substitution effects need to be monitored carefully.

More employment protection needed in SMEs

Many non-regular workers, including older workers, are deprived of basic social protection and employment rights, as regulations and legal requirements are often not respected or well enforced. This is most notably the case among SMEs, which record the most violations of labour regulations. By contrast, employees in larger firms may enjoy higher employment protection than basic social protection through collective labour agreements. It is also difficult for large firms to carry out dismissals for managerial reasons, which could cause severe resistance from employees and social partners.

These considerations suggest that the rules governing the use of fixed-term contracts, TWA employment and in-house subcontracting in Korea need to be reformed while also strengthening their implementation and enforcement. In particular, further effort is needed to shift towards a more equal treatment of employment protection regulation for regular and non-regular workers. The enforcement of employment protection regulations for workers in SMEs should also be a priority.

The progress of recent reforms

Korea has recently taken a number of significant policy steps towards securing better employment outcomes for older workers. While these initiatives largely go in the right direction, some could achieve more if they were strengthened further.

Minimum mandatory retirement at 60

Regulations on employers' mandatory retirement rules gradually came into force in 2016 and 2017 under a new law enacted in Korea in 2013. Under the new rules, age limits for mandatory retirement must not be lower than 60 years. The new law encourages collective dialogue on shaping mandatory retirement and wage-setting rules. The new law also introduces a comprehensive incentive scheme for enterprises that restructure their wage-setting mechanisms to better accommodate older workers.

Prior to 2013, the Korean government already had incentives in place for employers to rehire workers they previously terminated under mandatory early retirement schemes. As from 2008, subsidies were provided for firms to rehire their early retirees, provided the age of mandatory early retirement set by the firm was at least 56 years old. Eligibility criteria were gradually strengthened over time: the minimum age of mandatory early retirement was raised to 58 years in 2013 and 60 years in 2016, for firms to be eligible for the rehiring subsidy. The aim was to encourage firms to rise their mandatory retirement age on a voluntary basis. The reforms had a significant effect as the average age of mandatory early retirement increased by three years, from 57.1 in 2008 to 60.2 in 2016.

At the same time, the new regulation triggered concerns among employers around the need to negotiate new wage-setting mechanisms in view of the prospect of having to retain low-performing workers up to the age of 60. Government concerns were also raised that the legislation might create obstacles for youth to enter the labour market in case wage-setting mechanisms fail to properly adjust away from a seniority-based model. Concerns were also raised about a knock-on effect in some economic sectors regarding higher incidences of honorary retirement and (potentially) non-regular employment.

Alongside other issues, such worries led to the launch of a social dialogue in September 2014 led by Korea's Tripartite Commission composed of employers' and workers' representatives as well as spokespersons for the public interest. The Commission's vast agenda confronted various issues around reforming wage-setting mechanisms. One key recommendation focused on the need to make so-called "wage peak systems" a common practice in enterprises.

Wage peak system

The short-term reform of Korea's seniority-wage practices mainly concerns the use of the wage peak system. According to this system, the employer commits to maintain older workers in their job in exchange for a wage cut that is partly compensated by government subsidies granted to the employee. However, to change the wage system, including the introduction of the wage peak system, the consent from trade unions is necessary if such change may adversely affect employees, whole or in part, even in the case of conflicts of interest among employees. The only exception is the case where such change is reasonable and inevitable in light of established social norms and all relevant circumstances. After much discussion and upheavals, the Tripartite Commission reached an agreement on the labour market reform on 15 September 2015.

The agreement includes a broad range of labour market reforms to alleviate the dual structure of the labour market, extend the social safety net and eliminate uncertainties in work organisation and pay by addressing a number of key issues such as the definition of ordinary wage, the reduction of working hours and improvements in the wage system. It contains the introduction of the wage peak system without the consent of trade unions or majority of workers in a firm. It also encourages companies to adopt a wage-setting mechanism based on job duties or skills, and reduces the uncertainty of employment protection rules in respect of under-performing workers. However, the trade union (KFTU) declared the breakdown of the agreement and its withdrawal from the Tripartite Commission after the government announced the guidelines on the procedure of the introduction of the wage peak system and the dismissal of under-performing workers on 22 January 2016.

Without a wage peak system, the extension of the mandatory retirement age in Korea may not accomplish its goal of encouraging employers to retain older workers longer because their wages could not be aligned with their productivity. The additional burden for firms could be substantial in terms of their competitiveness (see Figure 4.4 above). It would prompt them to continue to push older workers out of the workplace before the mandatory retirement age through more frequent use of honorary retirement. The social partners need to co-operate in the introduction of the wage peak system in order to prolong the current retirement age from the main job.

However, in the long run reliance on the wage peak system is not desirable. It should be seen as a transitory measure to compensate for strong seniority in wage-setting practices which should ultimately be replaced by a job-based mechanism for setting wages. In addition, it may have a negative impact on older workers' motivation to improve their skills or productivity due to a lower wage. At the same time, good practice in retaining older workers and in wage setting should be better rewarded while non-compliance with the minimum mandatory retirement age should be monitored closely and penalised.

Removing mandatory retirement

The difficult move away from a low mandatory retirement age in Korea should be seen in the context of an international trend to eliminate mandatory retirement altogether. Organisations representing older people are generally favourable to eliminating any reference to age when it comes to retirement. For instance, the American Association of Retired Persons, a non-profit, non-partisan social welfare organization based in Washington with a membership of nearly 38 million people supports the elimination of maximum hiring and mandatory retirement ages for all workers (AARP, 2016). Qualification for employment should be based on competency and fitness rather than age.

AGE Platform Europe, a European network of around 150 organisations of and for persons aged 50 years and over, representing more than 28 million older people in the European Union, has also defended this position since its creation in 2001. With the removal of the Default Retirement Age in 2011, the United Kingdom has prohibited the setting of a mandatory retirement age. This is also the case in four other OECD countries (Australia, Canada, New Zealand, and the United States).

Getting rid of mandatory retirement altogether is not without controversy. In particular, employers often argue that their businesses could not be run as efficiently without mandatory retirement practices. As it is difficult to objectively measure the performance of older workers, mandatory retirement provides an easy mechanism to get rid of unproductive workers. But ultimately it comes down to a point of fairness. Why should someone still performing well be forcibly retired just because of age? The United States eventually got rid of mandatory retirement progressively by raising the minimum age of mandatory retirement. This would seem a sensible approach for other countries, including Korea. Difficulties for employers will be greater in countries with rigid employment protection rules but this should be another reason for reforming these rules and allowing greater flexibility for employers in dismissing workers for poor performance.

Laws against age discrimination

Following a recommendation by the OECD in 2004 (OECD, 2004), in 2009 Korea has passed the Act on Prohibition of Age Discrimination in Employment and Aged Employment Promotion, prohibiting various forms of unfair treatment for older workers in terms of hiring, firing, remuneration, training, promotion and other aspects of professional life. Legal provisions discount all those cases of discrimination where: bona fide occupational qualifications play a role[5]; seniority-based wage-setting or promotion practices are in place; a mandatory retirement policy is operated; and in cases of positive discrimination in favour of older workers. Adjudication falls under the responsibility of Korea's National Human Rights Commission and enforcement is carried out under the MOEL.

In general in OECD countries, individual victims of discrimination face strong barriers to bringing a case to the courts, as legal action remains a costly, complex, time-consuming and adversarial process. This is also the situation in Korea, where very few cases are brought before the relevant body. Records from the National Human Rights Commission (National Human Rights Commission, 2014) reveal that 1 498 cases of age discrimination were brought forward between 2001 and 2014. Of these, 76% were employment-related – most of them related to recruitment and hiring (Figure 4.7). This implies that only around 100-150 cases are brought forward every year. Of the completed caseload between 2001 and 2016, only 11.2% were accepted; 59.2% were rejected and 29.1% were dismissed.

Figure 4.7. Reporting of age discrimination is still relatively low in Korea

Number of cases brought before the National Human Rights Commission related to age discrimination in employment in Korea, 2001-16

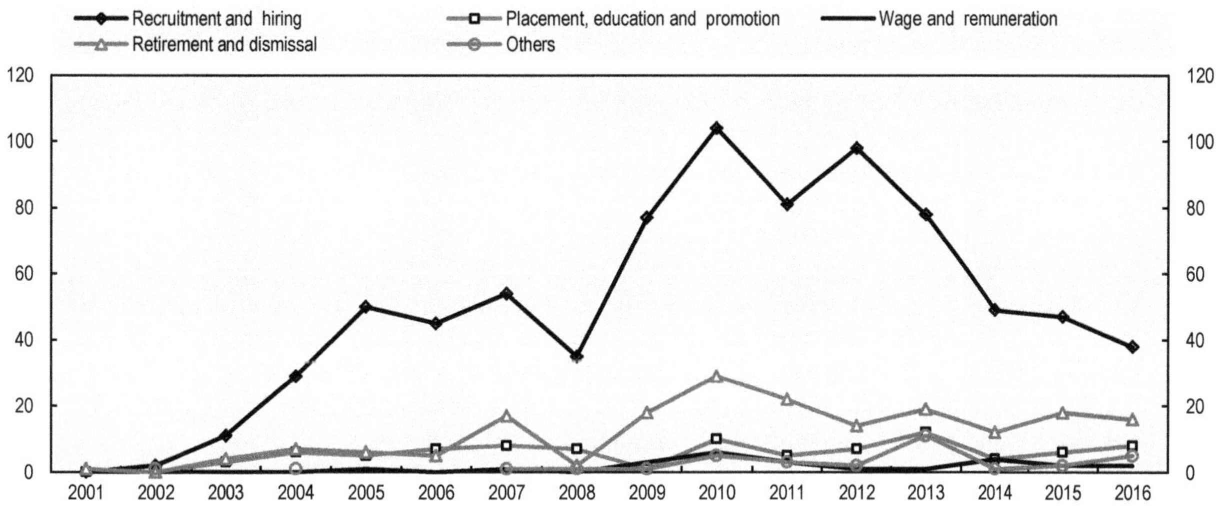

Source: National Human Rights Commission.

StatLink http://dx.doi.org/10.1787/888933832305

The 2009 Act has yet to fulfil its potential impact. While age restrictions are seldom stated explicitly on job advertisements, subtler obstacles remain in place for many older workers throughout the recruitment process. It will take more effort on behalf of policy makers to overturn the business culture and mentalities that continue to endorse such obstacles. In 2016, MOEL monitored 6 836 cases of suspected age discrimination, which resulted in 244 official warnings or remedial orders being issued. As the enforcement of legal rules is based on the willingness of victims to claim their rights, public awareness and incentives for victims to lodge discrimination complaints are crucial elements of an effective anti-discrimination policy. MOEL thus complements its monitoring activities through awareness raising campaigns aimed at transforming current attitudes towards older workers and promoting positive business practices. Since 2006, every third week in September has been designated Elderly Employment Week in Korea, with workplace and media campaigns promoting the message that workers' abilities are more important than their age and prizes going out to companies and workers demonstrating best practices in promoting employment of the elderly. Korea's Job Centres organise a complementary activity about twice a year in the form of an *Employer-Employee Meeting Day for the Aged*, where best practices are shared and positive examples of re-employment are highlighted, including rewards for companies with innovative solutions.[6]

Moving from age discrimination to age diversity

Stereotypical views about older workers could give rise to discrimination by age in the hiring, firing, compensation, training and promotion of older workers (OECD, 2006). Most OECD countries have launched a number of ad hoc initiatives for the prevention of age discrimination to change attitudes of employers towards older workers. Initiatives include legislation, awareness campaigns, development of "tool kits", promotion of best practices, and consultation and co-operation with the social partners (Sonnet et al., 2014).

In Norway, for example, the social partners participate actively in the activities of the *Centre for Senior Policy* to raise awareness of the value of older workers' resources, identify what is needed to motivate workers to remain at work longer, and stimulate age diversity at work (OECD, 2013a).

Age discrimination alone tends to be insufficient to change deeply-rooted workplace cultures linked to age. According to Davey (2014), for example, legislation against age discrimination in the workplace in New Zealand has had limited success "because much of it is not overt, and discriminatory practices are deep seated in business culture". It is thus crucial that legal rules are complemented by initiatives to promote age diversity. In an overview of good age-management practices among OECD countries, Duell (2015) finds that in general implementation remains poor, particularly in SMEs. Guidance for SMEs, as well as coaching, mentoring and guidance for older workers and jobseekers, should be provided on a wider scale. Social partners should introduce age-management issues in collective bargaining. Training the social partners at local level can help with the implementation of good age-management practices but the "knowing-doing gap" is wide. Guidelines and consultancy need to take into account the different management styles and conditions, and available resources of companies of different size.

Reducing age discrimination in Korea can only come about through changing labour market cultures. This will require a shift away from businesses' current hierarchical structures towards more horizontal ways of working. It will also require movement away from the current tenure-oriented, age-based human resources management practices towards more job-oriented, performance-based ones. Such changes will require time to take hold although a range of different measures and approaches could probably do much to speed things up.

Access to flexible work

More flexible work arrangements could be helpful to employers and workers, improving business efficiency and labour market performance. Under a rapidly changing business environment, more flexibility in working-time arrangements may be a better strategy than numerical work force adjustment in that firms could retain skilled workers and avoid the costs for hiring, firing and skills formation. It could also enhance the employability of some groups of workers, particularly those with family responsibility or limited ability to work long hours because of health problems.

Part-time work could be such a type of rewarding flexible work, in particular for older workers opting for phased retirement. However, in Korea, the incidence of part-time work among workers aged 55-64 in total employment was only 11.7% in 2015, well below the OECD average of 17.7% and with little change since 2000. Under Korea's labour law, part-time workers are protected from discrimination, working conditions should be the same and wages proportional to the hours worked, relative to full-time work. Recently, Korea has decided to take a range of measures to encourage part-time work as a way of raising the female employment rate. As specified in the "Roadmap to achieve a 70% employment rate" launched in June 2013, these measures include: subsidies for the creation of quality part-time jobs[7]; counselling services for the introduction of part-time jobs; and the establishment of the right to shorter working hours according to life stages (e.g. participation in apprenticeships for youth, child care for women, and preparation of retirement for older workers). According to Ministry of Employment and Labour (2016), subsidies were provided to 13 074 employees for an amount of KRW 51 billion (e.g. 1.04% of the total expenditure on unemployment benefits). Around three-fourths of subsidised part-time employees are women and only 11% of subsidised part-time employees of both genders are older than 50. According to the Additional Economically Population Survey, 43.6% of all part-time workers in 2014 were aged 50 or older, but there is no information available on the quality of their jobs in terms of pay and benefits, job security and working condition. More should be done to monitor the job quality of part-time workers as well as the impact of the part-time job subsidy programme on different age groups.

If the government intends to use quality part-time jobs as a tool to prevent career interruption, a right to demand shorter working hours needs to be introduced as indicated in the roadmap. For older workers, part-time work may be helpful to facilitate phased retirement and prepare for retirement, including possibly embarking on a second career after retirement. Some barriers hinder older workers from voluntarily working on a part-time basis. Along with reduced wages, in many cases jobs attached to part-time work are different from the full-time jobs that older workers previously held. Thus, if older workers opt for a part-time job, they are likely to be transferred to a lower position. This may not be acceptable to older workers under Korea's workplace culture, which is affected by hierarchical order based on age and seniority. As mentioned in Chapter 5 the retirement pension system (defined-benefit retirement pension and retirement allowance) is another barrier as reduced wages following a transfer to a part-time job lower the value of an old-age pension. To overcome such barriers, part-time work in the main job needs to be encouraged and benefit entitlement rules adjusted accordingly, e.g. by allowing continued contributions on the basis of a full-time job.

Health reasons also drive early retirement. According to labour force survey data, in 2014 respondents retired from their main jobs at an average age of 51; for 19% of them, this was because of health problems. This large share is likely to be related to the fact that the Labour Standards Act has no provisions on sick leave which would provide workers with the right to request sick leave for having a health-related treatment. While workers in big firms or public organizations can use paid sick leave thanks to employment rules or collective labour agreements, many workers in SMEs have no sick leave. Many workers in SMEs have no choice but to leave their company when facing health problems. If sick leave could be guaranteed by law, many workers, especially older workers who are more vulnerable to illness, would be able to return to their main job after a necessary treatment.

Korea's labour code stipulates various flexible working-hour rules. They include:

- A *flexible* working-hour system that may adjust regular working hours upwards or downwards in every three-month period while leaving regular hours unchanged.
- A *selective* working-hour system that allows employees to select when to start and finish their work day under the same regular working hours.
- A *discretionary* working-hour system that assumes employees work regular hours although their actual hours vary from day to day; this is applicable to employees who work outside the workplace such as press reporters, for example.

Flexible work arrangements require an agreement between the employer and the trade union or an employees' representative. However, flexible work arrangements are not broadly used in practice: in 2013, among employees in firms with at least 10 permanent employees, only 4.8%, 3.5%, and 6.9% were covered by, respectively, the flexible, the selective and the discretionary working-hour system. Telework or home-work is also negotiable – the government has encouraged both work arrangements under the name of "smart work" to help promote a better work-life balance – but coverage is even lower, reaching only 0.6% and 0.9% of employees, respectively, in 2013.

No information is available on the degree to which older workers benefit from flexible work arrangements. It is likely that older workers have less access to such arrangements or to quality part-time work. In particular, as older workers in Korea have poorer ICT skills than in many other OECD countries (see Chapter 5) they are not likely to opt for telework and home-work. To promote longer and better working lives for older workers it will be important to tailor flexi-time arrangements to their needs. The government should provide technical services and disseminate good practices to stimulate flexibility.

Subsidising older workers' wages

Another way of making it more attractive to employers to retain older workers longer is to subsidise their wages. Effective subsidies need to be well targeted. Age alone is not likely to be a useful target given the diversity of older workers in terms of employment prospects and capacities. Subsidies should be targeted at disadvantaged older workers, such as low-wage earners and jobseekers who have been unemployed for a long time, e.g. more than six months for the least skilled and more than a year for the others. In addition, the question remains as to whether it is more appropriate to give wage subsidies to employers or to older workers themselves in the form of an earnings top-up.

In Korea, three types of wage subsidies are available: the subsidy for the wage peak system, a working-hour reduction subsidy and a subsidy for extended employment of older workers (Table 4.2). The subsidy for the wage peak system was introduced in 2006 to tackle early retirement practices. It assumes that the seniority-based wage system drives early retirement practices and that a wage cut for older workers provides incentives for firms to retain older workers also after the mandatory retirement age. However, in the longer term the subsidy is likely to deter firms from reforming the seniority-wage system towards a performance-wage system. In 2016, the subsidy provided KRW 30.8 billion to 6 683 employees (e.g. 0.63% of the total expenditure on unemployment benefits).

The working-hour reduction subsidy is a new allowance for workers aged 50 or more beginning in 2016. It could be a significant channel not only to promote the reduction of working hours, but also to retain older workers longer in their main job. This subsidy should be combined with a skill development programme to enhance older worker's productivity and a worker's right to request the reduction of working hours.

To promote and retain employment of older people, the government has also provided subsidies to employers who i) hire workers who have retired because of the mandatory retirement age, ii) raise the retirement age above age 60, or iii) abolish the mandatory retirement age. In 2016, 2 496 companies received KRW 23.1 billion as subsidies.

Finally, all subsidies could be increased for low-wage earners. The redistributive effect of the wage peak systems needs to be assessed, and fine-tuning measures are necessary to ensure that vulnerable workers benefit most. A well designed system of in-work benefits is likely to be more effective in this respect while also being sustainable in the long term, unlike a wage peak system that should remain transitory in nature.

Table 4.2. Wage subsidies for older workers in Korea

Three key wage subsidies programmes for hiring and retaining older workers in Korea, 2017

	Subsidy for the wage peak system	Working-hour reduction subsidy	Subsidy for extended employment of older workers
Target group	Employees to partially compensate the wage cut	Employers	Employers
Entitlement conditions	a) Firms must introduce the wage peak system with the consent of the employees' representative or a trade union (if the trade union covers the majority of the entire employees). b) The stipulated mandatory retirement age must be 60 or more. c) The wage-cut must be 10% or more from a certain age after 55.	Workers must be aged 50 or above.	a) Firms with less than 300 permanent employees. b) Re-employment of workers having retired because of the mandatory retirement age. c) Raise the retirement age above 60 or abolish the mandatory retirement age.
Duration	Up to 5 years.	Up to 2 years.	Between 6 months and 2 years.
Benefit value	Difference between the peak wage and the reduced wage taking into account the ceiling of KRW 10 800 000 per year.	Supports 50% of reduced income if work 32 hours or less a week up to a maximum value of KRW 3 600 000 per year per worker.	Maximum KRW 3 600 000 per year per worker.

Source: OECD compilation based on programme-level information from MOEL.

Conclusion

The large majority of workers in Korea retain their main job only up to their early-50s. Upon retiring early, or on an "honorary" basis, many either become self-employed or enter low-quality, precarious and low-paid jobs in sectors ill-suited to the skills and expertise they have built up over their working lives. Many maintain a so-called second career for a decade or two, if not longer, before effectively stopping to work and retiring in their early 70s.

These retirement dynamics among older workers are somewhat unique to Korea among the OECD countries. They are driven, in large part, by the prevalence of seniority-based professional appraisal systems that act to reward job tenure and age over any other variable. As discrepancies between workers' pay and their productivity grow and become more obvious, many face severance from their main job and limited opportunities for suitable re-employment. Reforming Korea's deeply-entrenched seniority-based wage-setting mechanisms will be an important first step towards enabling longer retention that could benefit workers and employers alike.

In the short term, reform could be achieved through promotion of the wage-peak system alongside potential additional subsidies for low-wage earners. In the longer term, Korea's entire human resources culture will need to move towards more performance-based or job-specific professional appraisal techniques, away from the current focus on seniority. Important first steps are being taken in this regard.

To this effect, more could be done to build a strong consensus around the positive impacts job-specific appraisal and wage setting could have for all stakeholders. From a legislative point of view, more could also be done to i) reduce employers' uncertainty around dismissal costs and what might constitute an unfair dismissal; ii) reform in-house subcontracting alongside the development of a more mature TWA sector; and iii) properly implement existing laws against age discrimination.

Notes

[1] A survey implemented by a Korean newspaper (JoonAng Daily) for 1 000 adults aged 40-59 well illustrates this fact. The main reason why saving for retirement is difficult is the cost of education for 49% of respondents and the cost of children's wedding for another 30% (released on January 21, 2015).

[2] Despite conditioning on observable differences across individuals, it nevertheless may be the case that individuals with higher tenure have other (unobservable) characteristics that make them particularly attractive to firms.

[3] www.businesskorea.co.kr/news/articleView.html?idxno=9768 (accessed 10 December 2017).

[4] The OECD index on protection of permanent workers against individual dismissal includes the following components: notice periods and severance pay for no-fault individual dismissal, procedural inconvenience, and difficulty of dismissal.

[5] The Article 4-5 on Exception to Prohibition of Discrimination of the Act stipulates that any of the following cases shall not be considered as age discrimination: a) where a certain age limit is inevitably required in consideration of the characteristic of the duties; b) where wage, and other money and valuables, and welfare benefits are reasonably differentiated to length of services; and c) where a retirement age is set under labour contracts, work rules, collective agreements, etc. pursuant to this Act or other Acts.

[6] For example, one such winner was a construction company that continued to hire career workers, leading to a substantial increase in the proportion of older workers. The company conducted job analysis with the help of a consulting institute and selected three areas where the skills and experience of older workers are important: project management, expert committees, and technical committees. In addition, it introduced a mentoring system whereby older workers provide on-the-job training to new recruits during three months. This has contributed to enhancing labour productivity and team work between younger and older workers (Ministry of Employment and Labour, 2016).

[7] The quality part-time job in the roadmap is defined as a job which meets voluntary personal needs (study, child care, phased retirement), is free of discrimination, and guarantees basic working conditions such as minimum wage, the basic social insurances, etc. The subsidy programme stipulates five requirements for eligibility: open-ended contract, 130% of the minimum wage or more (120% for SMEs), 15 to 30 weekly working hours, guarantee basic working conditions including four basic social insurances, and no discrimination.

References

AARP (2016), The Policy Book: AARP Public Policies 2015-2016, Washington.

ABU (2012), Temporary Agency Work Works! The economic and social role of temporary agency work in the Netherlands, Badhoevedorp.

Age Platform Europe (2010), "AGE position paper: why the mandatory retirement age should be banned", Brussels.

Bovenberg, A.L., A.C.J.M. Wilthagen and S. Bekker (2008), "Flexicurity: Lessons and Proposals from The Netherlands", CESifo DICE Report, (6) 4, 9-14.

Davey, J. (2014), "Age Discrimination in the Workplace", *Policy Quarterly*, Volume 10, Issue 3, Institute for Governance and Policy Studies, New Zealand.

Duell, N. (2015), "Local economic strategies for ageing labour markets. Management practices for productivity gains of older workers", *OECD Employment Policy Paper*, No. 11, LEED, Paris.

Hwang, S.K, J.H. Jeong, S. T. Kim and J. R. Nam (2005), "Korea's Wages and Labour Market", Korea Labour Institute (KLI), Sejong.

Hwang, S.K. (2012), "Changes in the Labour Market in the Transition Period of Baby-boomer Generation", Korea Development Institute (KDI), KDI Publishing, Sejong.

Joeng, J.H, J.H. Kim, D. B. Kim and I. J. Lee (2011), "Ageing of Labour Force and Innovation of Wage System", Korea Labour Institute (KLI), Sejong.

Kim, S.U., J.H. Jeong and S. Y. Ryu (2015), "International Comparison of Wage and Productivity", Korea Labour Institute (KLI), Sejong.

Kim, D.B., I. J. Lee and J.H. Kim (2007), "Factors influencing the Employment of the Elderly – Comparison between Regular and Non-regular Workers", presented to the Korea Industrial Relations Association.

Korea Development Institute (2011), "Paradigm Shift for Building a Virtuous Cycle of Growth and Employment", Korea Development Institute (KDI), KDI Publishing, Sejong.

Lee, B.H. (2012), "Reason for Using In-house Subcontract and its Impacts on Employment", Korea Labour Institute (KLI), Sejong.

Marvel, R. and A. Cox (2017), "Fulfilling work: What do older workers value about work and why?", Centre for Ageing Better, Institute for Employment Studies, Brighton.

Ministry of Employment and Labour (2016), *Best Practices for Making Older Workers Friendly Workplaces*, MOEL Publishing, Sejong.

National Human Rights Commission (2014), Human Rights Statistical Yearbook 2014, Seoul.

OECD (2004), *Ageing and Employment Policies/Vieillissement et politiques de l'emploi: Korea 2004*, Ageing and Employment Policies, OECD Publishing, Paris, https://doi.org/10.1787/9789264017382-en.

OECD (2006), *Live Longer, Work Longer*, Ageing and Employment Policies, OECD Publishing, Paris, https://doi.org/10.1787/9789264035881-en.

OECD (2013a), *Ageing and Employment Policies: Norway 2013: Working Better with Age*, Ageing and Employment Policies, OECD Publishing, Paris, https://doi.org/10.1787/9789264201484-en.

OECD (2013b), *OECD Employment Outlook 2013*, OECD Publishing, Paris, https://doi.org/10.1787/empl_outlook-2013-en.

OECD (2015a), *OECD Skills Strategy Diagnostic Report: Korea 2015*, OECD Skills Studies, OECD Publishing, Paris, https://doi.org/10.1787/9789264300286-en.

OECD (2015b), *Ageing and Employment Policies: Poland 2015*, Ageing and Employment Policies, OECD Publishing, Paris, https://doi.org/10.1787/9789264227279-en.

OECD (2016), *Skills Matter: Further Results from the Survey of Adult Skills*, OECD Skills Studies, OECD Publishing, Paris, https://doi.org/10.1787/9789264258051-en.

OECD (2018), Working Better with Age: Japan, Ageing and employment policies. OECD Publishing, Paris.

Phang, H.N., Uh, S.B., Yoo, K.C., Lee, S.M., Ha, G.R. (2012), "Practices of the Mandatory Retirement Ages and Retirement Management in Enterprises", KLI, Sejong.

Sonnet, A., H. Olsen and T. Manfredi (2014), "Towards More Inclusive Ageing and Employment Policies: Lessons from France, the Netherlands, Norway and Switzerland", *De Economist*, Vol. 162.

Chapter 5. Addressing poverty among Korean older workers

This chapter examines the availability and adequacy of income support for older workers. While the main pillars of a comprehensive social protection system are in place, one-half of Korea's population aged 65 and over lives in relative poverty. The chapter discusses options to extend and improve the different programmes. In particular, limited coverage and low payments reduce the impact of social welfare policies on poverty reduction. In addition, further reforms are needed to develop an effective three-pillar pension system based on the National Pension Scheme, company pensions and individual savings.

The statistical date for Israel are supplied by and under the responsibility of the relevant Israeli authorities. The use of such data by the OECD is without prejudice to the status of the Golan Heights, East Jerusalem and Israeli settlements in the West Bank under the terms of international law.

Due to labour market failures discussed in previous chapters, many older workers are pushed outside the core labour market before reaching the retirement age with a double penalty as a result: poor quality jobs and little or no social protection. Changes in the labour market and vocational training are needed to improve outcomes for older workers but these changes will take time to materialise and may only be visible in the longer run. In the meanwhile, significant efforts are needed to address the high poverty rate among older people also in the short run. With one in two persons of age 65 and over living in relative poverty, the urgency of the social problem cannot be neglected.

While the main pillars of a comprehensive system of social protection are in place in Korea, they are still in most cases at an early stage of implementation, compared with many other OECD countries. This chapter discusses the strengths and weaknesses of the various programmes and makes recommendations to improve the system. A difference is made between urgent and structural reforms.

Towards effective social security for older workers

Public social spending as a percentage of GDP is still low in Korea, compared with other OECD countries, despite a continuous increase since the Asian financial crisis in the late 1990s. In 2016, gross public social spending stood at 10.4% of GDP – the second lowest in the OECD, well below the OECD average of 21% and only one-third of the level in many European countries (Figure 5.1, Panel A).

Pensions and health care are the largest and fastest increasing components of Korea's social expenditure (OECD, 2018). Even without further social benefit reform, social expenditure in Korea is projected to increase rapidly to at least 26% of GDP by 2050, because of the shift in the age structure and the gradual maturing of the current social protection system (Won and Kim, 2013). In 2015, public expenditure on old-age and survivor benefits amounted to 3.0% of GPD, still the second lowest in the OECD area and well below the OECD average of 8.5% (Figure 5.1, Panel B).

As a result of the overall low level of social spending and the importance of services rather than cash transfers, the Korean benefit system has almost no impact on poverty and inequality outcomes in the country. Data from the OECD Income Distribution database show that 10.5% of Koreans aged 18-65 had a market income below 50% of the median income in 2014 (Figure 5.2, Panel A). The tax and benefit system reduced the relative poverty rate by only 1.2 percentage points to 9.3%. For people aged 66 and above, the reduction in relative poverty is higher (14 percentage points), but one in two of older Koreans are still living in relative poverty after transfers (Figure 5.2, Panel B).

These results are in stark contrast with most OECD countries. Tax and transfer systems reduce poverty among people aged 66 and over by 56 percentage points on average in the OECD, from 68% to 13% (Figure 5.2, Panel B). Only in Mexico and Turkey, there is less redistribution towards older people than in Korea (Figure 5.2, Panel C).

As discussed in OECD (2014), the high elderly poverty rate reflects a decline in family support before other private and public sources of old-age income have matured. In contrast to many OECD countries, where population ageing and the development of a public pension system occurred over a long time span, rapid population ageing in Korea has left the country poorly prepared for a long period. Many elderly had assumed that their children would care for them, thus making it unnecessary to prepare financially.

Figure 5.1. Social expenditure in Korea has increased but remains low in an international comparison

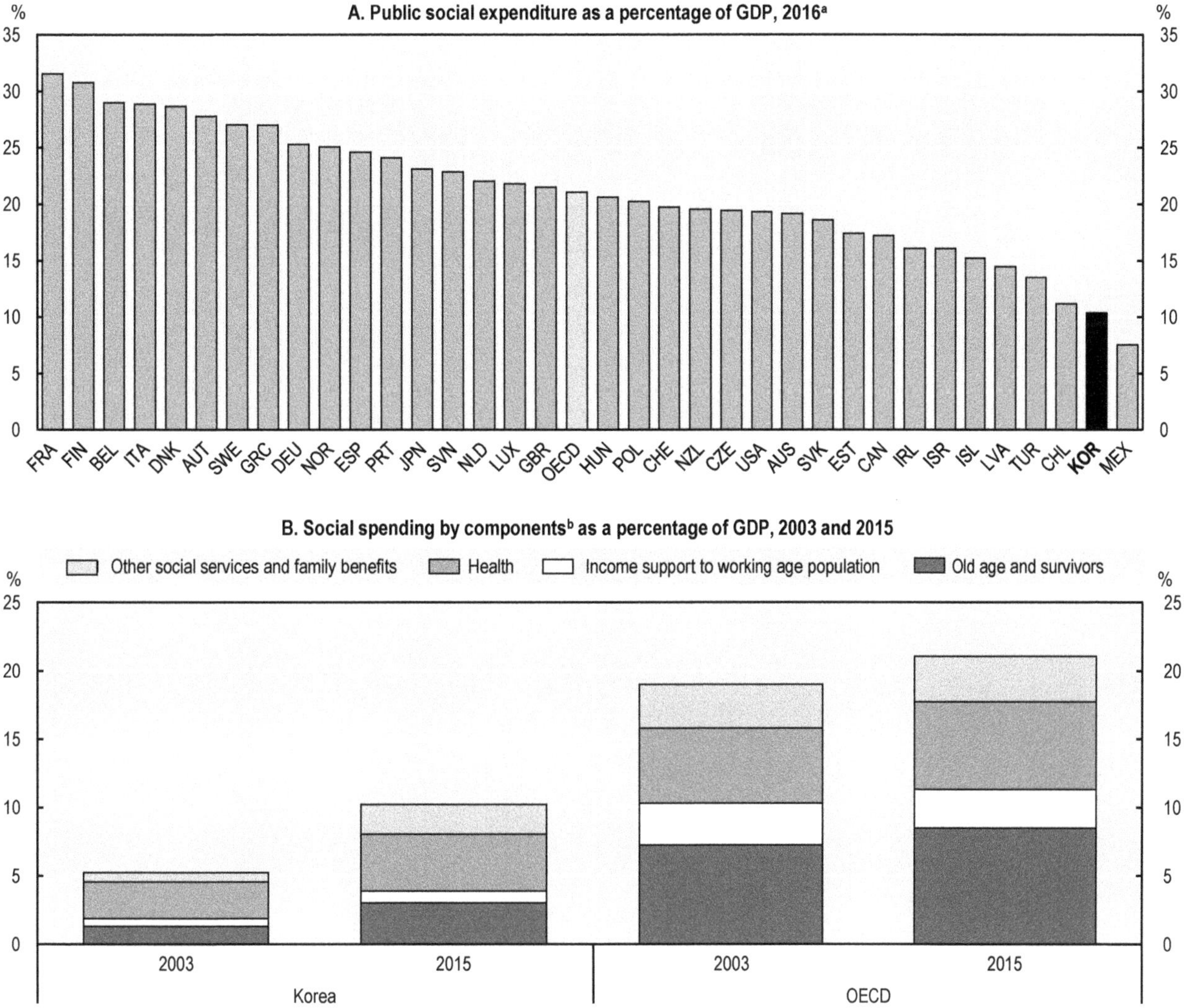

Note: OECD is the unweighted average of the 35 member countries.

a) Data refer to 2012 for Mexico, 2013 for Japan, 2014 for Turkey and 2015 for Canada, Chile and New Zealand.

b) Income support includes incapacity related benefits and unemployment. *Other social services and family benefits* includes active labour market programmes and housing.

Source: OECD Social Expenditure Database, https://data.oecd.org/socialexp/social-spending.htm.

StatLink http://dx.doi.org/10.1787/888933832343

Data from the OECD Income Distribution Database show that public transfers account for only 30% of older people's income in Korea in 2015, whereas in a typical OECD country public transfers account for nearly 60% of their income (Figure 5.3).[1] In order to escape poverty, many older people in Korea have no other choice than to work. Korea is the country with the second highest share of work income in total household income of older people, accounting for half of their total income. Data from the Korean Survey of Household Finance and Living Conditions also illustrate that private transfers (accounting for only 5% of total household income in 2016) have been declining in the past five years

(Table 5.1). At the same time, public transfers are gradually increasing as a share of total household income.

Figure 5.2. The Korean benefit system does little to lift older people out of poverty

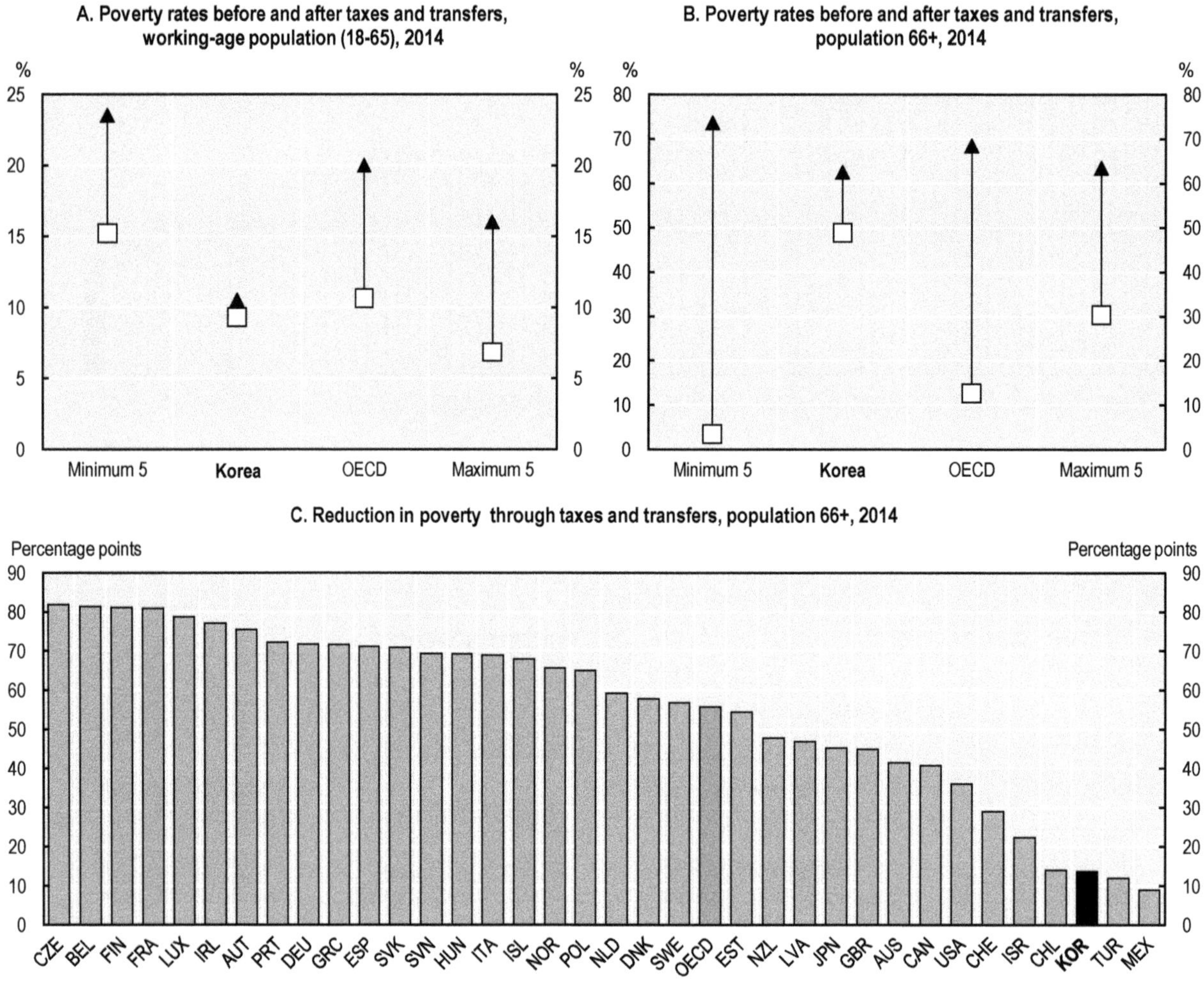

Note: The Minimum 5 is the average of the 5 countries with the lowest poverty level after taxes and transfers and the Maximum 5, the average of the 5 countries with the highest poverty level after taxes and transfers. OECD is an unweighted average. Data for Chile refer to year 2015 and to 2012 for Japan.

Source: OECD Income Distribution Database, http://stats.oecd.org/Index.aspx?DataSetCode=IDD.

StatLink http://dx.doi.org/10.1787/888933832362

Figure 5.3. Work accounts for half of older people's household incomes in Korea

Income sources of households with a head aged 66 years and over, 2014[a]

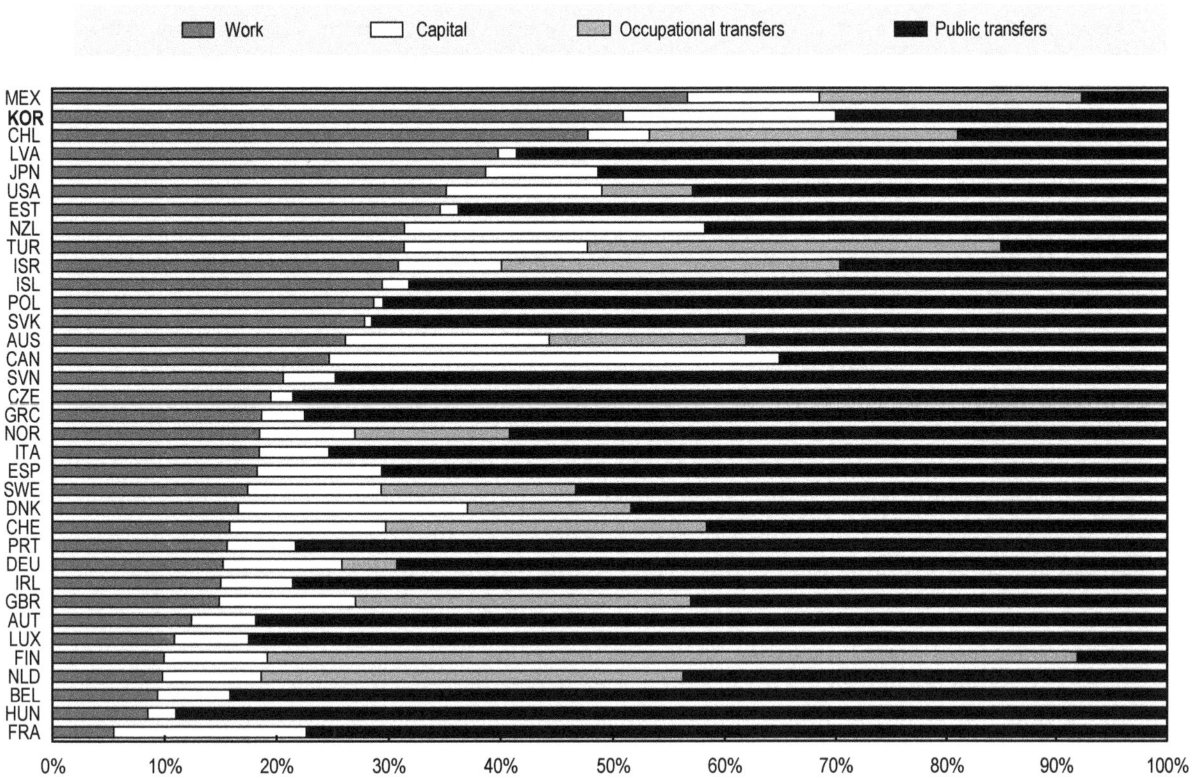

a) Data refer to 2012 for Japan and to 2015 for Chile, Finland, Israel, Korea, the Netherlands, the United Kingdom and the United States.

Source: OECD Income Distribution Database (IDD), www.oecd.org/social/income-distribution-database.htm.

StatLink http://dx.doi.org/10.1787/888933832381

Table 5.1. The share of public transfers in older people's household income is increasing while private transfers are declining

Income sources of households with a head aged 60 years and over, 2012-16 (in percent)

	2012	2013	2014	2015	2016
Total income	100	100	100	100	100
Work income	35	38	39	40	41
Business income	25	24	24	24	21
Asset income	12	12	11	10	11
Public transfer income	19	19	20	20	22
Private transfer income	8	7	6	5	5

Source: Statistics Korea (2016), "Results of the Survey of Household Finances and Living Conditions in 2016".

StatLink http://dx.doi.org/10.1787/888933832552

The evidence shows that the social security system in Korea is currently insufficient to reduce poverty among older people. Comparing Korea with other OECD countries reveals that policy can do much more in financially supporting older people. An effective multi-pillar approach is necessary to ensure adequate retirement income and reduce poverty among older workers. The following sections discuss and evaluate each of the existing policy programmes and presents recommendations to improve their effectiveness.

Reducing in-work poverty among older workers by the Earned Income Tax Credit

With the intention to support the large number of people not able to earn a decent living despite being in employment, the Korean government introduced an in-work support scheme in 2008, the *Earned Income Tax Credit* (EITC). By reducing the income tax bill or providing cash refunds when the resulting tax deduction is larger than the actual tax to be paid, the scheme raises the take-home pay for working households with low incomes. Similar income tax credit schemes are used in many OECD countries and were shown to contribute to poverty reduction and to increase employment (OECD, 2005). Empirical evidence also suggests that the effectiveness of such tax credits is greatest in countries with low income tax rates and low social benefits for the non-employed – both being characteristic of the situation in Korea (Bassanini, Rasmussen and Scarpetta, 1999).

Since the introduction of the EITC scheme in 2008, the scope and coverage of the programme have been repeatedly expanded to include more and more workers. Initially, the EITC targeted families with children, but it was then expanded to childless couples and, eventually, also to single-member households aged 40 and over, and self-employed people.[2] Income and asset thresholds and the maximum pay-out were also augmented repeatedly and varied with the composition of the household (see Table 5.2 for an overview of the eligibility criteria as they apply in 2017).

Table 5.2. Eligibility criteria for the Earned Income Tax Credit in 2017

Criteria	The eligibility requirements
Recipient	• Employed or self-employed • No entitlement to Basic Livelihood Security Programme in March of the application year
Household	• To have a spouse, or • To have at least one child under 18 or • To be aged 40 or above
Total income threshold	• Single person: KRW 13 million per year (38% of the average wage in 2016) • Single-income family: KRW 21 million per year (62% of the average wage in 2016) • Dual-income family: KRW 25 million per year (74% of the average wage in 2016)
Assets	• Total asset (house, and, savings, etc.) of all household members must be below KRW 140 million

Source: Korean National Tax Service website, https://www.hometax.go.kr.

The various changes in the eligibility criteria over the past few years led to an increase in the total number of benefiting households from around 0.5 million in 2008 to nearly 1.4 million in 2016, accounting for about 7% of the total number of households in Korea. Two-thirds of all EITC households have a head aged 50 or more (Figure 5.4), and a large proportion (47%) of these older households consists of single-person households, without a spouse or children at charge. While overall one in three EITC households has a self-employment income, this share decreases from age 50 onwards (Figure 5.5). In the age group 70 and over, only one in seven EITC households are self-employed. This finding is surprising given the high incidence of self-employment among older workers. Possibly, some older workers receive benefits from the Basic Livelihood Security Programme (see below), making them ineligible for EITC benefits. Another reason could be unawareness among older self-employed people about the EITC system. Since most self-employed people tend to register their business with the tax authorities, informality does not seem to be a plausible explanation. To address this issue, a better understanding is needed of the low incidence of self-employment among older EITC beneficiaries.

Figure 5.4. Two thirds of all EITC recipiency households have a head aged 50 or more

Distribution of recipients by household type and age, as a percentage of all EITC recipients, 2016

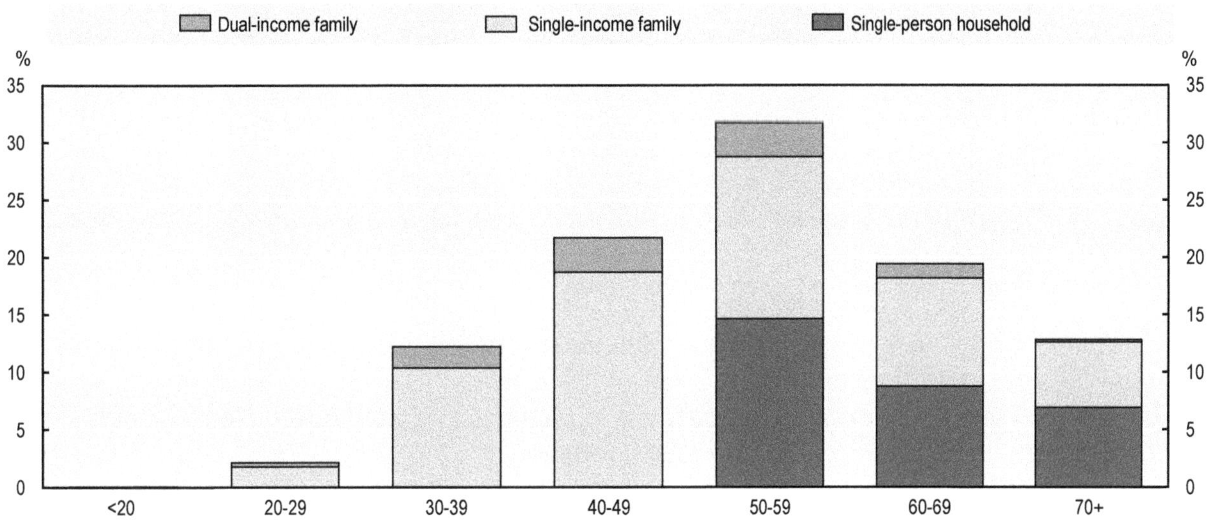

Source: Administrative data from the National Tax Service.

StatLink http://dx.doi.org/10.1787/888933832400

Both the maximum tax credit and the income level at which EITC is phased out are comparable with similar in-work tax credit schemes in other OECD countries.[3] In 2016, the maximum tax credit ranged from 2.1% of the average wage for singles to 5.0% for childless single-earner couples and 6.2% for childless dual-earner couples (Table 5.3). These maxima put Korea in the middle range in an international comparison for singles and on the higher end for couples without children. Only the United Kingdom allows significantly higher maximum credits for childless couples. In regard to the wage level at which in-work benefits are phased out, Korea ranks in the middle of countries for singles and towards the higher end for couples without children.

Figure 5.5. Very few of the older recipients of EITC are self-employed

EITC households by age and employment status, as a percentage of all EITC recipients, 2016

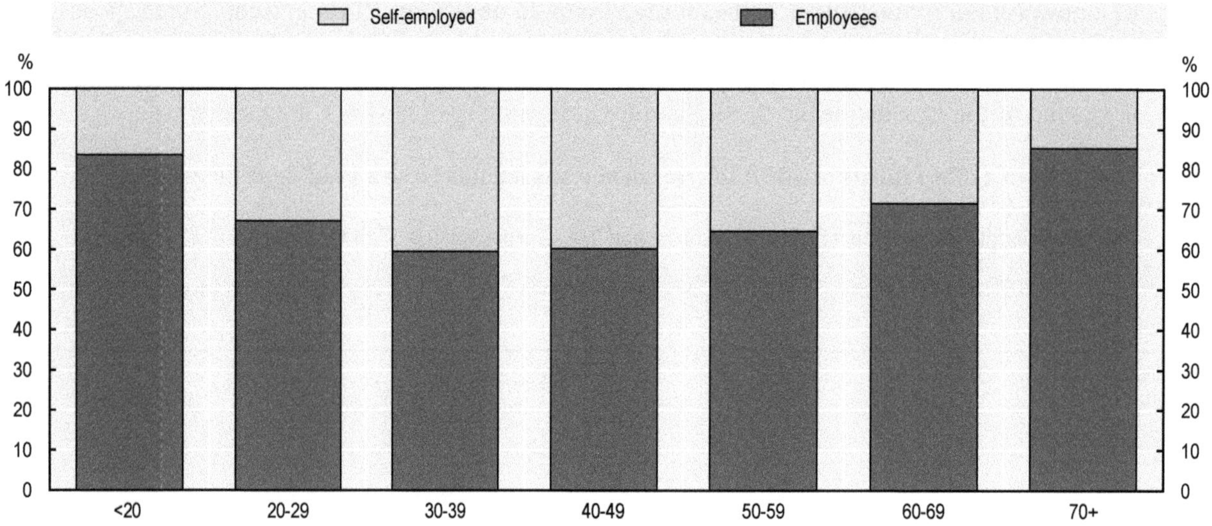

Source: Administrative data from the National Tax Service.

StatLink http://dx.doi.org/10.1787/888933832419

Table 5.3. EITC benefits for households without children are comparable to those in other OECD countries

Maximum benefit amounts and phase-out levels for EITC and in-work benefits in selected OECD countries for households without children, as a percentage of average wages (AW)

	Maximum benefit (% of AW)		Benefit phased out at (% of AW)	
	Single	Couple	Single	Couple
Korea	2.1	5.0 – 6.2	38	62 – 74
Canada	2.1	3.8	37	57
Finland	1.6	3.2	220	440
France	2.4	2.6	62	92
New Zealand	1.5	1.5	21	21
United Kingdom	7.9	13.4	39	54
United States	1.0	1.04	29	40

Note: Data refer to 2016 for Korea and to 2010 for the other countries.
Source: Update based on OECD (2013), *Strengthening Social Cohesion in Korea*, OECD Publishing, Table 2.3, http://dx.doi.org/10.1787/9789264188945-en; and Kim, M.J (2016), "The Current Status of the Earned Income Tax Credit in South Korea and the Implications for Japan – Earned Income Tax Credit or Reduced Tax Rate?", NLI Research Institute Report.

StatLink http://dx.doi.org/10.1787/888933832571

Despite the relatively high maximum benefit levels in an international comparison, the average EITC payment in 2016 was only around 2.2% of the average wage, with around one-third of all participants receiving less than KRW 500 000 or 1.5% of the average wage (Table 5.4, Panel B). Among older EITC households, and especially in the age group of 70 years and older, there are significantly more recipients with annual incomes of less than KRW 5 million (i.e. below one-third of the minimum wage) than among younger EITC households (Table 5.4, Panel A).

Table 5.4. Older EITC recipient households are over-represented among low-earners

	Total	<20	20-29	30-39	40-49	50-59	60-69	70+
A. Percentage distribution of EITC recipients by wage level and age, 2016								
Total	*100*	*100*	*100*	*100*	*100*	*100*	*100*	*100*
Under KRW 5 million	32.9	54.3	22.1	18.7	19.0	29.7	37.3	73.3
KRW 5 < 10 million	24.1	16.5	19.7	18.8	20.1	29.7	30.5	13.3
KRW 10 < 15 million	21.4	15.9	22.5	25.4	25.2	22.6	20.6	9.2
KRW 15 < 20 million	15.8	9.1	25.4	26.8	26.0	12.7	9.3	3.7
KRW 20 < 25 million	5.8	4.3	10.3	10.4	9.6	5.3	2.3	0.6
B. Percentage distribution of EITC recipients by benefit amount received and age, 2016								
	Total	<20	20-29	30-39	40-49	50-59	60-69	70+
Total	*100*	*100*	*100*	*100*	*100*	*100*	*100*	*100*
Under KRW 5 million	36.2	43.0	25.6	24.1	23.5	36.9	36.6	68.9
KRW 0.5 < 1 million	27.9	22.6	24.9	24.3	24.2	34.0	32.2	16.4
KRW 1 < 1.5 million	18.1	16.8	25.0	26.7	26.8	14.4	15.1	7.3
KRW 1.5 < 2.1 million	17.8	17.7	24.6	25.0	25.5	14.7	16.0	7.5

Source: Administrative data from the National Tax Service.

StatLink http://dx.doi.org/10.1787/888933832590

Because of the relatively short history of EITC in Korea, evaluation studies are still rare. Available findings are mixed but, overall, point to a positive impact on labour supply – in terms of both participation and working hours – especially of households at the phase-in range of EITC; i.e. the range within which EITC benefits increase as earnings increase and therefore the range when work incentives are strongest (Lee, Kwon and Moon, 2015; and Song and Bahng, 2014). However, while Jeong and Kim (2015) found positive effects on the poverty rate of couple families, they found no significant effects on the poverty rate for elderly single-member households, largely because the benefits are too small to lift people out of poverty. So far, there seem to be no studies that looked at the impact and implications of the inclusion of self-employed people.

Overall, findings suggest that EITC has a positive impact on labour supply and poverty for certain groups. Yet, EITC alone is insufficient to reduce the high level of in-work poverty among older workers in Korea and thus can only be one element in a broader strategy. For older workers, the most pressing issue is to ensure that all those who are potentially eligible for EITC are reached. Especially among self-employed older workers, EITC coverage seems far below actual in-work poverty rates.

The high poverty rate among older people – including those who are in employment – calls for a stronger focus on this target group. It may be worth to raise the benefit levels of EITC for persons over 50 to reduce in-work poverty in this group, like in Sweden. Sweden introduced an in-work tax credit in 2007 and extended it several times for specific age groups, with the aim of increasing their labour force participation. The credit for those older than 65 is substantially larger than for other age groups.

Insuring older workers against the risk of unemployment

Employment Insurance (EI) is a comprehensive labour market and social security measure in Korea that includes: i) employment security and vocational skills development programmes; and ii) unemployment insurance providing income support to displaced workers. However, as discussed at length in various OECD publications, including *Back to Work: Korea* (OECD, 2013b), *Strengthening Social Cohesion in Korea* (OECD, 2013a) and *Connecting People with Jobs: Korea* (OECD, 2018), EI suffers from both low coverage and relatively low payments for average-wage workers.

Low coverage of employment insurance

In principle, EI covers all employees on a mandatory basis, except for most persons working less than 60 hours a month or 15 hours a week, and family labour. Most self-employed people can opt in on a voluntary basis. To be entitled to EI, a beneficiary must have at least 180 days of coverage during the last 18 months, be registered at an employment security office, capable of work and available for work. In addition, unemployment must not be due to voluntary leaving, misconduct, a labour dispute, or the refusal of a suitable job offer. Overall, Korean EI eligibility conditions are towards the stricter end of the regulations found across OECD countries, largely due to the sanctions for voluntary unemployment (Figure 5.6).

Figure 5.6. Korea has rather strict eligibility criteria for employment insurance

Strictness of OECD's unemployment benefit indicator, scored from 1 (least strict) to 5 (most strict)

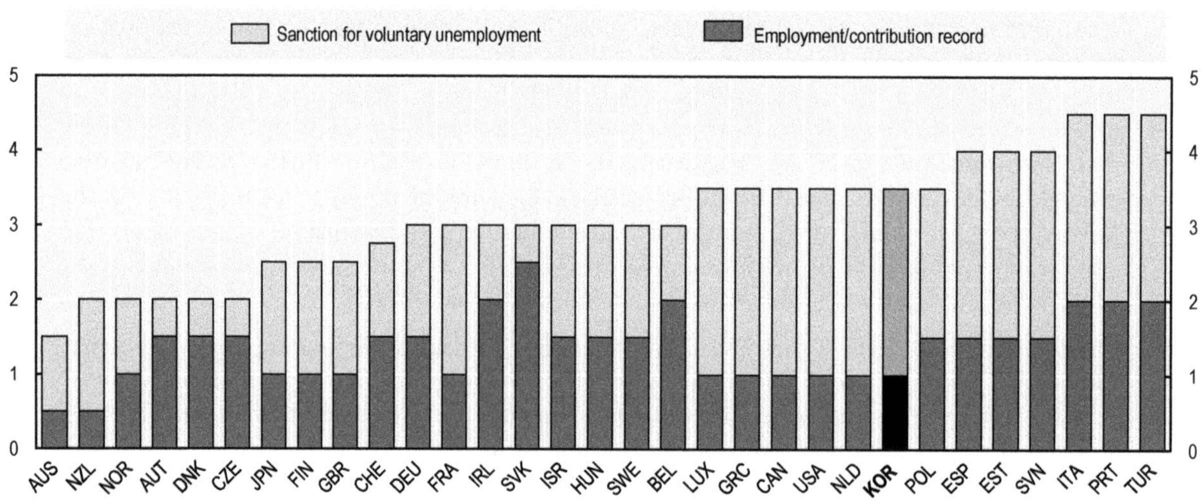

Source: Venn, D. (2012), "Eligibility Criteria for Unemployment Benefits: Quantitative Indicators for OECD and EU Countries", OECD Social, Employment and Migration Working Papers, No. 131, OECD Publishing, Paris. http://dx.doi.org/10.1787/5k9h43kgkvr4-en.

StatLink http://dx.doi.org/10.1787/888933832438

While there are substantial grey areas between voluntary and involuntary separations, "honorary retirement" (i.e. voluntary retirement before the mandatory retirement age; see Box 4.1 for details) is a justifiable reason for separation. As such, people who go on voluntary retirement are, in principle, entitled to EI. Workers aged 65 and over who are newly employed are excluded from receiving unemployment benefits although they can still participate in employment security and vocational skills development programmes.

In 2016, less than half of all workers aged 50-64 (43.5%) had access to an employment safety net (Table 5.5). The share of covered older workers is considerably lower than for other age groups. This can be explained by two factors: the high share of only voluntarily insured self-employed in the age group 50-64 (21.8%) and a high share of non-enrolled older wage workers (18%). The drop in EI coverage with age is directly related to the switch in occupation after honorary retirement discussed in Chapter 2 of this report. While many older workers are covered by EI during their main job, they are much less likely to be covered in the jobs they take up afterwards.

Table 5.5. Less than half of all older workers have access to an employment safety net

Distribution of workers with and without employment safety net by age and employment status, 2016

Age	Wage workers *with* employment safety net	Wage workers *without* employment safety net						
		Not enrolled	Legally excluded (wage workers)	Non-wage workers				
				Employer		Self-employed	Unpaid family workers
				Firms with 5 or more employees	Firms with less than 5 employees		
Total	53.2	14.9	5.8	1.7	4.4	15.5	4.5
15-29	67.3	24.6	1.8	0.1	0.8	3.4	2.0
30-49	63.5	12.5	2.4	1.8	5.0	11.6	3.2
50-64	43.5	18.0	2.6	2.4	5.6	21.8	6.1

Note: This figure adapts and updates calculations similar to those published by Yoo, G. (2013), "Institutional Blind Spots in the South Korean Employment Safety Net and Policy Solutions", KDI Focus.
Source: Supplementary results of the Economically Active Population Survey by employment type, 08/2016.

StatLink http://dx.doi.org/10.1787/888933832609

The drop in EI eligibility among older workers is unfortunate, as it happens at a moment that they have much more volatile employment conditions and are in higher need of an adequate employment safety net. As discussed in detail in *Connecting People with Jobs: Korea* (OECD, 2018), strong efforts are needed to i) boost EI coverage among those who are currently (voluntarily) excluded from the system; and ii) better enforce EI regulations to ensure better coverage among undocumented workers. These recommendations particularly hold for older workers, who are over-represented in both categories.

To expand EI coverage, OECD (2018) recommends to seek effective ways to ensure coverage among self-employed workers, possibly by making EI contributions mandatory for this group; and to allow workers who voluntarily leave their jobs to access EI after a suitable waiting period, rather than disqualifying them outright.

For instance, several OECD countries have resorted to mandatory EI registration for self-employed workers to improve coverage among this group of workers. Indeed, the voluntary approach used in Korea has not resulted in significant coverage rates, nor did it in other OECD countries. Greece and Slovenia are two countries that have recently switched from voluntary to mandatory coverage for self-employed persons (OECD, 2018). Mandatory coverage would also have the advantage that older workers are more likely to contact the Employment Centre and make use of the available employment services, hereby increasing the likelihood that they find better jobs and avoid poverty.

Value and duration of unemployment benefits

While benefit recipients receive in principle 50% of their previous wage, in reality EI has become a flat-rate payment. Since its introduction in the 1990s, the maximum EI payment has remained largely unchanged. In contrast, the minimum EI payment, fixed at 90% of the minimum wage, has gradually increased in line with the minimum-wage increase. Today the minimum EI payment is almost equal to the maximum, which implies that the link between previous earnings and benefit amounts has largely disappeared.

As a result, while being relatively generous for low-wage workers, the EI system pays rather low benefits for the average worker in Korea. As discussed in *Connecting People with Jobs: Korea* (OECD, 2018), the EI benefit floor as a percentage of the average wage for full-time employees is higher than in any other unemployment benefit system across the OECD. Korea is also the only country that brings all primary-tier unemployment beneficiaries above the relative poverty threshold of 50% of the average wage.

However, for a worker earning the average wage, benefit levels are rather low due to the binding maximum EI level. When considering family benefits as well as income taxes and mandatory social security contributions paid on unemployment benefits, the net replacement rate for an average-income earner, at 50%, is in the bottom quarter among an OECD ranking (Figure 5.7). As a comparison, the ratio of net income out of work to net income while in work is 65% in the OECD on average.

Figure 5.7. Employment insurance benefits in Korea replace a low share of previous income

Net replacement rates of entitlements for an average-income earner in international comparison, calculated at three different points of time (initially, averaged over one year and averaged over five years), 2015

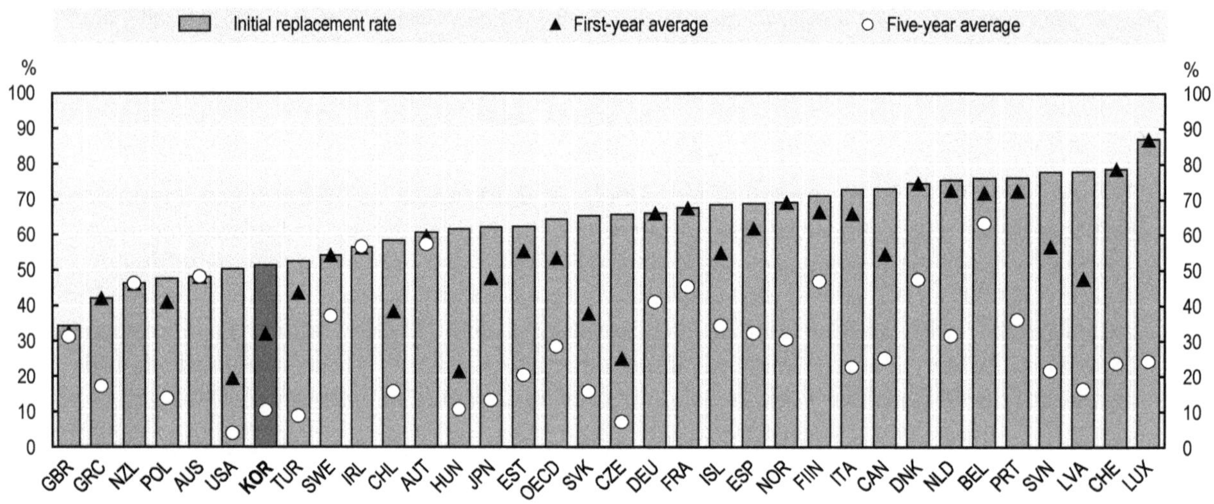

Note: The net replacement rate (NRR) is the ratio of net income out of work to net income while in work, considering income taxes and mandatory social security contributions paid by employees. Social assistance and housing-related benefits are not included, while family benefits are included. NRRs are calculated for a 40-year-old worker with an uninterrupted employment record since age 22. They are averages over four different stylised family types and two earnings levels. OECD is an unweighted average of the 34 countries shown (excluding Mexico).
Source: OECD Tax-Benefit Models, www.oecd.org/els/social/workincentives.

StatLink http://dx.doi.org/10.1787/888933832457

In addition, the maximum duration during which beneficiaries can receive an EI payment in Korea is one of the shortest in the OECD. The duration of benefits increases with age at the time of job loss and the length of the contribution record, ranging from 90 days for people insured for less than a year (irrespective of age) to 240 days for people aged 50 or older. Only four OECD countries have benefit durations that are shorter than 8 months. As a result of the short duration, the net replacement rate averaged over the first year is only 32%; the third-lowest share in the OECD (again, Figure 5.7).

Enhancing social benefits for elderly people

Basic Livelihood Security Programme

The Basic Livelihood Security Programme (BLSP) is a comprehensive means-tested social assistance programme in Korea. Introduced in 2000 in the aftermath of the Asian financial crisis, the programme provides various cash benefits to eligible persons living in absolute poverty (including a living benefit, housing benefit, medical benefit, education benefit, child-birth benefit, funeral benefit and self-support benefit).

In order to receive one or more of the benefits, an applicant has to meet the income and family requirements. The income requirement has been drastically reformed in July 2015 to tackle the "all or nothing" principle: Before reform, either all benefits were available to the beneficiary or none. More specifically, the threshold income level (income and assets converted into income) was diversified across benefits: it is now 30% of the standardised median income (derived from a household survey and similar to the minimum cost of living) for living benefit, 43% for housing benefit, 40% for medical benefit and 50% for education benefit. Today, people not eligible for the main payment (living benefit) may still receive other benefits, reducing the risk of poverty traps that discourage work.

The family requirement implies that applicants cannot receive benefits if they have a close family member (child, spouse or parent) capable of supporting them – the so-called *family support obligation* rule. However, eligibility does not depend on whether such family support is actually provided. The capacity of family support is measured by the family members' income and assets. While the threshold income to be accepted as an incapable legal supporter was raised from 130% of the minimum cost of living to 100% of median income in July 2015, it still means that relatives with a relatively low income are supposed to help their income-poor family member.

Income requirements and the family support obligation both keep the BLSP caseload below the actual poverty numbers. In 2016, about 1.7 million Koreans received one or several BLSP benefits, corresponding to around 3.2% of the population. About 76% of them received a living benefit and 85% received a housing benefit. The caseload is similar to the OECD average but low in comparison with OECD countries with immature overall social protection systems. Not even half of all Korean people living in absolute poverty (estimated at around 7-8%) are covered by the programme.

The largest beneficiary groups are those aged 40-64 and 65 and above (Figure 5.8). When compared with the overall population numbers by age group, people aged 65 and above are over-represented in the BLSP programme. However, compared with the total share of elder people living in absolute poverty (estimated at around one-fourth), a recipiency rate of 6.9% among older people is very low. The low coverage is largely related to the strict family eligibility criteria. While people with the possibility of assistance from family members are not eligible for the benefit, many children cannot or will not help their elderly parents nowadays in Korea.

Figure 5.8. BLSP recipiency in Korea is highest among youth and older people

Percentage of BLSP recipients by age group, number of recipients and share of the population, 2015

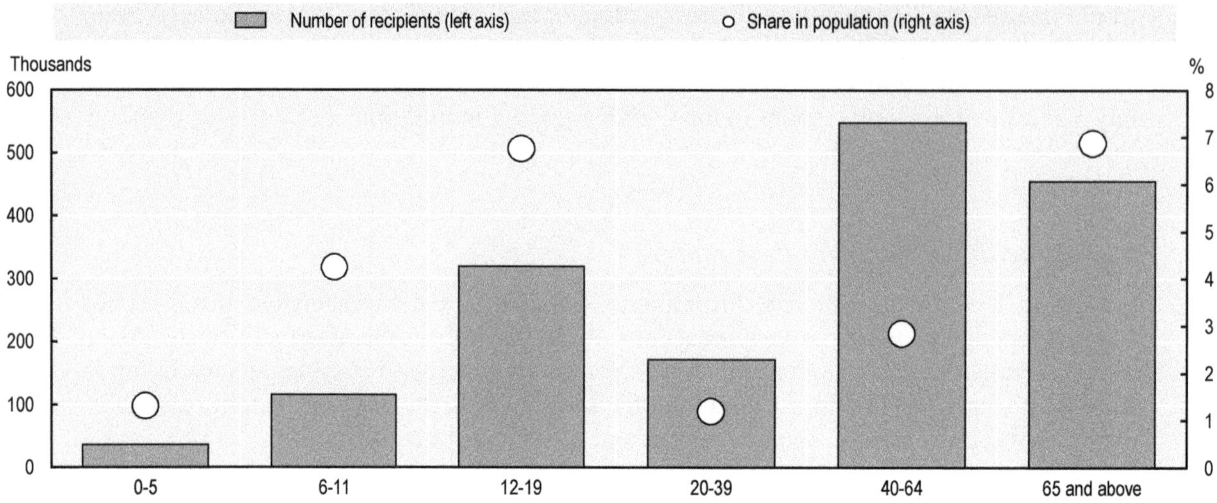

Source: 2015 Annual statistics on BLSP recipients (Ministry of Health and Welfare, 2017), UN Data, UNSD Demographic Statistics (http://data.un.org).

StatLink http://dx.doi.org/10.1787/888933832476

The government recently announced a plan to abolish the family support obligation for the housing benefit as of 2018 and to exclude, as of 2019, the application of the family support obligation for the living benefit and health benefit to the households of the lower 70% of the income distribution with household members aged 65 or above or a severely disabled person. These reforms would be particularly welcome for the large group of older people living in absolute poverty without support from their relatives.

Apart from the coverage, also the benefit level of the BLSP programme is rather limited. Estimates based on the OECD tax and benefit model for cash minimum income benefits show that Korea ranks among the bottom third of OECD countries with respect to the level of living and housing benefits (taken together) as a share of the average income in the respective country. Taking into account net income taxes and social contributions, a single person eligible for the living and housing benefits would receive only about 24% of the median household income in Korea (Figure 5.9). The comparable median payment value across OECD countries for people eligible to both payments is around 40%; housing benefit in particular is significantly higher in many OECD countries.

In sum, it would be important to take further steps to broaden the coverage and increase the generosity of BLSP, especially in view of much higher than average poverty rates in Korea for some groups of the population. Benefit levels are low by OECD standards and eligibility conditions – notably those regarding the absence of so-called "supporting persons" – may still prevent many poor older persons from receiving BLSP benefits.

Figure 5.9. Payments provided by minimum income benefit are relatively low in Korea

Net income value of social assistance payments (main benefit plus housing benefit) for a single person in percent of the median household income, 2015

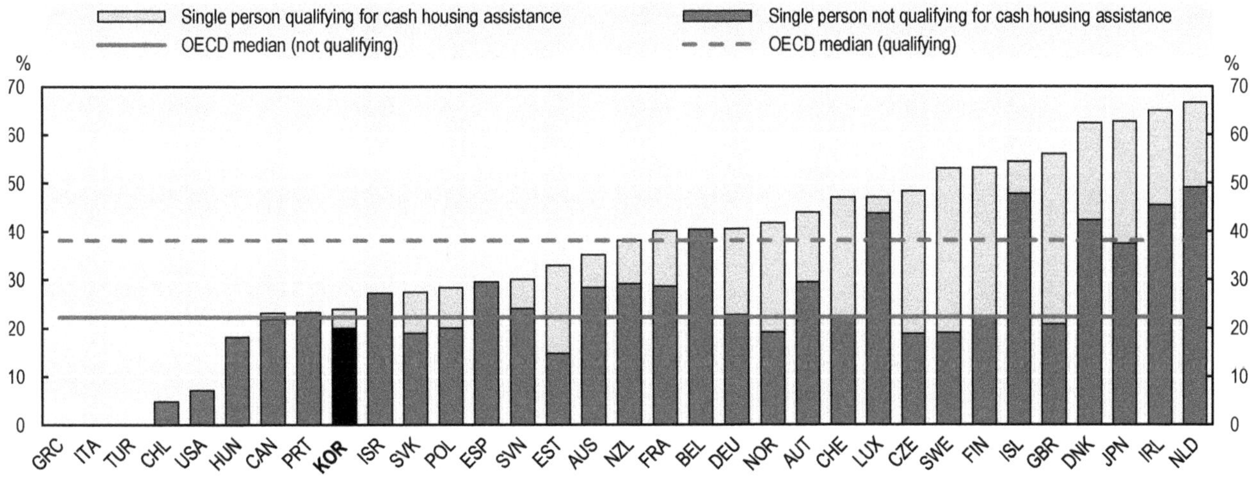

Note: Median net household incomes are from a survey in or close to 2011, expressed in current prices and are before housing costs (or other forms of "committed" expenditure). Results are shown on an equivalised basis and account for social assistance, family benefits and housing-related cash support, net of any income taxes and social contributions. US results include the value of Food Stamps, a near-cash benefit. Where benefit rules are not determined on a national level but vary by region or municipality, results refer to a "typical" case (e.g. Michigan in the United States, the capital in some other countries). In countries where housing benefits depend on actual housing expenditure, the calculation represents cash benefits for someone in privately-rented accommodation with rent plus charges equal to 20% of the average gross full-time wage.
Source: OECD Tax-Benefit Models, www.oecd.org/els/soc/benefits-and-wages.htm.

StatLink http://dx.doi.org/10.1787/888933832495

Basic Pension

In addition to its Basic Livelihood Security Programme, Korea has a social welfare programme targeted at individuals aged 65 and above. This Basic Pension is a non-contributory means-tested benefit for people who have not contributed for long enough to be entitled to a contribution-based pension payment. The maximum monthly benefit level has been KRW 200 000 since 2014, equivalent to 5.5% of the average earnings in 2016 and lower than any other non-contributory basic pension benefit across the OECD (Figure 5.10). The new government, which began its term in May 2017, announced a plan to increase the maximum benefit level to KRW 250 000 in April 2018 and thereafter gradually to KRW 300 000 by April 2021. Even at the new level, the Basic Pension would still be amongst the lowest in the OECD,[4] where the average benefit equalled 20% of average earnings in 2016.

Figure 5.10. The value of Korea's Basic Pension is lower than in any other OECD country

Basic, non-contributory pension payments in OECD countries as a percentage of average earnings and share of persons aged 56 and over receiving a basic pension, 2016

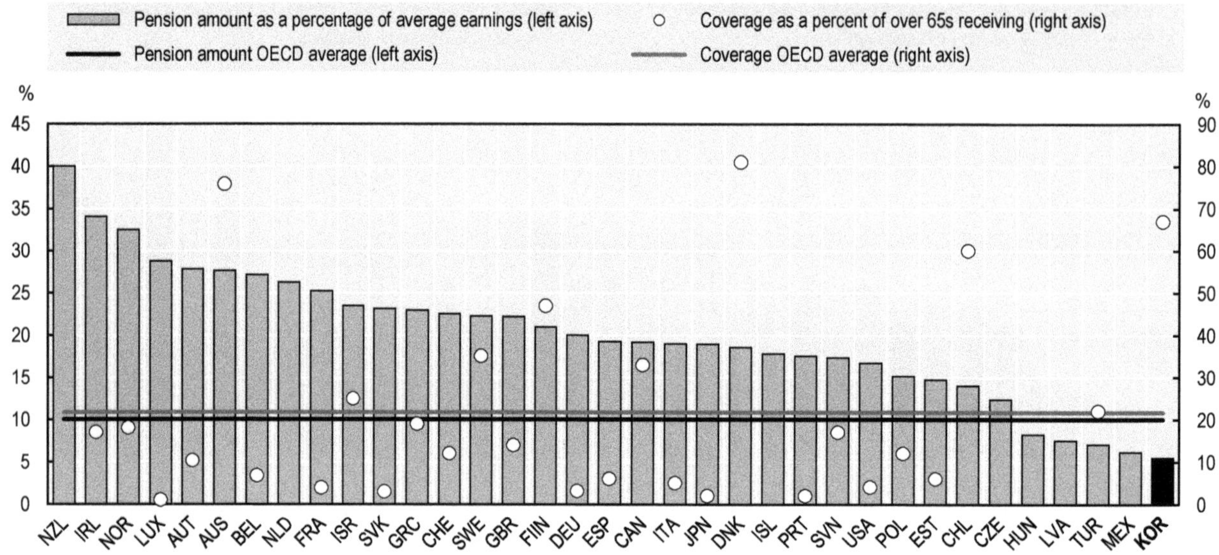

Source: OECD (2017), *Pensions at a Glance 2017: OECD and G20 Indicators*, OECD Publishing, Paris, http://dx.doi.org/10.1787/pension_glance-2017-en.

StatLink http://dx.doi.org/10.1787/888933832514

At the same time, the Basic Pension covers an exceptionally large proportion of the Korean population aged 65 and over. Nearly 70% of the elderly population receives a Basic Pension. This is similar to the shares found in Australia, Chile and Denmark but a multiple of the OECD average of only 22% for similar non-contributory basic pension schemes across 28 OECD countries (Figure 5.10). In other words, the Basic Pension in Korea spreads out resources very thinly over a large segment of the older population.

The Basic Pension could play a more important role in reducing the high poverty rate among older people in Korea, by better targeting scarce government resources to those with the highest need. More specifically, narrowing the coverage of the Basic Pension to people aged 65 living in absolute poverty would leave room to increase the benefit level for these people significantly, without affecting government's overall budget.

Strengthening the multi-pillar pension system

In addition to social welfare programmes, Korea has a multi-pillar pension system for its elderly population which includes the following pillars:

- Pillar 1: Public pension schemes including the National Pension Scheme and Occupational pension schemes
- Pillar 2: Company pension system
- Pillar 3: Individual, voluntary pension savings for retirement

Improving the National Pension Scheme to reduce old-age poverty

The National Pension Scheme (NPS) was created in 1988 to establish a major income support system for the elderly population. Its coverage was initially limited to regular employees in firms with at least ten workers and then gradually expanded to include all workplaces and eventually all types of employees as well as the self-employed. The pension age for the NPS is currently 61 years with at least ten years of contributions. This is gradually going to be increased to 65 years by 2033. A reduced early pension can be withdrawn from the age of 56 years (this age will be increased in parallel to 60 years).

The NPS is a defined-benefit programme, combining earnings-related and redistributive components. The income an insured person earns during the insured period is converted to the present value, and the benefit is annually adjusted based on national consumer price fluctuations. The target replacement rate after 40 years of contributions was 46% in 2016 and is being reduced by 0.5 percentage points for every year until reaching 40% in 2028 to improve the financial sustainability of the system. The contribution rate started at 3% of monthly income in 1988 and was increased to 6% in 1993 and to 9% in 1998 (shared equally between the worker and the employer). People above the age of 60 do not pay contributions and benefits do not accrue after this age.

By the end of 2016, the NPS insured 21.8 million people and had KRW 558.3 trillion worth in assets, accounting for 38% of GDP (National Pension Service, 2017). The NPS offers five types of benefits: old-age pension, disability pension, survivor pension, lump-sum refund, and lump-sum death payment (Table 5.6).

Table 5.6. Types of benefits offered in Korea's National Pension System

Types of Pension	Eligibility conditions
Old-age pension	The old-age pension is the major benefit in the National Pension program. People who have been insured more than 10 years can be paid the old-age pension as of age 61.
Disability pension	The disability pension is paid if the insured has a disability, and the benefit level is determined based on the severity or conditions of physical or mental illness.
Survivor pension	The survivor pension is designed to guarantee the income of the spouse and eligible family, whose livelihoods had been maintained by the deceased, when the insured person dies.
Lump-sum refund	A lumps-sum refund is payable when a person can no longer be covered under the NPS because of age, emigration or death, etc., while failing to qualify for other types of benefits.
Lump-sum death payment	When an insured person dies, and there are no eligible survivors for a Survivor pension or Lump-sum refund, a funeral grant is given to the extended-family.

Source: National Pension Service.

The NPS has a number of weaknesses as a major source of income for the elderly population, including a low coverage rate, a low actual replacement rate and financial instability. First, although participation has been mandatory by law since 1999, a large number of people are not insured, especially non-regular workers and self-employed. While 85% of regular workers are registered with the national pension system, the rate is only 36.5% among non-regular workers (Statistics Korea, 2017). Overall, around 60% of the working-age population was insured under the national pension system at the end of 2016 (National Pension Service, 2017). The low coverage reflects a lack of trust in the pension system as well as evasion by self-employed and non-regular workers. In addition, some self-employed workers are exempted from paying premiums due to low income. According to government's projection in 2013, only 41% of the elderly are expected to receive NPS benefits in 2030 (OECD, 2016). Second, given the recent introduction of the NPS, the average contribution period is still short and the actual pension benefit low. At KRW 353 thousand per month in 2016, the average benefit equalled only about 10% of the average wage (National Pension Service, 2017). Even looking ahead, the actual replacement rate would still be less than 20% in 2030-40. As a result, the impact of the NPS in reducing poverty is limited by its recent introduction and a slow acceptance by the public. Third, NPS spending is set to rise faster than NPS revenues, despite the gradual cut in the replacement rate to 40% and the planned hike in the pension eligibility age from 61 to 65 in 2033. The reform in 2007 cannot solve the structural imbalance between expenditures and revenues: if the current system is maintained, the NPS fund is expected to be fully depleted by 2060 (Ministry of Health and Welfare, 2014).

Addressing the low NPS coverage requires more rigorous policies to increase compliance of self-employed and non-regular workers. In a similar vein as for the EI system, NPS coverage could be improved by increasing the penalties for employers who do not enrol their workers and expanding the resources and mandate of the labour inspectorate to control compliance of employers (see OECD, 2018). Combining the collection of taxes and social insurance contributions as is currently planned will improve identification of the self-employed and transparency about their income.

The best option to achieve financial sustainability of the NPS is to raise the contribution rate (Jones and Urasawa, 2014). Set at 9%, the current contribution rate is the second-lowest among the 22 OECD countries where pension contributions are mandatory for both private and public pensions (Figure 5.11). The adjustment of the contribution rate should begin as soon as possible, as delays would make the necessary increase larger.

Figure 5.11. Contributions to the National Pension Scheme are very low in Korea

Mandatory pension contribution rates for an average worker in per cent of the gross wage, 2016

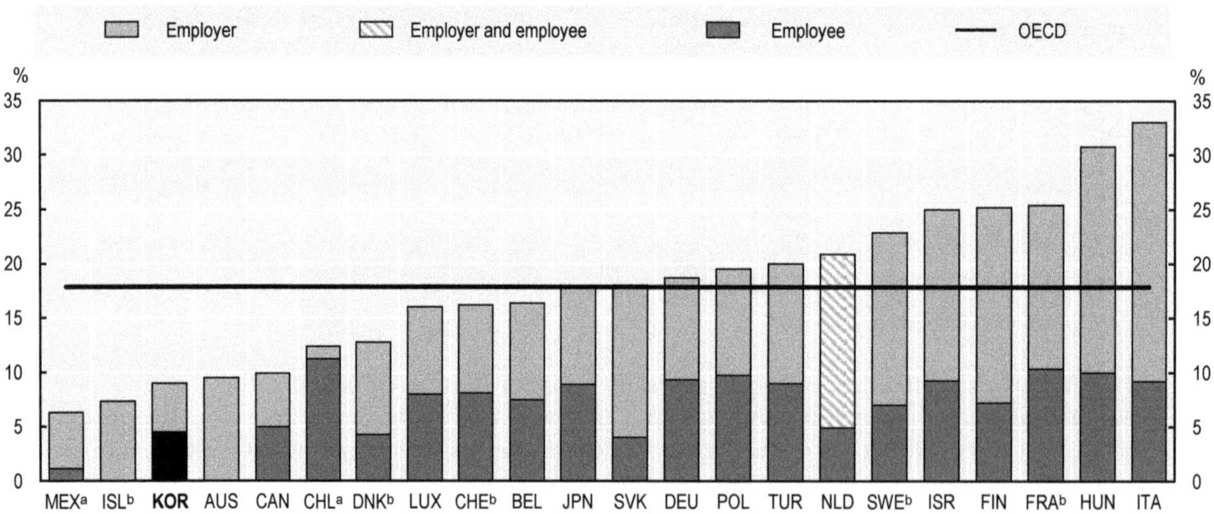

Note: OECD is the unweighted average of the 22 countries shown in the chart.

a) Data refer to private contributions.

b) Data refer to both public and private contributions.

Source: Table 7, OECD (2017), *Pensions at a Glance 2017: OECD and G20 Indicators*, OECD Publishing, Paris, http://dx.doi.org/10.1787/pension_glance-2017-en.

StatLink http://dx.doi.org/10.1787/888933832533

Limiting the financial burden of occupational pensions

The three occupational pension schemes for civil servants, military personnel and private-school teachers insure more than 1.5 million workers, with the scheme for civil servants accounting for more than two-thirds of the total. The occupational pensions have similar benefit structures and a rather generous replacement rate (76%) compared with the NPS, intended to compensate civil servants for relatively low wages and to attract a competent work force with a long-term commitment to public service.

Occupational pension benefits were increased repeatedly under political pressures without corresponding financing measures, forcing them to rely increasingly on government subsidies. Two reforms, in 2009 and 2015, aimed at enhancing the financial viability of the civil service pension scheme by raising the contribution rate, reducing the accrual rate and raising the minimum age of eligibility (Table 5.7). The reforms also had a roll-over effect on the pension scheme for private-school teaches since both are linked by the Private School Teachers and Staff Pension Act. Nevertheless, the outlook remains difficult as both the number of retirees and their life expectancy are rising. The gradual application of the contribution and accrual rates reduces the impact of the reform. For the military pension no reform has taken place so far.

Table 5.7. Features of Korea's occupational pension scheme for civil servants

	Old system	2009 Reform	2015 Reform
Contribution rate	5.5%	7%	9%
Accrual rate	2.1%	1.9%	1.7%
Eligibility age	60 years old	60 if employed before 2009, 65 years if employed after 2010	Gradual increase from 60 to 65 by year of retirement

Source: Government Employee Pension Service.

StatLink http://dx.doi.org/10.1787/888933832647

Promoting company pension systems

The weakness of the NPS and the decline in family support left a void that is to be filled in part by company pensions. In 2005, the government launched a plan to encourage the conversion of the mandatory retirement allowance into a company pension to provide better income security for retired workers. The retirement allowance, which was introduced in 1953 and became legally mandatory in 1961, requires firms to pay departing employees a lump-sum equivalent to at least one month of wages per year of work. It was initially intended to be a support for the unemployed and the retired in the absence of unemployment insurance and pensions, similar to a severance payment. Nevertheless, given high labour turnover – average job tenure in Korea is only six years – most workers receive the retirement allowance numerous times during their working life. About 70% of workplaces that offer retirement allowances have paid the allowance prior to retirement at least once (Jones and Urasawa, 2014).

The company pension system introduced in 2005 allows firms to transform the retirement allowance into a defined-benefit (DB) or a defined-contribution (DC) scheme, in which the contribution is predetermined and the benefit depends on the investment returns. The decision is based on an agreement between management and employees. Companies that introduce a pension are exempt from paying retirement allowance, although many still do.

To promote the shift to a company pension system, the government has launched several measures since 2005 to make the retirement allowance less attractive. First, tax deduction for internally-funded retirement allowance plans has been phased out by 2016. Second, withdrawal of a worker's retirement allowance before leaving the company (including for retirement) is limited to specific purposes since 2012. Third, employees moving between jobs are required to place their retirement allowance in an Individual Retirement Pension (IRP). Fourth, the government expanded the tax credit for the IRP at the workers' own expenses from maximum KRW 4 million to KRW 7 million. Fifth, since July 2017 all workers including the self-employed are allowed to join an IPR scheme.

The company pension system has grown steadily in the past ten years, covering nearly 6.2 million employees and KRW 147 trillion of the total asset in 2016 (National Pension Service, 2017). However, the system's impact remains limited. By 2016, only 17% of the firms in Korea had introduced a company pension system, with the percentage increasing with firm size, from 15% of firms with less than 30 employees to 90% of firms with 300 or more. Among workers eligible for company pension plans – those with more than one year of job tenure – 47.7% were enrolled at the end of 2016. Regular workers account for the vast majority of those enrolled in the company pension system. Only 1.6% of those who received the retirement benefit received the payment as an annuity during 2016, while all others still received a lump-sum payment.

It is important to accelerate the shift away from the lump-sum retirement allowance in order to supplement the weak National Pension Scheme. Additional measures are needed to strengthen this second pillar of the Korean pension system. Most importantly, while retirement pension plans apply to all workers in all firms irrespective of their size, more should be done to ease restrictions on the grounds of employment duration and types thereby expanding the target of mandatory enrolment. Various discussions are ongoing in this regard between the National Assembly and the government, including a suggestion to include all workers with three months of tenure and plans to limit the maximum amount and the permitted causes of early withdrawals. Consideration should also be given to aligning the age when the retirement pension can be drawn with the NPS pensionable age.

Encouraging private-sector savings for retirement

Voluntary individual pension accounts, which are open to individuals regardless of their employment status, were introduced in 1994. Various personal pension accounts are offered by insurance companies, banks, and asset management companies. Individuals who contribute a specified amount of money for more than five years are entitled to receive monthly pensions starting at age 55. They are allowed a tax credit of up to 13.2% of the amount placed in such accounts up to a ceiling of KRW 4 million a year. Taxation, which is deferred until the individual begins receiving benefits at age 55, is set at a rate of 3.3% to 5.5%, depending on the recipient's age and the amount of annual pension.

Coverage of voluntary individual pension plans remains somewhat limited in Korea, accounting for about 24% of the working-age population (Table 5.8). In addition, a substantial number of individuals withdraw their funds before reaching age 55: the share of investors closing their account rises from 28% after five years to 48% after ten years (Jones and Urasawa, 2014). The total amount of assets in Korea's private pension plans including both company pension plans and voluntary individual pensions reached 26.9% of GDP in 2016 which compares with an unweighted OECD average of 50% and a weighted average of 83%.

In sum, despite recent reform efforts individual pension accounts remain underdeveloped in Korea and effort is needed to continue reform and further strengthen this third pillar of the pension scheme. It is important to increase the penalties for early withdrawal of funds and provide more favourable tax credits for people's individual accounts.

Table 5.8. Coverage and assets for private pension plans in Korea could be expanded

Coverage as a percentage of the working-age population (15-64 years) and total assets as a percentage of GDP and in millions of USD, latest year available

	Coverage		Assets	
	Occupational	Personal	% of GDP	USD million
Australia	x	..	123.9	1 523 302
Austria	13.9	18.0	6.0	21 980
Belgium	59.6	..	6.9	30 612
Canada	26.3	25.2	159.2	2 403 874
Chile	..	..	69.6	174 480
Czech Republic	x	52.6	8.4	15 684
Denmark	x	18.0	209.0	611 895
Estonia	x	12.3	16.4	3 656
Finland	6.6	19.0	59.3	134 867
France	24.5	5.7	9.8	230 184
Germany	57.0	33.8	6.8	223 906
Greece	1.3	..	0.7	1 254
Hungary	..	18.4	4.3	5 105
Iceland	x	45.2	150.7	32 359
Ireland	38.3	12.6	40.7	118 322
Israel	..	..	55.7	177 293
Italy	9.2	11.5	9.4	165 238
Japan	45.4	13.4	29.4	1 354 754
Korea	x	24.0	26.9	364 634
Latvia	0.3	11.4	12.7	3 340
Luxembourg	5.1	..	2.9	1 659
Mexico	1.7	..	16.7	156 503
Netherlands	x	28.3	180.3	1 335 227
New Zealand	6.8	74.8	24.4	45 109
Norway	..	26.7	10.2	36 899
Poland	1.6	66.6	9.3	41 038
Portugal	3.7	4.5	10.8	21 092
Slovak Republic	x	19.0	11.2	9 523
Slovenia	..	..	7.0	2 963
Spain	3.3	15.7	14.0	164 241
Sweden	x	24.2	80.6	389 264
Switzerland	x	..	141.6	904 380
Turkey	1.0	13.9	4.8	35 217
United Kingdom	..	..	95.3	2 273 713
United States	40.8	19.3	134.9	25 126 592
OECD		**Simple:**	50.0	38 140 159
		Weighted:	83.0	

Note: "x" = Not applicable; ".." = Not available.
Source: Adapted from OECD (2017), *Pensions at a Glance 2017: OECD and G20 Indicators*, OECD Publishing, Paris, http://dx.doi.org/10.1787/pension_glance-2017-en.

StatLink http://dx.doi.org/10.1787/888933832666

Conclusion

High poverty rates among older people, including those who are in employment, call for significant improvements in social security. While the main pillars of a comprehensive system of social protection are in place, many programmes are still immature and only gradually capturing the population of older workers. Recent reforms have contributed to improving the situation but more is needed to financially support older people.

First, general protection systems should be expanded. The *Earned Income Tax Credit* which intends to support people not able to earn a decent living despite being employed would be more effective, notably for older workers in second careers, if eligibility criteria and benefit amounts were to be revised. Similarly, the Basic Livelihood Security Programme, Korea's social assistance measure, could be more effective in reducing poverty. While recent reforms have put an end to the "all or nothing" nature of payments, the benefit level itself remains low by OECD standards and eligibility conditions – notably the "family support obligation" – still affect older persons disproportionately.

Secondly, further pension reform is needed to ensure those entering retirement have an adequate standard of living while those who still want to work are rewarded in doing so. Korea's Basic Pension could be better targeted and the payment value increased to provide a more solid safety-net. This is all the more important as benefits paid under Korea's National Pension have been significantly reduced to ensure financial sustainability. In addition, measures could be taken to extend both the institutional and effective coverage of the National Pension itself. For many non-regular workers, employers are still managing to evade their obligations to document their workers formally and pay into the measure, similar to EI. In addition, the contribution rate should be raised to achieve financial sustainability of the National Pension.

Finally, further measures could be taken to foster the implementation of retirement pension plans notably among small and medium-sized enterprises. Despite several government initiatives over the past decade to encourage the conversion of the mandatory retirement allowance into a retirement pension, the allowance continues to be used as severance payment throughout workers' careers. More radical measures need to be taken to transform the allowance into a second pillar of the pension system.

Notes

[1] It should be noted that incomes measured for households and older people are assumed to draw on the earnings of younger family members with whom they may live. For older people who live in multi-generational households work is likely to be a more important income source.

[2] The extension of the EITC to single-member households was done in several stages: in 2013 single-member households aged 60 years and above became eligible; the age threshold was further reduced to 50 years in 2015 and to 40 years in 2017.

[3] As discussed in OECD (2018) and OECD (2013a), EITC is less generous than comparable in-work schemes in OECD countries for households with children as these countries tend to have higher child top-up benefits.

[4] Assuming a constant inflation rate between 2016 and 2021 – the core inflation rate was 1.6% in Korea in 2016 (https://stats.oecd.org/) – the maximum monthly benefit would equal 7.6% of the average earnings by 2021. If other countries do not increase their monthly benefit, Korea would become the fourth-lowest in the OECD ranking.

References

Bassanini, A., J. Rasmussen and S. Scarpetta (1999), *The Economic Effects of Employment-Conditional Income Support Schemes for the Low-Paid*, http://dx.doi.org/10.1787/083815484206.

Jeong, C. and J. Kim (2015), "The redistributive effects of EITC and of CTC on one-earner and dual-earner household", *Korean Social Security Studies*, Vol. 31/1.

Jones, R. and S. Urasawa (2014), "Reducing the High Rate of Poverty Among the Elderly in Korea", *OECD Economics Department Working Papers*, No. 1163, OECD Publishing, Paris, http://dx.doi.org/10.1787/5jxx054fv20v-en

Kim, M.J (2016), "The Current Status of the Earned Income Tax Credit in South Korea and the Implications for Japan – Earned Income Tax Credit or Reduced Tax Rate?", NLI Research Institute Report.

Lee, D., G. Kwon and S. Moon (2015), "Studies on policy effects of the EITC", *The Korean Association for Policy Studies*, Vol. 24/2.

Ministry of Health and Welfare (2014), 2013 Yearbook of Health and Welfare, Sejong-si.

National Pension Service (2017), 2016 National Pension Statistics Facts book, National Pension Research Institute, Jeonju-si.

OECD (2018), *Connecting People with Jobs: Korea*, OECD Publishing, Paris.

OECD (2017), *Pensions at a Glance 2017: OECD and G20 Indicators*, OECD Publishing, Paris. http://dx.doi.org/10.1787/pension_glance-2017-en.

OECD (2016), *OECD Economic Surveys: Korea 2016*, OECD Publishing, Paris, http://dx.doi.org/10.1787/eco_surveys-kor-2016-en.

OECD (2014), OECD Economic Surveys: Korea 2014, OECD Publishing, Paris, http://dx.doi.org/10.1787/eco_surveys-kor-2014-en.

OECD (2013a), Table 2.3 in *Strengthening Social Cohesion in Korea*, OECD Publishing, Paris, http://dx.doi.org/10.1787/9789264188945-en.

OECD (2013b), *Korea: Improving the Re-employment Prospects of Displaced Workers*, OECD Publishing, Paris. http://dx.doi.org/10.1787/9789264189225-en.

OECD (2005), *OECD Employment Outlook 2005*, OECD Publishing, Paris, http://dx.doi.org/10.1787/empl_outlook-2005-en.

Song, H. and H. Bahng (2014), "The Effect of EITC on Job Creation in Korea", *The Korean Economic Review*, Vol. 62/4.

Statistics Korea (2017), Supplementary Results of the Economically Active Population Survey by Employment Type, Daejeon.

Statistics Korea (2016), Results of the Survey of Household Finances and Living Conditions in 2016, Daejeon.

Venn, D. (2012), "Eligibility Criteria for Unemployment Benefits: Quantitative Indicators for OECD and EU Countries", OECD Social, Employment and Migration Working Papers, No. 131, OECD Publishing, Paris. http://dx.doi.org/10.1787/5k9h43kgkvr4-en.

Won, J. and T. Kim (2013), "Projecting Social Expenditure and Total Tax Burden in Korea -A Study on Forecasting Social Expenditure for OECD Countries and Corresponding Total Tax Revenue for Korea", http://repository.kihasa.re.kr:8080/handle/201002/10893 (accessed on 27 April 2017).

Yoo, G. (2013), "Institutional Blind Spots in the South Korean Employment Safety Net and Policy Solutions", KDI Focus No. 28 (eng.), September 2013, Seoul, https://www.kdevelopedia.org/download.do?timeFile=/mnt/idas/asset/2014/09/17/DOC/PDF/04201409170134127079951.pdf&originFileName=13273_2.pdf.

ORGANISATION FOR ECONOMIC CO-OPERATION AND DEVELOPMENT

The OECD is a unique forum where governments work together to address the economic, social and environmental challenges of globalisation. The OECD is also at the forefront of efforts to understand and to help governments respond to new developments and concerns, such as corporate governance, the information economy and the challenges of an ageing population. The Organisation provides a setting where governments can compare policy experiences, seek answers to common problems, identify good practice and work to co-ordinate domestic and international policies.

The OECD member countries are: Australia, Austria, Belgium, Canada, Chile, the Czech Republic, Denmark, Estonia, Finland, France, Germany, Greece, Hungary, Iceland, Ireland, Israel, Italy, Japan, Korea, Latvia, Lithuania, Luxembourg, Mexico, the Netherlands, New Zealand, Norway, Poland, Portugal, the Slovak Republic, Slovenia, Spain, Sweden, Switzerland, Turkey, the United Kingdom and the United States. The European Union takes part in the work of the OECD.

OECD Publishing disseminates widely the results of the Organisation's statistics gathering and research on economic, social and environmental issues, as well as the conventions, guidelines and standards agreed by its members.

OECD PUBLISHING, 2, rue André-Pascal, 75775 PARIS CEDEX 16
(81 2016 31 1 P) ISBN 978-92-64-06483-6 – 2018

www.ingramcontent.com/pod-product-compliance
Ingram Content Group UK Ltd.
Pitfield, Milton Keynes, MK11 3LW, UK
UKHW051505290926
15471UKWH00008B/1439

9 789264 064836